HOMELAND INSECURITY

How Washington Politicians Have Made America Less Safe

Terry D. Turchie

Kathleen M. Puckett, Ph.D.

Published in the United States by
History Publishing Company
Palisades, New York

Library of Congress Cataloging-in-Publication Data
Turchie, Terry D.
    Homeland Insecurity: how Washington politicians have
    made America less safe / Terry D. Turchie, Kathleen M.
    Puckett.—1st ed.
       p.cm.
    Includes bibliographic references and index.
    LCCN 2008929466
    ISBN-13: 978-1-933909-33-2
    ISBN-10: 1-933909-33-1
    SAN: 850-5942

    1. United States—Federal Bureau of Investigation—
       History. 2. Internal security—United States—History—
       20th century. 3. Political corruption—United States—
       History— 20th century. 4. United States—Politics and
       government—20th century. I.
       Puckett, Kathleen M.
       II. Title.

    HV8144.F43T87 2008   363.25'0973
                                          QBI08-600165

Printed in the United States on acid-free paper

9 8 7 6 5 4 3 2

First Edition

CONTENTS

DEDICATION

We dedicate this book to the men and women of the Federal Bureau of Investigation, who have served our country with integrity and allegiance to the rule of law for more than 100 years.

ACKNOWLEDGMENTS

This book is the result of over 60 years of combined experience in federal law enforcement, counterintelligence, and counterterrorism. But it is also shaped by the observations of hundreds of our coworkers, friends, family members, and by the shared experience of millions of our fellow countrymen.

We are grateful for the confidence Don Bracken at History Publishing Company has shown in our ability to tell this critical and possibly very controversial story, and to our Editor, Tom Cameron, for so expertly shepherding us through the telling.

We are especially grateful to, and want to express our great affection and regard for, the wonderful Cynthia Riggs, author of the Martha's Vineyard Mystery Series. Not only is she a superb writer, but her penchant for making her historic Cleveland House available to writers and poets who are lucky enough to travel to that magical place led directly to the publication of our first book, the award-winning *Hunting the American Terrorist— The FBI's War on Homegrown Terror*. We can never thank her enough, but we are determined to do it in person, and yearly, if possible!

INTRODUCTION

Think of this book as a warning bell.

At this writing, early in the U.S. Presidential Election Year of 2008, the sound it makes is faint to most ears. In the waning months of the presidency of George W. Bush, Americans are preoccupied with the long and complex war in Iraq, a possible looming economic recession, and a prevailing level of continual anxiety and fear about the next terrorist attack on American soil. In the midst of the turmoil, media outlets worldwide are documenting the growing intensity of the battle between Democrats and Republicans for the second presidential administration of the 21st Century.

There seems to be no general awareness of the bell that is tolling the steady and impending destruction of a uniquely protective American institution. The danger is, because the sound of the bell is faint, an American institution will be destroyed long before the impact of its destruction is realized.

The consequences will be devastating to American public life. An historic instrument of the checks and balances outlined by the Constitution is in danger of being lost to Americans without their ever being aware of the critical role it has played in the past 100 years of American history, and what its absence will mean to American democracy in the 21st Century and beyond.

We sound the alarm in this book, to bring to light the critical damage that over three decades of the exercise of unfettered political power has had on the role of the Federal Bureau of Investigation—the FBI—in ensuring transparency in government, the pre-eminence of the rule of law, and the guardianship of civil liberties.

It all began with Watergate.

As the war in Vietnam raged throughout the 1960s and into the 1970s, many Americans lost confidence in the integrity of their elected leaders. Just as they began to hope for a breakthrough that would end the war, they awoke to the sounds of the Watergate burglars, working under cover of darkness to help one political party damage another in the constant game to acquire and maintain power at any cost.

The Watergate era was as much about personal loyalties, political alliances, and long-standing feuds between political dynasties as it was about lying, corruption, bribery, and obstruction of justice. The underlying motivation for all of it was power.

The dangers presented to societies by the seductive and addictive nature of power have been evident for thousands of years. Christian Meier wrote in *Caesar, An Autobiography* that the Roman republic fell because:

> . . . *It could no longer contend with the social problems at home or the military and administrative problems abroad. For any attempt to solve them only increased the power of individuals, or at least the fear that they inspired among most of the senators. This led to fierce conflicts . . . to growing inefficiency and thus to the disintegration of the inherited order.*[1]

Just as in the years leading to the collapse of ancient Rome, the partisan warfare that has raged in Washington over the past three decades has polarized U.S. politics to a standstill on almost every issue. By the end of the 20th century, the emphasis on building political dynasties and maintaining and enhancing their political power blinded leading Democrats and Republicans alike to the looming danger of international terrorism directed against America. Partisan feuding and markedly different priorities for the country characterized every decision they made—or failed to make—prior to the terrible attacks on September 11, 2001.

When the attacks occurred, power and prestige in both political parties were seriously threatened. Neither party could afford to be labeled as the one that allowed the tragic events of 9/11 to occur. For a brief time, politicians of all stripes united in what appeared to be in the best interests of America's national security. The bipartisan 9/11 Commission appeared to begin in an atmosphere of partisan truce, to examine in detail what had been left unaddressed in the national security apparatus that had led to such a catastrophic breach.

In reality, however, what the 9/11 Commission did was rally politicians to protect exposure of the shortsightedness and complacency they had all exhibited for years relative to the growing danger of terrorism. Their strategy was to focus blame primarily on the FBI for the success of the al Qaeda attacks within the United States.

Why, despite the critical danger facing the country, have politicians in Washington interfered with securing its protection? The reason has far more to do with psychology than ideology. The pursuit and protection of their own political power drives them. The motivation behind their faulty analysis and ineffective strategy is preserving, protecting, and enhancing their own power.

As former FBI agents ourselves, we are well aware of mistakes and misdeeds that have been part of the Bureau's history since its earliest days, and the all-too-human natures of the agents, supervisors, administrators, analysts, and directors who have made up its ranks.

Continuous scrutiny by hundreds of historians, political scientists, and the media over its history only intensified after 9/11, and books harshly critical of the FBI have consistently been on the review lists of national publications both in the United States and abroad. As a result, there is an amazing dichotomy in the Bureau's public image. The FBI has been variously portrayed as effective or bumbling, professional or amateurish, blithely arrogant or unshakably determined, powerful or ineffectual. Since it is an institution made up of human beings, all these labels may have been correct at one time or another, and it is not the intent of this book to refute any of them.

Our intent is to demonstrate the devastating effect partisan political attacks on the FBI have had on the critical role this uniquely American institution has in ensuring the enforcement and protection of federal law regardless of whom it impacts, and in spite of which political party its investigations impact upon.

The FBI is the only government agency with the authority to conduct investigations in the interest of national security at the same time it addresses violations of federal criminal law. From bank robberies to public corruption, terrorism to civil rights, the FBI's dual mission—conducting both national security and "color of law" civil rights investigations—ensures protection under the law from both internal and external threats, while balancing that protection by enforcing laws that guarantee civil liberties under the Constitution. (In essence, color of law civil rights investigations concern the violation of an individual's civil rights by any law enforcement officer under the "color" of his official position.).

The FBI's culture of independence from political pressures and interference is the only guarantee to all Americans that its work will be thorough and impartial, regardless of the party or individuals in power.

The FBI's first Director, J. Edgar Hoover, saw and understood the corrosive effect of power on human nature. Whatever other motivations he may have had, his purpose in keeping mysterious "FBI files" on so many of America's political leaders ensured the Bureau's independence from political manipulation. There has never been any evidence that Hoover used the files to blackmail or extort. It's clear that the very rumor of their existence was enough to protect him and his organization from political intrusion.

After Hoover died, and in the midst of the Watergate scandal, the party in power tried to capitalize on the reach of the FBI and bring it under political control. Both parties and their machines have continued down that road ever since. But the FBI's strong culture of independence, coupled with its uniqueness as a law enforcement institution with a dual role—enforcing federal laws while preserving civil rights—has made it difficult for politicians to succeed.

After 9/11, the time was right. Assigning blame for the attacks to the FBI allowed both Democrats and Republicans to deflect criticism from themselves and to use fear to strengthen their power: over the FBI, over the civil liberties of every American citizen, and most importantly, to insure their protection from investigations of their own activities, many of which are prosecutable under public corruptions statutes in federal and state courts.

The Washington politicians highlighted in this book are representative of many not mentioned and of the invisible political forces at work in American politics today that have made America less safe.

How have they accomplished such an ignoble feat?

Three have exploited the fear of terrorism to gain greater control over the FBI and to interfere with FBI investigations. Five have used their positions to manage the FBI from afar, confusing oversight with political direction. Two have been involved in the passage of legislation and development of guidelines that restricted the FBI's efforts to protect the country from domestic threats—which had a direct bearing on the success of the 9/11 terrorist attacks. Two have fraternized with America's enemies, more to enhance their own power than to protect the national security. One has been accused of selectively leaking classified information to the media; the other is representative of a long, sad line of elected leaders who have looked the other way in the face of massive political corruption and bad behavior.

From Watergate to 9/11, they have all played a part in moving America from a nation governed by transparency and the rule of law to one governed by fear and the development of a military/industrial/intelligence model that is advertised as the answer to both internal and external threats. The model is ill-conceived and threatens our nation's democratic existence far more than the terrorists it seeks to eradicate. For when the war on terror is over, the insidious infiltration of former and current "spies" into many walks of life will be complete.

Imagine the danger posed to democracy when thousands of mercenaries with intelligence backgrounds who were trained to topple foreign governments become embedded in private corporations with invisible connections to their handlers in one political party or the other. Imagine the potential growth of that danger if politicians with interests in those corporations succeed in controlling or obliterating the only remaining federal agency powerful enough to follow the trail and disrupt their schemes.

Intent on securing their own power, both partisan and personal, politicians of all stripes have critically endangered national security by favoring their political allies in the Intelligence community—the CIA and the military—over the FBI in prosecuting the domestic "war on terror."

Neither the CIA nor intelligence agencies in the military are chartered to operate under the rule of constitutional law. Their post 9/11 involvement in "extraordinary rendition" and coercive interrogation techniques at both Abu Ghraib and Guantanamo Bay are clear evidence—with documented participation by and support of the U.S. Department of Justice that is always headed by loyalists to the party in power—of the slippery slope our nation is riding away from traditional American values and standards.

This is the real story of how pursuit of their own power has led Washington politicians to vie for control in remaking or destroying the only federal agency charged with investigation of their personal and public corruption as well as counterintelligence, counterterrorism, and the national security of the United States: the FBI.

This is the story of how, in crippling and possibly destroying the FBI, politicians have critically endangered American life in the 21st Century.

CHAPTER ONE

ADDICTED TO POWER
Why Politicians Do What They Do

Power is sweet; it is a drug, the desire for which increases with habit.

Bertrand Russell, 1951

In 1973, President Richard Nixon, deeply involved in the Watergate cover-up, was recorded discussing at length with his legal counsel, John Dean, the use of presidential power to destroy his political opponents. In 1969, Senator Edward Kennedy left the scene of a fatal accident and didn't appear in public again until he had his attorneys at his side. He had the power of privilege and the money to protect himself. By 1998, President Bill Clinton explained away his sexual exploits in the White House with a single phrase: "Because I could."

Why do politicians appear to believe they are above the laws that constrain the behavior of every other American?

They are literally addicted to the perks and pleasures of power. The political culture in Washington, D.C., just like the royal courts of monarchies and the ancient Roman Senate, operates on the same principle: power enables privilege. Privilege shared creates its own excepted, favored class, exempt from legal and social rules that govern other citizens. It feels good to

1

be a member of this class, so good that the pleasure centers of the brain are activated, and the process of addiction to power—and privilege—begins.

The opportunity to acquire power in America is not necessarily a consequence of birth or inherited wealth. Socioeconomic classes are remarkably porous when compared to those in the rest of the world. U.S. presidents have come from log cabins as well as landed estates; and despite undeniable social inequalities and prejudices, America provides opportunity to immigrants as well as those who are born here to pursue their dreams.

The opportunities are great, but so is the competition, and the climb to success in every endeavor depends on an ability to secure enough power to stay once you're there.

Inevitably, the battle to keep and extend political power results in compromise of even the loftiest of original values that bring politicians to public service in the first place.

In the iconic movie *Mr. Smith Goes to Washington*, the idealistic senator played by Jimmy Stewart dismays his mentor, the esteemed but secretly corrupt Senator Paine, with his ingenuous assumption that doing the right thing is the business of Washington. Paine's monologue to his naive protégé is a classic and cynical illustration of how business in the Capitol is really done:

> *I was hoping you'd be spared all this. I was hoping that you'd see the sights, absorb a lot of history, and go back to your boys . . . Now you've been living in a boy's world, Jeff, and for heaven's sakes, stay there! This is a man's world. It's a brutal world, Jeff, and you've no place in it. You'll only get hurt . . . I know it's tough to run head-on into facts but, well as I said, this is a man's world, Jeff, and you've got to check your ideals outside*

*the door, like you do your rubbers. Thirty years ago I had
your ideals. I was you. I had to make the same decision
you were asked to make today. And I made it. I compromised—yes! So that all those years, I could sit in that
Senate and serve the people in a thousand honest ways.
You've got to face facts, Jeff. I've served our state well,
haven't I? We have the lowest unemployment and the
highest federal grants. But, well, I've had to compromise.
I've had to play ball. You can't count on people voting.
Half the time they don't vote anyway. That's how states
and empires have been built since time began.*[1]

We all know that people with the best intentions often
betray them, and we all know the old proverb that the road to
hell is paved with good intentions. What we haven't fully realized is the particularly ruinous role that the addiction to power
has had in shaping the national security structure of the United
States.

Every politician acts to satisfy the interests of the group or
constituency that helped put him or her in power. Intense personal bonds are developed with a handful of people who are able
to implement a politician's visions and further his or her power.
The loyalties that develop reinforce the power politicians hold.

By expanding a politician's grip on power, political loyalists
within government and industry ensure they have support
when their interests eventually drive them into corrupt or inde-
fensible activities. Unethical and even illegal behaviors inevitably become part of the underlying fabric that supports the
continuation and enhancement of a politician's power, whether
the politician intends it or not.

The ability of political power to seduce well-intentioned and
even idealistic people into behaviors they might never have
believed of themselves was the subject of an address in Copen-

hagen by the recipient of the 1991 Sonning prize for his contribution to European civilization, then-President Vaclav Havel of Czechoslovakia:

Why is it that people long for political power, and why, when they have achieved it, are they so reluctant to give it up?

In the first place, people are driven into politics by ideas about a better way to organize society . . .

In the second place . . . it gives you a tremendous opportunity to leave your mark, in the broadest sense, on your surroundings, to shape the world around you in your own image, to enjoy the respect that every political office almost automatically bestows upon the one who holds it . . .

In the third place, many people long for political power and are so reluctant to part with it because of the wide range of perks that are a necessary part of political life—even under the most democratic of conditions.[2]

Havel went on to say that the seductive perks in his life included going to a special doctor, having a driver and special routes set aside for him throughout Prague, having a cook and a housekeeper and even someone to dial his telephone for him. A former playwright, Havel was inclined more than most to continuously reflect on the human condition. As a result, he was more conscious than most politicians of his own vulnerabilities, and the very human nature of the temptations he lived with in his exalted position.

Most people, including most politicians, are not as conscious of their vulnerability to temptation. Since they are human beings, however, they are inevitably seduced to some extent by the special perquisites of their offices that make life more comfortable and pleasurable for them. It seems more and more logical to take advantage of situations that enhance their efficiency, their productivity, their ability to focus on the important work in front of them, and unlike Havel, they do not state publicly that being in power makes them permanently suspicious of their own motives. Havel finished his speech in Copenhagen by characterizing politics as placing:

> . . . *greater stress on moral sensitivity . . . it requires especially pure people, because it is especially easy to become morally tainted . . . a less vigilant spirit may not notice it happening at all.*[3]

It's quite a stretch to propose that thoughtful introspection and humility should be part of every Washington politician's day. No one on a politician's staff is there to remind him or her that human vulnerabilities apply to everyone; a good staffer supports the politician in fair weather or foul. No one sits in the back seat of a town car with a politician and whispers, "Remember, thou art mortal," as Julius Caesar supposedly had a servant perched behind him on his chariot do. Politicians have full schedules and busy lives, and their support staffs are there to make their days flow as seamlessly and positively as possible, not to throw admonitions of human frailty after them.

The long days of Washington politicians and their staffers are spent rather in one primary pursuit: to preserve and extend the power they hold to accomplish what they and their constituencies expect of them. The longer they're in Washington, the more ingrained this behavior becomes. That's the way it is inside the Beltway, and in order to succeed there, everybody learns the rules of the game. The fact that the game includes a serious and debilitating addictive process is mostly unrecognized, especially by the players themselves.

The physiological and psychological process of addiction is increasingly well known to psychiatrists, psychologists, and neurologists. An addicted brain, regardless of its intelligence, is a changed brain. Addictive substances like alcohol, heroin, cocaine, and nicotine have recognizable effects on the pleasure centers of the brain, which become dependent on increased amounts and frequencies of those substances to function. The brain sends out powerful signals to repeat the pleasure-producing behaviors without consideration of future consequences or what values are important to a person.

Humans and many other species are hard-wired to adapt to and seek further pleasurable stimuli, since feelings of satiety and safety mean that nourishment is present, that danger is avoided, and that continuation of the species is assured.

The pleasure and pain mechanisms of the brain manage critical behaviors that perpetuate a species. Aggression is managed, while feeding and reproduction are rewarded. If these pleasure and pain elements—which operate on a simple "more" or "no more" basis—are unopposed, dangerous levels of conflict are likely as individuals struggle to gratify themselves at the expense of others.[4]

In a worst case scenario, the continuation of the species might be in jeopardy, as the elimination of too many in a population leads to eventual annihilation of the population itself.

Over millennia, human cultures have evolved structures like family and community to counter these primitive brain impulses towards pleasure and away from pain, but they always remain fixed and powerful underneath. They have to be; they're part of a basic biological survival strategy.

In all species of social animals, hierarchies of power develop naturally according to the physical and social abilities that make up the business of life. There are obvious advantages for an individual who is stronger, smarter, or quicker than average in any social group. Recent research has shown that high levels of what is described as "emotional intelligence" also provide a great deal of advantage in social situations.[5]

Unfortunately, neither intellectual nor emotional intelligence is of much help in combating demands from the pleasure/pain centers of an addicted brain. In fact, the more intelligent an addict, the more inventive and elaborate may be the lengths he goes to in order to get more of whatever it is he's addicted to.

Specialists in treating addiction are well aware of enhanced resistance to treatment in many highly intelligent patients. They are also aware that an alcoholic—or a heroin addict, or an amphetamine user—has permanently altered his or her brain by the physical process of addiction, and that the only tactic—there is no known cure—in these life-threatening addictions is abstinence coupled with social and professional support.

What does this have to do with politicians?

In general, politicians are ambitious, socially active strivers with moderate to high levels of intelligence, whose brains are uniquely and continually stimulated by their drug of choice: power.

There's a poignant accuracy in the old observation that it's possible to be "drunk on power." Interactive social activities between human beings, such as sex or politics, activate the same pleasure centers in the brain that addictive chemical substances stimulate. The same brain mechanism demands continued and increasing levels of the stimulus—in this case, political power. The privilege that comes along with political power provides additional sources of pleasure, such as fame, social position and increased access to other addictive substances (such as alcohol, drugs, and money). Politicians are continually plied with money and gifts for political favors, perpetuating their sense of power and importance as well as providing them a life of excitement and social and physical comfort.

The following chapters illustrate the dangerous toll that the unrecognized and untreated addiction to power in American politicians has taken on the national security of the United States—in one very specific case. The point of this book is to expose the toxic effect this addiction has had on the only force in American politics that can counter it: the rule of law.

In the U.S. government, one primary agency is chartered to enforce the law in opposition to political corruption: the FBI. For over three decades, politicians have sought to undermine the real threat the FBI presents to their power—and their addiction to that power—by doing what addicts always do to satisfy their cravings: eliminate the barriers that stand between them and their drug. In the case of Washington politicians, the FBI has long been the primary barrier to the corrupting influence of power.

CHAPTER TWO

RICHARD M. NIXON

From Watergate to 9/11

You can't trust the FBI.

Richard M. Nixon, 1972

. . . the FBI must be brought under brutal control.

Henry Kissinger[1]

In 1972, if you were crossing over the Potomac River on the Francis Scott Key Bridge, the Watergate glittered against the nighttime sky. The name of the luxury hotel had become synonymous with one of the most searing episodes in modern American history.

Both of us were attracted to the FBI that J. Edgar Hoover built. The FBI represented justice and the American way, a perfect fit for us kids who grew up in the early postwar 1950s, with our television heroes and safe and secure family neighborhoods. The Bureau had tackled bank robbery gangs in the thirties, Nazi spies in the forties, the Ku Klux Klan in the fifties, and the Mafia in the sixties. No one would have predicted that by the 1970s, the FBI would be pitted against the President of the United States.

Watergate defined the arrogance and abuse of power by those addicted to it during the Nixon Administration, from 1968 until the day Nixon resigned the presidency in August 1974. It has since become synonymous with political corruption of all sorts.

The eventual exposure of Watergate and its ruinous cover-up was enabled both by irrefutable evidence (the White House Watergate tapes) and the successful enforcement of the law as a result of an FBI investigation and the subsequent indictment and conviction of a number of the conspirators.

For most Americans, Watergate is distant history. In an ABC News Poll taken on June 17, 2002, 65 percent of those asked said they didn't know enough about Watergate to tell the basic facts to someone else.

The greatest number of Americans who do know something of Watergate got their information from a best-selling book that became a popular and thrilling movie about two *Washington Post* reporters named Bob Woodward and Carl Bernstein, whose inside source "Deep Throat" led them to information that toppled a president and *All the President's Men*.[2]

Bob Woodward had promised never to reveal the identity of Deep Throat. By 2005, however, the family of former FBI Associate Director W. Mark Felt finally disclosed that Felt was the mysterious source.

Although the FBI literally played a mere supporting role in the famous movie, the real story of the Watergate investigation illustrates the deliberate and even desperate lengths that powerful politicians went to in trying to control and even subvert the Bureau in order to preserve their hold on power.

When Director Hoover died suddenly in May 1972, President Nixon named L. Patrick Gray as Acting FBI Director. For the first time since Hoover's appointment to the obscure Bureau of Investigation in 1924, a president had the chance to put his own man in control of an organization that had proven to be a thorn in the sides of politicians for nearly half a century. Gray was a Naval Academy graduate and an officer of the line during World War II and the Korean War. He graduated from the George Washington School of Law and went to work in the Nixon Administration, eventually becoming the Assistant Attorney General in the Civil Division of the Department of Justice.

On the surface, the FBI appeared to be adjusting to the long-time director's sudden death. Some things changed overnight. Stylish colored dress shirts were breaking out across headquarters and at the Washington Field Office. The serious expressions that Bureau employees wore were now occasionally interspersed with smiles, sometimes even laughter.

Gray appointed Mark Felt as the FBI's Associate Director, the number two spot in the Bureau hierarchy. Felt was the most recognizable of the FBI's top leaders with his impressive looks, movie-star-thick silver hair, and expensive-looking dark blue suits with faint white pin stripes. He was tall, and he always stood erect.

The FBI had every reason to be optimistic about its future, even as storm clouds swirled around the White House.

Hoover's death and the prospect that the party in power could take hold of the FBI must have seemed like a godsend to the president and his men. President Nixon was just the latest Commander in Chief who'd been frustrated by FBI Director Hoover, whose reputed "secret files" on the rich and powerful in Washington had long insured his own as well as the Bureau's independence from political control.

Nixon had a specific bone to pick with the FBI. In 1970, he had met with Hoover and the directors of the CIA and NSA to form a committee to evaluate domestic intelligence operations.

Massive demonstrations and violence tore at the fabric of American society in the late 1960s, and halfway through his first administration Nixon anticipated more of the same. Hundreds of thousands of anti-Vietnam War protesters took to the streets in Boston, New York, San Francisco, and Washington, D.C., shouting slogans, blocking traffic, and crashing police barricades. Splinter groups of the anti-war movement became the domestic terrorists of their day, attacking police stations with improvised explosive devices and setting fires at universities and corporations supporting the war effort.

With the government stunned and put on the defensive by political unrest, and law enforcement overwhelmed by the unprecedented level of violence on American streets, both did a poor job at drawing a distinction between legitimate protest and domestic terrorism.

Within months of President Nixon's inauguration in 1969, his attorney general (and former campaign manager) John Mitchell had concluded that the president had the power to order wiretaps without court supervision of domestic groups seeking to "attack and subvert" the government.

Nixon subsequently approved a plan drafted by a political loyalist named Tom Huston that outlined extensive activities to disrupt domestic groups and enhance the gathering of domestic intelligence. The "Huston Plan" permitted surreptitious entries, covert mail coverage, and a variety of other invasive activities directed at American citizens.

But Director Hoover decided the FBI wouldn't play.

Nixon turned to White House Counsel John Dean to convince Hoover the Bureau should join the Huston Plan. In the end, Dean could never get past Hoover's number three man at the Bureau, Mark Felt.

In his book *Blind Ambition*, John Dean describes the Nixon Administration's frustration with Hoover and the FBI:

> *The President, I discovered, had ordered removal of most of the legal restraints on gathering intelligence about left-wing groups. He had authorized wiretaps, mail*

intercepts and burglaries. These were the hottest papers I had ever touched. The plan had the full support of the Central Intelligence Agency, the Defense Intelligence Agency, the National Security Council—of everyone except Hoover's FBI. Hoover had footnoted the document with an objection that the risk of each illegal method was greater than the potential return.

Tom Huston came to brief me. With rabid conviction, he told me the nation would surely crumble from within if the government failed to deal with the revolutionaries and anarchists who were bent on destroying it. He was incensed that the President's orders could be blocked by Hoover merely because Hoover 'wanted to ride out of the FBI on a white horse.'

Now, however, the Nixon Administration had an opportunity to bring the investigative power of the FBI under its own control. It couldn't have come at a more opportune time, since they needed all the cover they could get. They were sitting on a political powder keg that was becoming known as Watergate.

In mid-1971 *The New York Times* began publishing the "Pentagon Papers." Alarmed by leaks of classified information pertaining to his Vietnam War strategy, Nixon established a group from within the White House to identify those responsible. The group became known as the "Plumbers," and included G. Gordon Liddy, a staff member of the Finance Committee to Re-Elect the President (CREEP), and E. Howard Hunt, a former CIA employee and White House consultant. They were supervised directly by John Ehrlichman, assistant to the president for domestic affairs.

After the leaks were traced to Rand Corporation analyst Daniel Ellsberg, the Plumbers identified Ellsberg's Los Angeles psychiatrist, Louis Fielding. They burglarized Fielding's office, hoping to find information linking Ellsberg to the New Left anti-war movement. The Republican Party planned to use the information to launch a Congressional investigation of domestic groups opposed to the war, with the ultimate goal of linking those groups to their opponents in the Democratic Party.

The key to the Plumbers' success was absolute loyalty.[3] There could be no chance that the covert operations performed on behalf of the White House would become public.

Their service to the Nixon administration's pursuit of power is a classic illustration of the ease with which party loyalists entranced by their connections to power can be blinded to the boundaries of civil and even legal behavior:

> *The figures caught up in the drama–from the plumbers to the president's top advisers—acted on a combination of explicit orders from the president, or what his aides thought the president wanted or what the lower level operatives thought the president or his aides wanted.*[4]

In June 1972, the Washington Metropolitan Police Department arrested five men for burglarizing the headquarters office of the Democratic National Committee at the Watergate Hotel. Seven men were eventually implicated in the burglary. They included Liddy and Hunt as well as James W. McCord, the security coordinator for CREEP; Eugenio R. Martinez, who was receiving a $100 per month retainer from the CIA; Virgilio R. Gonzalez; and an attorney, Frank Sturgis. Another of the burglars, Bernard Barker, the owner of a real estate firm, had $25,000 with him at the time of his arrest.

The FBI traced the money to a Mexican bank and determined it had been contributed to CREEP by Dwayne Andreas, chairman of the board of First Inter-Oceanic Corporation—later Archer Daniels Midland Corporation, or ADM. The men had failed at an earlier burglary attempt and succeeded at a second where they installed wiretaps and took photographs. None other than the deputy director of the CIA provided former CIA employee Hunt with a false identity (the name Edward Warren), a wig, glasses, and a speech-altering device to facilitate the burglaries.

Nixon's legal counsel, John Dean, his chief of staff, H. R. "Bob" Haldeman, and John Ehrlichman handled the administration's response to Watergate. Their strategy was to keep the role of Nixon loyalists from both law enforcement and the media.

By the 1972 presidential election in November, the Watergate burglary had captured little of the nation's attention. With little initial information to capitalize on, Democrats tried to make the burglary an issue, hinting at the involvement of highly placed Republican officials. It didn't work. On Election Day, President Nixon carried 49 states, capturing 520 electoral votes and 61 percent of the popular vote to win re-election against his Democratic opponent, anti-war candidate Senator George McGovern.

The victory further enhanced the addiction to power of the president as well as the staff that surrounded him. They believed strongly that their own power and influence had been recognized and approved by a vast majority of Americans. And—after the convictions of six of the Watergate burglars in early 1973—they were furious that the FBI had turned its attention to campaign financing irregularities involving people in the White House.

The Senate Select Committee on Presidential Campaign Activities, headed by Senator Sam Ervin of North Carolina, began hearings on the matter. *The Washington Post* ran daily stories following trails of money, corruption, and cover-ups. *Post* reporters Carl Bernstein and Bob Woodward were assisted by a mysterious source they called "Deep Throat," who seemed to know a great deal about everyone involved in the investigation, and who encouraged them to "follow the money" to the ultimate revelation that the highest levels of the Nixon administration were complicit in the Watergate cover-up.

With the combination of intense investigative activity and public scrutiny, the dam had begun to break. John Dean decided to call on the man the Nixon White House had placed at the head of the FBI itself to assist in the cover-up.

But by April 1973, L. Patrick Gray resigned as FBI director after admitting that he had destroyed evidence related to Watergate on behalf of the White House.

Gray had little choice. He was facing a growing rebellion from within the Bureau, and the rumbling from FBI agents on the street was growing louder as they repeatedly ran into stumbling blocks thrown in their path by a White House that was intent on disrupting the Watergate investigation.

Unknown to anyone but *Post* reporter Bob Woodward at the time, Gray's complicity in the Watergate scandal on behalf of the administration had caused Gray's number two man, Associate Director Mark Felt, to personally overcome the burden of loyalty he'd given the director of the FBI for an entire career to prevent the Bureau, as an institution, from being involved in the scandal.

Gray had been providing FBI 302(s) or interview results from the FBI's investigation to John Dean. Dean decided to give Gray the contents of Howard Hunt's White House safe, which contained information that detailed administration spying on the Democrats. In his book *Blind Ambition*, Dean expressed great satisfaction in the manner in which he manipulated Gray into destroying Hunt's incriminating documents:

> *When Ehrlichman suggested I 'deep six' the sensitive materials from Hunt's safe by throwing them into the Potomac River . . . I came up with what I thought was a*

clever idea—to give the documents directly to L. Patrick Gray III . . . by this ruse, we could say we turned all evidence over to the FBI, and literally it would be true.

In February 1973, Gray tried to explain to the Senate Judiciary Committee how he had been persuaded by White House Counsel John Dean to destroy FBI documents implicating the Nixon White House in the Watergate cover-up. His feeble and confused words were striking evidence of the corrupting influence of power, and the unhappy fact that those in power, or influenced by people in power, are never wholly trustworthy:

You know, when you are dealing closely with the office of the presidency, the presumption is one of regularity on the conduct of the nation's business, and I didn't even engage in the thought process that would set up a presumption here of illegality and I didn't consider it.[5]

After Gray's resignation, Dean told the president that there was "really no control" the White House could impose on the FBI at that point. They decided to declare the events related to the Watergate break-in a national security matter, and arranged to solicit help from the CIA in containing the fallout and reining in the FBI.

On May 30, 1973, John Ehrlichman told the Senate Appropriations Subcommittee that President Nixon ordered him and Bob Haldeman to direct the CIA to let the FBI know that its Watergate investigation would interfere with ongoing agency activities important to national security.[6]

Nixon and his men were confident that the CIA could be relied on to support them in thwarting the FBI by providing false information, just as they had used Gray's political loyalty to corrupt his position as FBI director. The White House transcripts clearly show that the main worry on the part of Nixon and his executive staff was the FBI itself. The Bureau was too independent and was pursuing an investigation that was out of their political control and threatened to ruin them all.[7]

When the FBI investigation of Watergate pushed forward after Gray's resignation, Dean testified before the Ervin Committee that President Nixon was involved in the cover-up. It was his word against the president's, and Nixon made repeated assurances to the American public that he "took no part in, and was not aware of, any subsequent efforts to cover up the illegal acts associated with the Watergate break-in." The White House tape recordings showed otherwise; and in August 1974, President Nixon resigned.

In his book, *The Ends of Power*, H. R. Haldeman confirmed, "The President was involved in the cover-up from Day One, although neither he nor we considered it a cover-up at that time."

Many of the people who inhabited the political jungles of Washington, D.C., during the Watergate era are in powerful positions today. Some star on talk shows; others are regular contributors to entertainment news, delivering carefully scripted sound bites designed to proffer one agenda or the other. Even "hard news" channels have become corrupted by their desire to attract these long-famous big political names to bolster ratings. Both Democrats and Republicans have now mastered the manipulation of the public through media outlets, where truth is what they spin it to be. They push the same agendas and hold the same grudges they have for nearly four decades.

In their quest for power and influence, they foster the inevitable bad behavior and illegal conduct that develop and eventually attract the attention of the FBI. The pattern etched into the DNA of the nation during Watergate then repeats itself, and the Bureau is attacked by politicians on both sides who recognize it as the most overwhelming threat to their addictive need for power.

The parallel trails of power, corruption, and deceit walked by a succession of American political leaders that began with Watergate have persisted ever since. The same trails led directly to the flawed decision making and pursuit of political power over the needs of national security that enabled the successful terrorist attacks of 9/11. Many of the same people who were mentored in the Nixon White House now advise President George W. Bush in his strategy for a "War on Terror." The distaste for FBI involvement in national security matters that they acquired during the Watergate years has made them increasingly inclined to turn to their political allies in the CIA rather than to a Bureau that is chartered to operate—independent of politics—under the restrictions of constitutional law.

The scope of the Watergate investigation went far beyond the original burglary. American Airlines, Goodyear Tire and Rubber, Minnesota Mining and Manufacturing, Braniff Airways, Ashland Petroleum, Gabon Inc., Diamond International, Lehigh Valley Cooperative Farmers, Gulf Oil, Phillips Petroleum, Carnation Company, and Northrop Corporation were just a few of the well-known corporations that admitted to illegally contributing to Nixon's re-election. Chief executive officers of 12 of the corporations pled guilty instead of going to trial.

By mid-1974, 17 people, including members of the White House staff, either pled or were found guilty of obstructing justice and lying to the FBI. They included John Dean, H. R. Haldeman, John Ehrlichman, and two attorneys general, John Mitchell and Richard Kleindienst. Vice President Spiro Agnew, who resigned his office, was eventually convicted on corruption charges.

But the FBI also sustained serious damage from Watergate and its aftermath. Historical accounts of the FBI's role in the Watergate affair have been conspicuously inaccurate. Because of the movie *All the President's Men*, the majority of Americans who do know something about Watergate believe that the

Watergate convictions were the result of courageous actions by two aggressive reporters from *The Washington Post*. In fact, several factors contributed to bringing down the Nixon Administration. *The Washington Post* kept the public pressure on, buoyed by the relationship Bob Woodward had with the secret source "Deep Throat." Meanwhile, the FBI's criminal investigations spanned the nation and the world and were the most complex and trail-blazing of their time. The Watergate tape recordings, recorded inside the White House itself, acted like hidden wiretaps in an organized crime investigation. Together, all of these avenues converged to expose the damage the Nixon White House did to the nation in the arrogant pursuit of the drug of power.

As FBI agents, it was always painful for us to see references to the supposed complicity of the FBI itself in the Watergate scandal. This falsehood is everywhere. Encyclopedia.com asserts that:

> *. . . during the Watergate affair, it was revealed that the FBI had yielded to pressure from top White House officials, acting on behalf of President Richard M. Nixon to halt their investigation of the Watergate break-in.*

In fact, the FBI did not yield to White House pressure, and FBI agents across the country aggressively developed the evidence that would lead to the end of the Nixon administration and bring indictments and convictions to dozens of his loyal political advisers. Nixon's loyal men and the president himself had tried to control the FBI through the appointment of L. Patrick Gray, a Republican "loyalist" in the Department of Justice before he became Nixon's choice for FBI director. Gray indeed disgraced himself by his actions, but career FBI agents like Mark Felt had already recognized that Gray was a political ally of the Nixon administration and therefore unreliable as director.

For 36 years, official Washington played a guessing game as to the identity of "Deep Throat." In the book and movie version of *All the President's Men*, the source was portrayed as a shadowy hero. On every anniversary of Watergate, the speculation began anew. Numerous politicians close to the case were mentioned as possible "Deep Throat" candidates. The consistent implication of this long guessing game was that "Deep Throat" had played a major role in revealing the corruption, crime, and lawlessness of the Nixon presidency.

On May 31, 2005, Mark Felt ended the speculation when his family identified him as "Deep Throat." It had been the FBI's number two man who had helped the Bureau break the noose being wrapped around it by a desperate White House.

President Nixon was forced to leave the White House because of Watergate, but many Republican loyalists influenced and seasoned by the Nixon Administration continued their quest for power. They have never forgotten the critical failure of the Nixon administration to "control" the FBI investigation of Watergate.

Nixon stalwarts from the Watergate era were not kind in their reactions to the identification of Mark Felt as "Deep Throat." Henry Kissinger told Fox News:

> *Hero is not the first word that comes to my mind. I view him as a troubled man. I don't think it's heroic to act as a spy on your president when you're in high office. I could fully understand if he resigned . . . or if he went to the prosecutor. That would be heroic.*

The prosecutor Kissinger suggests Felt should have gone to would have been Attorney General John Mitchell. Mitchell was, of course, also involved in the White House cover-up.

General Alexander Haig was a Nixon staffer and subsequently became the secretary of state for President Ronald Reagan. Hearing the news about Felt, Haig told Fox News:

I don't think I would categorize him as a hero in any way. I live by a code that if you work for a president, you stay loyal to that president and if you can't for whatever reasons, then you have the obligation to resign and take whatever steps necessary in your power.

General Haig missed a critical detail. Felt didn't work for the president. He worked for an FBI that was sworn to uphold the United States Constitution and was seeing its independence in doing that eroded by an outlaw administration. Haig's follow-up comments to the press confirm his dismissal of the FBI's role in Watergate:

I think we're always tempted when these things happen to overblow the importance of Deep Throat in the overall outcome of Watergate. It's very important to remember it was the tapes that finally turned the country against the president and that was the real death blow to Richard Nixon, but it was politics that brought us there.

Haig was almost right. The real death blow to President Nixon and all of those who helped him subvert the United States government was their pursuit of power through corruption of the political process. Misplaced loyalties, arrogance, and a self-righteous attitude that the law did not apply to the White House contributed to Nixon's unraveling. The members of his staff who saw the coming tragedy and failed to speak up were all equally to blame. Like Kissinger, Haig appears to have learned very little in all of these years about the connection between power and corruption, arrogance and loyalty, and the potential ethical poison of long-standing political relationships.

President Gerald Ford received widespread acclaim for his pardon of President Nixon. Many believe that his decision helped the country move beyond Watergate and recover from the divisiveness it created. More than three decades later, however, the country hasn't recovered, and the pardon buried forever the opportunity to gather all the facts and return transparency to government.

Even worse, the pardon solidified the message that the powerful can engage in bad behavior and illegal acts and get away with it. It is this message that has set the tone for the conduct of both political parties ever since, inspiring continued bad behavior by politicians and consequently a spiraling distrust of government in America.

Lessons learned by Republican loyalists during Watergate paved the way for the lies and obstruction that characterized the Iran Contra scandal in the Reagan administration. By 1992, outgoing President George H.W. Bush pardoned Secretary of Defense Casper Weinburger, Lt. Colonel Oliver North, and three other Reagan administration loyalists who were indicted and/or convicted for their involvement in the Iran Contra scandal.

The FBI that investigated the Watergate scandal as well as Iran Contra for Special Prosecutor Walsh made bitter enemies within the Republican Party as a result. Party loyalists in power during the Republican administrations of the 1970s and 1980s are still bitter today. In their actions in service of their own addiction to power, Democrats would also find reasons to distrust and attempt to control the Bureau. The primary grievance for both is that the FBI presents the major obstacle to their quest for increased power.

Politicians and staffers implicated in and influenced by Watergate moved on with confidence that American memories of it would be short. Currently, former Nixon staffer Pat Buchanan speaks authoritatively on the Fox News Network, fear mongering about the plague that will hit America if we ever again elect a Democrat to the White House. G. Gordon Liddy has been out of jail for many years but still makes guest appearances on talk shows and radio stations. John Dean writes book after book about how bad Republicans in general—and the George W. Bush White House in particular—are, continuously trying to rewrite his own legacy of corruption. Nixon loyalists Dick Cheney and his close colleague, Donald Rumsfeld, respectively became vice president and secretary of defense for President George W. Bush.

Both Cheney and Rumsfeld carried with them decades of deep distrust of the FBI that set the stage for future conflict with the Bureau when history put them in charge of the nation when it was hit by the 9/11 terrorist attacks. They and their fellow politicians have used 9/11 as an opportunity to turn the public's grief into fear and blame. In using the tragedy to their political advantage, they are attempting to restructure the FBI's national security mission so that it will be forever under partisan political control. Failing that, they are proving forceful in their efforts to take responsibility for U.S. national security away from the FBI and to put it increasingly under the control of their longtime political ally: the CIA.

Chapter Three

FRANK CHURCH

Paving the Road to 9/11

I am satisfied that there was every reason in the world for the FBI to be investigating [Rev. Martin Luther] King . . . Of course, I want none of this talked about. None of this is to leave this room.

Senator Frank Church[1]

Watergate had fixed a national spotlight on domestic spying. Americans were tired of the war in Vietnam and what it had done to the country and repulsed by revelations of the despicable activities engaged in by their political leadership. Although several high-ranking Nixon administration officials had gone to prison for their involvement in the scandal, President Gerald Ford had pardoned President Nixon. The media was primed to move the spotlight further into the mechanisms of the executive branch of government, and the Democratic Party was spurred to grab maximum advantage and political power from Republicans in disgrace.

In January 1975, the Senate established an 11-member investigating body under Frank Church, a Democratic senator from Idaho, to look at allegations of unlawful conduct by U.S. intelligence agencies, including the CIA, NSA, and the FBI. Officially titled the "Select Committee to Study Governmental

Operations with Respect to Intelligence Activities," it was the forerunner for today's U.S. Senate Select Committee on Intelligence, which sits in oversight of the FBI.

Senator Church was eager to step into the breach. He was a respected, long-standing member of the Senate, who had battled cancer early in his life. With presidential aspirations leading to the 1976 elections, Church had every reason to believe that his chairmanship of the hearings, conducted in the post-Watergate environment, would attract significant attention and firm up his base of voters in a bid for the presidency.

The new FBI director, Clarence Kelley, had a stellar career in the FBI before and after military service in WWII. After his retirement from the FBI in 1961, he became chief of police in Kansas City, Missouri. In sharp contrast to the political functionary Gray had been, Kelley was a highly respected law enforcement professional.

After noting that the Bureau's Counterintelligence Program (COINTELPRO) had been ramped up by "additional effort" to address the violent actions of the New Left/Revolutionary movement in the 1960s, Kelley released a large number of previously classified documents concerning those efforts to the Church Committee.[2]

But by the time the Church Committee completed its investigation of intelligence community abuses, it had done more damage to the national security of the United States than the intelligence services of the Soviet Union or the People's Republic of China could ever have aspired to.

The Church Committee revealed the methods America's intelligence agencies used to counter the activities of people and countries that would do the nation harm. It published 14 reports on topics such as covert actions, mail openings, and other undercover activities of the FBI, IRS, NSA, and CIA.

Senator Church called America's intelligence agencies "rogue elephants."

He wrote that a dictator could use the National Security Agency (NSA) to "make tyranny total in America." Referring to the FBI's COINTELPRO, which had been aimed at disrupting the activities of radical domestic organizations, Church said:

> *The American people need to be reassured that never again will an agency of government be permitted to conduct a secret war against those citizens it considers a threat to the established order.*

Church and his committee saved their most damning criticism of the FBI for its investigation of the Reverend Dr. Martin Luther King. As a result, many Americans believe that the late FBI director, J. Edgar Hoover, had a vendetta against Dr. King and used the Bureau to harass him without cause.

The truth of this matter has become so convoluted that even significant policy decisions affecting today's terror war are being made against the backdrop of misinformation related to the investigation of Dr. King.

In reality, the FBI never opened a file on the civil rights leader in order to discredit him and his objectives.

The file was opened in the early 1960s to investigate the reasons for the intense interest in King developed by the American Communist Party (CPUSA) and King's close relationship with CPUSA functionaries Stanley Levison and Hunter Pitts O'Dell.

Both Levison and O'Dell had been cultivating King for years on behalf of the CPUSA, which saw an advantage in assigning "outstanding party members to work with the [Martin Luther] King group, and . . . to concentrate upon Martin Luther King."[3]

This information had a distinguished pedigree, coming as it did from a long secret and closely held FBI intelligence operation: Operation SOLO.

Assertions from politicians, the 9/11 Commission, the media, and academia that the FBI's law enforcement "culture" makes it incapable of its intelligence mission are utter non-sense. Most Americans don't know it, but with Operation SOLO, the FBI ran the most highly placed intelligence sources ever developed against the Soviet Union.

For several decades, because of Operation SOLO, American presidents were privy to the innermost thoughts of Soviet leaders. Although information from the sources was disseminated urgently, only a handful of people within the FBI ever knew the identities of these prized assets. Their work provides the real backdrop for the FBI's intense interest in Dr. King, and also explains how, despite intense effort and extensive funding by the U.S.S.R., the Bureau neutralized the Communist Party of the United States.

Over many years, KGB agents traveled to the United States for one specific purpose: to hold clandestine meetings with the president of the American Communist Party, Gus Hall.

Hall was invariably accompanied by his wife, Elizabeth, known as Liz. They lived in a two-story house in Westchester County, an hour's drive north of New York City. Each morning during the week, Hall was driven to his office in the Chelsea District of Manhattan where he worked a full day before heading home in the evening. Gus and Liz looked like everyone's healthy grandparents. On weekends they left their comfortable suburban house to buy fresh fruits and vegetables at a local farmer's market. No one would have suspected them to be any different than a hundred other families, but they were.

When he arrived at his office, Gus Hall directed the political and fund raising activities of the Communist Party of the United States (CPUSA) in his role as general chairman. Liz played an important role as his aide and confidant. Hall ran for president of the United States in every election between 1950 and the fall of the Soviet Union, with Liz as his potential "first lady." They made repeated trips to Russia, meeting with the ruling elite, and were treated as Soviet heroes.

Accordingly, and unlike with most grandparents, FBI agents assigned to the New York Office followed Gus and Liz everywhere they went. Their every move was watched because they were known agents of a foreign power hostile to the interests of the United States. Their trips to the Soviet Union, his run for president in each American election, their salaries for showing up each day to work at an office in an expensive area of Manhattan, and the fruits and vegetables Liz found at the market on weekends were all bought and paid for by money funneled to them by agents of the KGB. Money that was intended for use to bolster the recruitment drives of CPUSA often made its way to the pockets of Gus and Liz. At almost the same time the Soviet Union collapsed, a carpenter working on repairs in their Westchester house placed his hands in a darkened area above an attic door and watched as hundreds of dollars fell to the floor below. He discreetly left the house and called the FBI, which had long known that during all of the years Gus and Liz were fighting for the rights of the working class, they were stuffing money from the KGB into hiding spaces in their attic.

Hall and his CPUSA were the focal point of a massive Soviet intelligence operation to identify and recruit American citizens who had the potential to become influential in their business, church, union, or government employment. Setting up chapters throughout the country, the reach of the Soviet Union extended steadily as the KGB patiently developed Americans who would be able to cultivate public opinion and support causes in the interests of the Soviet government.

The KGB referred to this work as part of the "Political Branch" aimed at fashioning public opinion through a variety of clandestine means and the recruitment of agents of influence. Such a network of dedicated servants would be in a position to organize and coordinate anti-war protests, elect sympathizers to political office, and spot people with sensitive or classified access to military secrets who were worthy of cultivation.

CPUSA was the front line in the KGB's war inside America, and the FBI knew it.

However, unbeknown to the KGB, with Operation SOLO the Bureau already had penetrated CPUSA and was deeply involved in gathering critical intelligence about the internal politics and personalities of the Soviet Union itself.

Morris Childs was an idealistic young American communist who traveled to Moscow in 1929 to study revolutionary tactics at the Lenin School. He subsequently became leader of the Wisconsin branch of the American Communist Party and later headed the Chicago chapter of CPUSA.

After WWII, Morris again visited Moscow, but this time he was confronted by a very different reality. The U.S.S.R. was under the brutal regime of Joseph Stalin, and government repression of citizens was coupled with rampant corruption and anti-semitism. Disillusioned, Morris returned to the United States and volunteered along with his brother, Jack, to help the FBI in its investigation of CPUSA. Operation SOLO began.

By the late 1950s, the FBI had redirected the intelligence objective of Operation SOLO from CPUSA to the Soviet Union itself. Morris made over 50 trips to the U.S.S.R. and the Soviet Bloc, often meeting with the top Soviet leadership. For years, the Childs provided invaluable information about the inner workings and perspectives of the Soviet Union and its allies.

The FBI had morphed from the crime-fighting, gang-busting agency of the 1930s and the Nazi-hunting organization of the 1940s into a domestic security agency focused on the Soviet threat to U.S. national security. Inside the United States, the Bureau illustrated to successive presidents and Congress the threat posed by the ostensibly ideological CPUSA.

Funded by the Soviets who used KGB officers as bagmen, CPUSA was a closed society in need of penetration and disruption. The FBI took the job. Congress approved budget after budget and listened year after year as Director Hoover outlined the threat and the activities of the Bureau in dealing effectively with it.

Presidents and members of Congress, regardless of their party affiliations, joined in the declaration that the gravest threat to the national security of the United States was the Soviet brand of communism on the rise throughout the world. The proof did not have to come from FBI files. At the time, all anyone had to do was look at a world map.

The Iron Curtain separated the people of East and West Germany. Many of the nations of Europe suffered under the rule of the Soviet bloc. The Soviets influenced the Chinese government on their road to the Maoist brand of communism, and for a time the two nations appeared united in their commitment to defeat America.

The Soviets used the KGB to fund movements inside Latin America, taking advantage of years of poverty coupled with abuse and neglect from the United States, as well as the aspirations and the frailties of human nature. They realized early on that some Latin leaders who would be well-suited to masquerading as revolutionaries were in reality most effectively motivated by money and power. Cuba turned into an important and valuable military and economic ally of the Soviet Union, situated only 90 miles from Florida's tip.

President John F. Kennedy rallied the nation against the communist threat in his inaugural address, just minutes into his presidency. President Lyndon Johnson declared the war in Vietnam as critical to America's response to the spread of communism. President Nixon, first as a United States congressman and then as president, was a consistent opponent of communism, both inside and outside government.

Although there were few pieces of legislation designed to address the unique challenge faced from KGB political branch activities as opposed to the outright theft of classified information, the government was united in its response to a well-defined, universally accepted threat. No one in power in Washington was ignorant of what was going on, and that the FBI was dealing with the threat.

By 1961, the FBI alerted the new president and his attorney general that noted civil rights leader Martin Luther King was being secretly developed as an asset by two secret CPUSA members who had become his personal confidants and advisors: Hunter Pitts O'Dell and Stanley Levison. John F. Kennedy and his brother Robert were alarmed, and they spoke personally to King about the real sponsors of his relationship with Levison and O'Dell. Nevertheless, King continued his association with them.[4]

In the turbulent 1960s and early 1970s, as the nation was rocked by massive anti-war protests that turned to violent demonstrations and civil disobedience of an unprecedented nature, many in government believed that the same money funneled to the United States to support CPUSA and Soviet-style communist causes was supporting the violent protests. Domestic intelligence gathering and "domestic spying" took on a new and urgent meaning.

During the Watergate hearings, government officials had been hauled before the media as well as the investigative committee, and more and more information previously protected in classified files was being leaked to the press. Operation SOLO principals Morris and Jack Childs were justifiably worried about their personal safety. They were reassured that the security of Operation SOLO was the highest priority in the FBI.

Now, in the aftermath of Watergate, the Church Committee had demanded complete FBI files on 50 different subjects, including the one on Dr. King. Operation SOLO was in grave danger of compromise in the turmoil of the political backlash to Nixon's abuse of his own power and the unlawful actions of his staff. The complete King file would reveal that the FBI had penetrated the innermost sanctum of the American Communist

Party, that it was monitoring secret messages transmitted by the KGB to the party, and that it had a direct source of intelligence about the leadership of the Soviet Union.

FBI Director Kelley realized that he would have to authorize a briefing on SOLO to illustrate the critical sensitivity of the operation to Frank Church himself. FBI Assistant Director Ray Wannall requested a meeting with Church and his staff. In closed session, Wannall told Church that he was about to destroy the most important espionage operation the U.S. had ever directed against the Soviet Union, and that he was also about to kill the most valuable American spy. John Barron writes:

> *Visibly shocked, Senator Church asked, 'Can you explain?'*[5]

For nearly two hours Church and his staff were told the story of Operation SOLO and shown photographs of Morris Childs (neither he nor his brother were ever identified by name) with Soviet Premier Brezhnev and members of the Politburo. Wannall explained why the deliveries of Soviet money by the FBI assets (the Childs) to CPUSA had to continue, and he reiterated the facts that had caused the Kennedys to order the investigation of Martin Luther King for his continued association with the Soviet agents Levison and O'Dell. Barron describes the scene:

> *Church sank into his chair. 'You have put a terrible burden on me.'*
>
> *Wannall said, 'Yes. We are betting everything on your honor and patriotism.'*
>
> *Church thought for a while, then said, 'I only wish the American people could know. This certainly would open their eyes. It has opened mine . . .'*

Church pronounced the official verdict in two words:
'I approve.' He added, 'I am satisfied that there was every
reason in the world for the FBI to be investigating King'
(he later made the same statement to the entire commit-
tee). 'Of course, I want none of this talked about. None of
this is to leave this room.'⁶

In the end, however, despite substantial evidence that the
domestic intelligence activities of the FBI were known to,
approved by, and clearly understood by the leaders of both
major political parties, and that the King investigation was
linked to a much wider intelligence operation that had long provided critical knowledge of the Soviet Union's internal plans
and workings, the Church Committee fixed blame on the FBI
for "lawless and improper behavior."

In Book II of the Committee's conclusions, selective language allowed Republican and Democratic Party politicians to
claim they were unaware of the Bureau's measures to combat
domestic terrorism and lawlessness in the streets of America.

Senator Church had been provided with highly sensitive
information at the time that was known to only a handful of
people in government. Knowing that he possessed this information and still allowed his Committee to produce a false report on
the predication of the Bureau's interest in King severely undermined the integrity of his Committee and confirmed that his
motives were rooted far more in politics than in a concern for
the rule of law.

In the end, the prospect of Church attaining the office of
president himself made increasing his own political power and
position far more irresistible an objective than acknowledging
that the FBI investigation of King was based on information
from sensitive sources related to national security. Church
would not have been able to discuss publicly the reasons justifying the file on King, and so he chose to ignore what he couldn't

capitalize on for his own political gain. In fact, findings that incorrectly characterized the FBI investigation as a personal vendetta that attacked King's civil rights were highly useful for Church's image as a champion of civil liberties as a post-Watergate presidential candidate.

As the Church Committee hearings raged on, scoring more power for the Democrats (and for Senator Church) with each passing day, President Gerald Ford tried to stem the tide of public disclosures of classified information related to years of intelligence activity.

When the Church Committee issued a call to Acting CIA Director William Colby to testify, several of President Ford's top advisers, including Henry Kissinger and Donald Rumsfeld from the Nixon days, intervened in an effort to protect information important to the national security from being disclosed. Church would have none of it. President Nixon had tried to misuse and abuse government agencies to weaken the Democratic Party, and now the Democratic Party would try to destroy the image of those agencies with the American public both to get even and to secure its own political power.

The Church Committee produced thousands of pages of documents collected in 14 separate reports. They concluded that the FBI had illegally spied on American citizens, including Dr. Martin Luther King. J. Edgar Hoover was branded as responsible for the vendetta and harassment of Dr. King, as if the FBI's activities had been conducted entirely in the dark and independent of the knowledge of either the United States Department of Justice or a long succession of congressional committees.

The Church committee reports published in 1975 were received with great acclaim by the media and politicians from both parties, who had themselves dodged the bullet for their complicity in sending U.S. Intelligence Agencies on missions they now disavowed.

At the peak of his own political power, Senator Frank Church sought the 1976 Democratic nomination for president. He won primaries in Nebraska, Idaho, Oregon, and Montana, ultimately withdrawing in favor of former Georgia governor Jimmy Carter, who considered naming Church his running mate. Carter chose Minnesota Senator Walter Mondale instead, and Church was eventually narrowly defeated for re-election in Idaho in 1980. He died in 1984 of cancer, at age 59.

The political turbulence that prevailed during Frank Church's turn on the national stage propelled him into a prominent and powerful position, and put the brass ring of the U.S. presidency within his realistic grasp. Taking a more measured view of COINTELPRO and other intelligence operations, and remembering his acknowledgment of the implications of real-world endeavors like Operation SOLO, would not have put him on the road to a presidential run. He grabbed at the ring and the national spotlight when he saw his opportunity, regardless of the consequences to national security.

In effect, the Church Committee began the process of changing the rules of the road for intelligence gathering. Their conclusions were based on information they cherry-picked to support their positions, correspondingly inaccurate analysis, and a lack of understanding of real threats to national security that faced America at the time. Day after day, high-ranking Bureau officials were made to look as if they didn't care about civil liberties and were willing to stampede over the rights of Americans in the quest to counter illusory threats to national security.

The hearings did little to place the FBI's actions in context with the times in which they occurred, and made even less effort to acknowledge the prominent role that both the legislative and executive branches of government had played in demanding those FBI actions. Every effort was made to blame intelligence agencies for overstepping their legal authority in their defense of America while insulating both parties from the fallout.

In the aftermath of the hearings, two high ranking FBI officials, Mark Felt and Edward Miller, who had signed off on COINTELPRO activities aimed at disrupting the ability of groups and individuals to commit violence and to provide information to hostile intelligence services, were themselves indicted and then convicted of violating the civil liberties of American citizens.

Felt, Miller, and the FBI were caught in the middle of the struggle for power between Democrats and Republicans. One party, wounded by its conduct and commission of felonies during Watergate was pitted against the other, determined to gain power by appeasing thousands of citizens who would vote for Democrats if they perceived the possibility that they could change the country at the polls. The question of what was good for the country was not the issue; the issue was securing partisan political power.

Three critical results that issued from the Church Committee's conclusions about domestic spying would have a profound and lasting impact on the FBI and the nation's ability to defend against future threats like the tragedy on September 11, 2001.

First, as a direct result of the Committee's hearings, the FBI abolished its Domestic Security Division. Before the congressional legislation that followed had even become law, the FBI acted promptly—in the face of the intense public furor the hearings had generated—to end its work directed at a variety of potential domestic threats. Significantly, the new legislation would only allow investigations of U.S. citizens if the case could be predicated on information that there was already a relationship with a foreign power.

Putting this in context, someone might notice that a coworker is spending more money than he makes, works at a visible national security facility with access to classified information, drives a BMW, drinks heavily in the evening, but has never been known to travel outside the United States. Given the fact pattern, the FBI would not have sufficient justification to do anything but ask for an interview.

Second, the indictments and convictions of Felt and Miller sent a clear message to all FBI employees to stay away from counterintelligence ("Security") work. Job satisfaction was lacking, the rules of the game were dictated by political appointees, and any mistakes made might well end up in criminal indictments for the agents, not the bad guys. It's no surprise that the FBI had difficulty building an effective counterintelligence force within the organization after the Church hearings and their follow-up. That difficulty persists today, characterized by early retirements, failure to fill critical positions at FBI Headquarters, and growing control of the FBI's counterintelligence function by politicians and their allies in the CIA.

Third, the Church hearings focused exclusively on attacking the FBI for its domestic security role. They neglected entirely the fact that a large number of terrorist acts were perpetrated by violent groups and individuals, and didn't seem to understand or care to address the danger these actions posed to national security as a whole. The Church Committee heard no witnesses nor produced any reports that fully evaluated the attacks on America's police by organizations like the Black Panther Party, the anarchy promulgated by groups like the Weathermen, or the influence of radical elements of the American Indian Movement in promoting violence on Indian reservations.

When the Church Committee ended its inquiries, the nation heard one main conclusion: the FBI illegally spied on American citizens and for no apparent reason harassed and spied on Dr. Martin Luther King, Jr. Not a single piece of legislation to protect Americans from the homegrown anti-war violence that had swept America or from homegrown terrorism was proposed.

The American public was left to sort out political misinformation from fact in an ongoing struggle to decide what—and who—to believe when it came to significant threats to America's security. The Democratic and Republican Parties used their loyalists and elected officials to color the threat in shades that only appealed to their specific constituencies. In the process, they gained the power they sought to solidify their base, but the country as a whole was left far more vulnerable.

With a future age of terror looming, such wide disparities in thinking and deep political divides among elected leaders set the stage for a critical national disaster that has the potential to test the survival of American democracy. This terrible fork in the road began with Richard Nixon and the Republicans as well as Frank Church and the Democrats, and was in the end about the arrogance of political elites and their grasping for their drug of choice—political power—rather than the actual threat of violent acts of terror on American soil.

Both parties were aware of the actions the FBI took to combat terror in America in the 1960s and 1970s. Both looked the other way when those actions were challenged. In true political fashion, the reports issued by the Church Committee left plenty of room for both parties to evade responsibility and place blame squarely on the Bureau for actions that had been consistently condoned and encouraged by America's leaders until Watergate and its aftermath ruptured the structure they themselves had built.

CHAPTER FOUR

JAMIE GORELICK

FISA and the Wall

Someday someone will die—and wall or not—the public will not understand why we were not more effective and throwing every resource we had at certain 'problems'... the biggest threat to us now (Osama bin Laden) is getting the most 'protection.'

Email to FBIHQ from a New York agent
August 2001[1]

Senator Edward M. Kennedy proposed the legislation that became The Foreign Intelligence Surveillance Act of 1978—or FISA. It was a direct result of the Church Committee conclusions that the FBI and CIA had violated the civil liberties of Americans in the course of domestic spying. After an agreement with the Ford Administration, Kennedy took the lead in requiring that a special court have oversight over warrantless wiretapping in foreign intelligence investigations.[2]

Since the late 1970s, FISA courts have been part of the legal framework that allowed the FBI to conduct investigations in national security matters while restricting the collection of domestic intelligence.

The act severely limited collecting intelligence on American citizens residing inside the country. Although the FBI already had shut down its Domestic Security Section during the Church Committee hearings, FISA conclusively marked an end to all "domestic spying" by the Bureau.

Counterintelligence investigations use information obtained under FISA to collect evidence of foreign intelligence service targeting of Americans, as well as to identify methods and patterns in their operations inside the United States. FISA requires a lesser "standard of proof" than a Title III; supporting evidence is required to show that a foreign national or entity is engaged in intelligence activity, but not necessarily in the commission of an actual crime (such as espionage).

The FISA legislation represented the continuing evolution of political jockeying for power in the aftermath of Watergate and the Church Committee. Domestic "spying" on Americans had to be stopped, but at the same time, both Democrats and Republicans also needed to demonstrate their concern for protecting the national security interests of the United States. By allowing the investigation of foreign services and the identification of their efforts to collect classified or otherwise sensitive information, FISA appeared to address this issue.

In the same apparently bilateral spirit that had enabled both parties to collude in the Church Committee findings that absolved them from blame from COINTELPRO and shady CIA and NSA operations, Republican President Gerald Ford and Democratic Senator Edward Kennedy agreed to put legislation in place that favored individual privacy over national security.

But FISA presented a kind of "lose-lose scenario" for the FBI.

The Bureau needed to show the FISA court that the target of an investigation had an actual relationship or connection with a foreign intelligence service. There was no provision for proactive investigation and evaluation of such relationships, even those between intelligence officers and Americans with access to sensitive or classified information. Unless or until a third party provided specific information that a particular individual was engaged in a clandestine relationship with an agent of a hostile foreign power, no predication for an investigation existed.

The same situation applied in counterterrorism investigations, where no investigation of terrorist activity could be assisted by a FISA request unless the same standard could be applied. Even then, the FBI only had authority to investigate circumstances involving "international terrorism." In fact, FISA did not address domestic or "homegrown" terrorism at all. There was very little in FISA that allowed the FBI to be preventive in its approach to counterterrorism matters, especially if they related to domestic issues.

Within the FBI, the careful preparation of requests to the FISA court became a cottage industry. A FISA "package" began with the case agent in a field office and often took weeks to prepare. It went to the agent's squad supervisor for review and a signature and then through the top brass (special agent in charge or SAC) via the primary legal advisor of the office.

From the FBI field office, a FISA request went to the appropriate desk supervisor at Headquarters. That supervisor reviewed it and sent it along to headquarters lawyers and through a variety of supervisory layers until it was finally heard by the FISA court judge. On a prearranged date and time, the headquarters supervisor discussed the case with the judge and waited for approval. Once approved, a FISA order was good for 90 days only, after which time it expired unless it was updated with new information. Invariably, this meant that the renewal process had to be initiated before the original order had even been implemented in the field and before any potentially useful information had even been obtained.

The long and tedious FISA process before 9/11 held significant drawbacks for agents and supervisors trying to use it to mitigate hostile foreign threats to the United States.

There was constant conflict between agents in the field, pushing for urgent action to address national security issues, and the massive bureaucracy that grew up to support the FISA process. As a critical backbone of national security investigations, the FISA process became the victim of legal wrangling, powerful judges, and Department of Justice miscommunications and bad management. In addition to its failure to allow for the investigation of any type of domestic intelligence gathering, the FISA process became a barricade to the proper communication of national security information between agents and agencies.

This barricade was built higher and stronger when President Ford—a true believer in the privacy rights of Americans—instructed Attorney General Edward Levi to develop further guidelines for FBI national security investigations in addition to FISA. Ford signed an executive order to ensure that the guidelines were institutionalized and would prevent even the perception of "domestic spying" in the aftermath of Watergate.

By 1980, President Ronald Reagan restated Ford's guidelines with what became Executive Order 12333, also known as the Levi Guidelines:

1. Information obtained as a result of a FISA request was not to be shared with prosecutors involved in criminal cases.
2. FBI agents working on foreign counterintelligence investigations could not share information obtained via a FISA request with FBI agents assigned to criminal investigations, even though there might be some common crossover or connection between the targets of the investigations.
3. FBI agents involved in foreign counterintelligence investigations could not share or discuss any information they gained with colleagues in the criminal side of the FBI,

regardless of how it was collected and whether a FISA request was involved.

These were the rules of the road leading up to 9/11, and they were clear to everyone involved in the FBI, the Department of Justice, the FISA courts, and legislators from both political parties. Had an FBI agent violated any of these rules, he or she would have been subject to significant disciplinary action. FISA was heralded as providing protection to the American public from further abuses of civil liberties such as those identified in the Church Committee hearings, and it was rigidly adhered to. The Levi guidelines ensured a rigid separation between information obtained in counterintelligence and criminal investigations.

The combination of the restrictions posed by both the FISA rules and the Levi guidelines came to be referred to as the "Wall." In effect, the Wall severely restricted sharing information between criminal and intelligence components of the same government.

By 1995, Deputy Attorney General Jamie Gorelick developed formal procedures to further restrict sharing information between the criminal and intelligence sides. The already formidable Wall was now set in concrete, and further cemented by Gorelick's order:

> . . . *We believe that it is prudent to establish a set of instructions that will clearly separate the counterintelligence investigation from the more limited, but continued, criminal investigations. These procedures, **which go beyond what is legally required**, will prevent any risk of creating an unwarranted appearance that FISA is being used to avoid procedural safeguards which would apply in a criminal investigation.*

Incredibly, Jamie Gorelick became a member of the 9/11 Commission after the international terrorist attacks on America. The role she had played in cementing the Wall six years earlier should have kept her from serving on the Commission, since her conflict of interest was so blatantly evident.

But everyone on the 9/11 Commission had a role to play, and the dividing lines were clear and simple: Democrats were there to protect their party and its leaders and Republicans were there to protect theirs. The Commission would twist the facts whatever way it could to re-frame years of history and to conceal from or at least confuse the public about the political machinations that led to the terrible events of 9/11. It was imperative that politicians race to place blame for those events on inadequacies in the FBI and the CIA.

Just two weeks prior to 9/11, the FBI in New York City was in hot pursuit of Khalid al-Mihdhar, identified as a principal in the bombing of the *U.S.S. Cole* in Aden Harbor in Yemen in October 2000. The National Security Law Unit at Headquarters refused to allow the case agent to use information gleaned from intelligence investigations to pursue and find al-Mihdhar. The following written exchange resulted between the Headquarters supervisor and the New York agent respectively:

> *This case, in its entirety, is based on (intelligence). If at such time as information is developed indicating the existence of a substantial federal crime, that information will be passed over the Wall according to the proper procedures and turned over for follow-up criminal investigation.*

> *Someday someone will die—and Wall or not—the public will not understand why we were not more effective and throwing every resource we had at certain 'problems.' Let's hope the National Security Law Unit will*

stand behind their decisions then, especially since the biggest threat to us now (Osama bin Laden) is getting the most 'protection.[3]

The terrorist attack on the *U.S.S. Cole* was a wake-up call for many of us in the FBI, and it is not surprising that the New York agent was putting together the pieces from one incident in a race against time to prevent another one. But politics, lawyers, and the Wall were constant barriers to effectiveness and repeatedly slowed the pace of investigations when urgent actions were required.

The George Herbert Walker Bush Strategic Information Operations Center (SIOC) was located on the fourth floor of the J. Edgar Hoover FBI Building. Prior to the 9/11 attacks, the Center was the premier law enforcement command center in the world, designed to handle multiple national and international crises wherever they might occur. Admission to the Center beyond the reception area was off limits to anyone who did not have urgent business there. The place was divided into a number of breakout rooms, some of which could be joined to become larger conference rooms or provide additional space to create a command center. Several of the rooms were designed to accommodate command centers to coordinate the law enforcement response to individual emergency situations.

On a normal day, the Center was staffed by analysts who maintained communication links with other agencies 24 hours a day. Contrary to popular opinion, prior to 9/11 the FBI and CIA continuously shared information related to worldwide terrorism. Some of that information was shared via the Center. Counterterrorism Division managers used one of the breakout rooms to have frequent meetings during the week to discuss all aspects of the domestic and international terrorist threat as they were developed through investigations, tips, and information from other agencies.

The FBI's Counterterrorism Units that focused on Osama bin Laden and al Qaeda were continually behind the restricted access doors, near the information portals that were so vital to their ongoing interests.

The population of the Center swelled during any crisis, particularly when the FBI's Hostage Rescue Team was deployed to deal with a critical field situation. During these times, the reception staff increased, analysts were joined by additional colleagues, and men and women from a number of agencies took their places at the crisis table to address matters of urgent concern. Computers were brought in, experts in topical areas stood by, FBI and high-ranking officials from other U.S. government agencies assessed, negotiated, and debated with one another about appropriate moves, strategies, and the range of potential outcomes to any given action.

Within minutes of the October 10, 2000, terrorist attack on the *U.S.S. Cole*, the Center was in full operation. FBI Rapid Deployment Teams from the New York and Washington Field Offices were readying for departure to Yemen to begin their investigation. FBI Counterterrorism Assistant Director Dale Watson and Director Louis Freeh assembled a command structure to guide those teams and their efforts.

At the 8:00 a.m. director's briefing on the *Cole* attack, Director Freeh, Deputy Director Tom Pickard, and Attorney General Janet Reno sat at the rectangular conference table, accompanied by their respective staffs and FBI agent supervisors who had various responsibilities related to the crisis. They were joined by an assistant director from the Naval Criminal Investigative Service (NCIS).

This Navy executive, like others present, saw three stacks of documents in the center of the conference table. Each of the stacks had different-colored cover sheets. The colors marked the classification level of each of the series of papers. One color stood for unclassified information and another for information classified at the Secret level, available for distribution to all those at the table. A third color was reserved for Secret/ Restricted Information and available only to selected individuals. This latter information was obtained through investigations that involved FISA.

The NCIS executive had been told by an FBI headquarters supervisor that he could not have the information because it was restricted from dissemination by the Wall.

Despite the exigent circumstances—we were in emergency session concerning a terrorist attack on a United States Naval vessel, there were other Navy ships in ports across the world that might be in danger, and the terrorist attacks had resulted in the deaths of Navy personnel—Department of Justice official Fran Townsend confirmed that no exception could be granted to allow the Navy executive to see critical information.[4]

The Wall was the Wall.

The fatal flaw in Jamie Gorelick's carefully worded memo— and with FISA itself—is that neither recognizes the true nature of working on the front lines, where law enforcement, terrorism, and intelligence analysis collide.

In their zealousness to be seen as the guarantors of the civil liberties of Americans, Senator Kennedy and the Congress that approved FISA after Watergate and the Church Committee hearings—and later Gorelick as well—didn't understand or care how investigations work, and how analysis needs to be integrated into every aspect of the FBI mission if crimes are to be prevented and intelligence services neutralized. They also did not understand or pay any heed to the nature of the "insider" threat, which made it difficult for the FBI to justify developing sources of information in those areas where only early and tenuous indicators of intelligence, terrorism, or criminal issues might be present.

The allure of public recognition for politicians who champion the civil liberties of Americans was too irresistible to Senators

Church and Kennedy, as well as to Deputy Attorney General
Gorelick, to consider the negative implications that would leave
the country vulnerable in a time of crisis.

Despite this, the FBI adhered religiously to the guidelines
provided. As a result, however, many FBI agents refused to
work counterintelligence and counterterrorism. They believed
the constraints imposed on the Bureau by politicians created an
environment where they would be blamed for violating someone's civil rights if they were perceived as too aggressive, and
blamed for the tragic outcome if they failed to prevent a major
espionage affair or terrorist act.

When the 9/11 Commission heard the testimony of many
experts inside and outside of government, it became apparent
that the cumulative effects of FISA, the attorney general guidelines devised under President Ford and Executive Order 12333,
had played a major role in impeding the FBI's ability to prevent
terrorist activities. Instead of laying the blame where it
belonged, however, the commission blamed the FBI:

> These procedures were almost immediately misunder-
> stood and misapplied. As a result, there was far less
> information sharing and coordination between the FBI
> and the Criminal Division in practice than was allowed
> under the department's procedures. Over time the proce-
> dures came to be referred to as the Wall. The term the
> 'Wall' is misleading, however, because several factors led
> to a series of barriers to information sharing that devel-
> oped.

Jamie Gorelick chose to defend herself in an opinion she
wrote to *The Washington Post* in April 2004. She denied that
her memo had built a wall between criminal and counterterrorism investigations, and said that she was only establishing
clear and appropriate procedures for the use of information
obtained through FISA requests.

But Gorelick and everyone else associated with the FISA process knew that the practical and clearly understood effect of her memo was to prevent FBI agents from communicating and sharing critical information received in counterintelligence investigations to FBI agents handling criminal and domestic anti-terror investigations.

This was the field of play as the world watched jets strike the World Trade Center and the Pentagon on 9/11. Over two decades of political legislation, judicial interpretations, and Department of Justice policies had effectively prevented the FBI from maximizing its ability to prevent the attacks on that day.

The country would have been far better benefited if the 9/11 Commission and its conclusions had been the product of a jury of American citizens rather than the 9/11 Commission members, politicians all, who were intent on holding anyone's feet to the fire but their own.

Although it was important in establishing civil liberties boundaries to guide intelligence and terrorism investigations, FISA, as it was written, seriously damaged the FBI's capability to defend against a variety of threats, both internal and external. The legal monstrosity of the Wall did less to protect innocent Americans than it did harm to the intricate process of "connecting the dots" that is part of any effective national security apparatus. No politician from either party, however, will admit publicly that it was their legislation and its applications that helped set the stage for 9/11 by short-stocking the FBI's intelligence collection arsenal.

Nineteen years after the passage of FISA legislation, and seven years after the worst terrorist attacks on American soil, politicians on one side of the political spectrum continue to maintain and enhance their power by resorting to warning of the abuse of civil liberties in the war on terror. On the other side, politicians have gone overboard in actually trampling civil rights without making the country any safer from the threat of terrorism.

Politicians seem to relish describing the "war on terror" as an "asymmetric war." But images of helicopters vulnerable to shoulder-fired rockets, army tanks, and soldiers cautiously treading through towns and villages in 120-degree heat, remind us more of Vietnam. News stories of politicians and their staffs lying to FBI agents and federal grand juries sound more like Watergate. And the bitter public debates that occur everyday in Washington, D.C., where civility in the political process has been totally eclipsed by vicious personal attacks and scapegoating, are expressions more of the severity of the addiction to power than the rational consideration of public policy.

CHAPTER FIVE

DON EDWARDS

Of Terrorists, Spies, and Libraries

The FBI has a sordid history in many ways: the COINTELPRO program of harassment and some criminal conduct where they would target different people; the ABSCAM, where they would get people drunk and confuse them. . .

Former Representative Don Edwards[1]

Don Edwards served in the United States Congress for 32 years, representing the Silicon Valley area of California. During 23 of those years, Edwards was the powerful chairman of the House Judiciary Subcommittee on Civil Liberties and Civil Rights. When the Church Committee hearings ended, Edwards aligned his subcommittee into orbit with the Senate and House Intelligence Committees. Together, they assumed an oversight role relative to the FBI.

Edwards carried the Church Committee torch forward more effectively than most of his peers and became known as a champion of civil rights in America.

In the aftermath of the Church Committee hearings, however, championing civil rights increasingly meant opposition and hostility to the FBI. The message from politicians was that the FBI was a greater threat to the country than those it investigated, and flying that flag was an effective avenue to getting headlines in the media.

Edwards took his committee far beyond oversight of the Bureau; and in his zeal to develop his reputation as a fearless warrior for civil liberties, he literally diminished the ability of the FBI to defend against a variety of future threats, including international and homegrown terrorism.

Edwards always stressed that his background as an FBI agent gave him special insight into the workings of the Bureau, and he used his former employment to give him credibility in its oversight. But contrary to the image he sought to project, he spent only one year in the FBI, as a probationary agent, from 1940 to 1941. The FBI of that era was heavily involved in the pursuit of bank robbers, unlawful flights of interstate criminals, and trying to identify Nazi saboteurs landing on America's shores.

Years later, the organization that was subjected to Edwards' oversight was a vastly different and more mature FBI. Its mission had grown considerably and so had the complexities of crime and espionage. Successfully placing a high-echelon informant inside an organized crime family that had existed for decades, analyzing the patterns of the Soviet KGB and its collection and targeting efforts within the United States, and addressing political corruption at the local, state, and federal levels was light years away from what Edwards experienced in his brief time as an FBI agent.

Nevertheless, Edwards' carefully developed image as an insider with unique insight into the inner workings of the FBI added considerable weight to his opinions about the Bureau, which gained him far more attention in the media when they were negative rather than positive.

By the mid 1970s, the Senate and House Intelligence Committees were receiving regular briefings on threats to America's security, but increasingly those threats were exclusively foreign in nature. The FBI was losing its capability to gather domestic intelligence on internal threats. The political environment, coupled with the legal and policy guidelines imposed on the FBI in 1976 by then Attorney General Edward Levi, had effectively ended the FBI's domestic intelligence role. In the post-Watergate and Church Committee years, that is exactly what Congress wanted.

By 1978, then FBI director William Webster, a former federal judge of impeccable integrity and independence, testified in a hearing that the Bureau was "practically out of the domestic security field."

A September 2005 Special Report of the Department of Justice Office of the Inspector General states about this period:

> . . . *within the FBI, however, there was concern that the Levi Guidelines would unduly limit authorized techniques and would not permit the FBI to be proactive, to collect intelligence before disaster struck, and to develop an adequate intelligence base.*[2]

Representative Edwards did not confine his version of FBI oversight to guidelines for foreign counterintelligence. He used his subcommittee to conduct hearings into and to publicly attack the Bureau over the sweeping political corruption investigation of Congress called ABSCAM in the early 1980s.[3]

According to Edwards, the conduct of congressmen who sold their positions of public trust for money was explained by their being "drunk and confused." Hearing this, every foreign intelligence service targeting American interests should have been clamoring to buy rounds of drinks for the uniquely vulnerable crowd on Capitol Hill.

Of course, guidelines imposed on the FBI by Congress and politicians would have prevented FBI agents from following their KGB adversaries up the stairs and into the Capitol.

Since the ABSCAM offenses were recorded on videotape, it was a difficult public sell even at the time that the politicians involved were lured against their will into accepting bribes for political favors. A post-Watergate public was not inclined to be indulgent towards politicians who abused their offices.

In October 1982, a month-old *Washington Post* editorial, "Are Scams and Stings Out of Control?" was reprinted in the *Kansas City Star*. It captures the tone of the response of the general public to ABSCAM:

> *Ever since we learned that the FBI had been filming politicians pocketing bribes . . . there have been tirades from politicians criticizing not only the callous equanimity with which members of Congress took monies in violation of their sworn oath, but also the methods used to snare the culprits. . .*

> *. . . never has the clamor about legal, ethical, and procedural issues been so loud as since ABSCAM. The seven members of Congress who walked into a trap initially set for art swindlers provoked a storm that put most of them in jail, but also the FBI in the dock. The Bureau has been subjected to one hostile hearing, chaired by Congressman Don Edwards (D. Cal.), and another, hardly supportive, chaired by Senator Charles Mathias (R. Md.) . . .*

> *In the face of Congress's continued extreme reluctance—to put it mildly—to clean up its own affairs, the FBI should be directed to concentrate on crooked politicians rather than being driven out of this business . . . American distrust of public officials and authority has many historical roots, but given the present high level of distrust, the last thing the country needs is for politicians*

*to slam the FBI instead of welcoming and augmenting
efforts to straighten out our public life.*

Nevertheless, the final report of the House Judiciary Sub-committee on Civil and Constitutional Rights concluded in 1984 that "ill-conceived and poorly managed undercover operations" like ABSCAM were likely to undermine the public's faith in their political institutions.

Following Watergate, Republicans regarded the Bureau—which had resisted control by the Nixon White House during the investigation of both the burglary and the cover-up—as a danger to their future political power. Democratic politicians, sensing election victories and a re-capture of the White House from the Republicans in the aftermath of Watergate, focused on condemning aspects of the FBI's disgraced domestic security program (COINTELPRO) as an avenue and platform to increase their own power.

To politicians of all stripes, the fact that the FBI was not under their control meant that the Bureau was out of control altogether. Besides, a weakened FBI would be easier to control and would pose less of a threat to politicians in need of their power fix. Both parties rushed to establish oversight and impose restrictive guidelines on the Bureau's methods and operations.

Neither party wanted any notable public discussion that would show they were fully aware of the FBI's activities before the Church Committee. They have never admitted it. The parties protected each other, blamed the FBI and to a lesser degree the CIA for abuses in the years preceding Watergate, thus sparing themselves the embarrassment and political scandal that would have attached to identifying their complicity.

Representative Edwards and his subcommittee established the behavioral ground rules for the "Blame the Bureau" game that is still a feature of the sound bites and grandstanding by politicians that claim a great deal of national media coverage.

In an ironic and somewhat eerie foreshadowing of the past connecting with the present, *The Nation* magazine featured an article on August 11, 1997, titled, "The F.B.I.: A Special Report." The article drew heavily from Edwards' subcommittee hearings on the FBI and its conduct in undercover corruption probes. A section of the report called, aptly enough, "National Insecurity," had this to say:

> *Fears that America's national security interests are threatened by spies, traitors, or subversives have led a long line of presidents and Congress to gradually enlarge the bureau's powers. In the past few years the perceived menace of international and domestic terrorism has provided the rallying flag . . . F.B.I. Director Freeh told the Senate Appropriations Committee in June that extra funding would allow the FBI to double its 'shoe leather' for the investigations of domestic and international terrorist groups. And in his requests for additional legal authority to conduct more electronic surveillances, Freeh always cites the growing menace of terrorism.*

The terrorist threat alluded to by Director Freeh was growing. But Edwards and his subcommittee were preoccupied with the possible violations of the civil rights and liberties of United States congressmen caught taking bribes. They had little time to listen to FBI warnings about terrorism. Edwards perceived the Bureau itself to be the bigger threat to American democracy. In April 1997 he said:

> *. . . Congress should pay attention on a daily basis to the FBI. It has a history of problems, and it's a powerful,*

dangerous organization. It's a good organization in many ways, but Congress should have oversight by the hour on everything the FBI is doing.

In the Fall of 1987, a New York report regarding patterns of contact of librarians in the New York City area by known Soviet Line X (Scientific and Technical branch) officers in search of unclassified, emerging technologies was sent to FBI Headquarters. The line was highly active—in America's technological wonderland, the Silicon Valley, on the campuses of the country's major scientific universities, and in scientific and technical libraries across the country.[4]

New York wanted Bureau approval for an initiative they called the Library Awareness Program, so that they could contact librarians at selected scientific and technical libraries in an effort to find out what the known Soviet intelligence officers were up to. The New York request was approved.

Shortly afterward, FBI Headquarters officials received notice that Congressman Don Edwards had placed a call to the assistant director of the National Security Division of the FBI, James Geer. Edwards wanted to know why the FBI in New York—and apparently in other locations, as well—was talking to librarians about who was reading what in scientific and technical libraries.

Geer called a meeting with his staff and confirmed from Don Stukey, who headed the Soviet Section, that the purpose of the New York Library Awareness Program was specifically to monitor Soviet intelligence officers from Line X of the KGB who were using the libraries to identify unclassified documents early in their development that would be likely to lead to classified U.S. government projects. A couple of New York agents had gone to the Mathematics and Science Library at Columbia, and their visit had been reported to the press.

Stukey had successfully guided the FBI through a number of Soviet espionage cases during the 1980s. During 1985, which had been dubbed the "Year of the Spy," the FBI took several landmark espionage cases to trial, illustrative of the growing problem of the theft of classified information and the aggressive Soviet effort at the time. He was concerned when the soft-spoken Geer said:

> *Well, Don Edwards wants the FBI to put an immediate end to the Library Awareness Program, to stop contacting librarians, and wants to have hearings to look into the reasoning behind this.*[5]

At the hearing some days later, the lights were dim in the room prior to the proceedings. Edwards was standing alone near the podium reserved for the subcommittee members, while cameramen moved about straightening, shuffling, and wrestling cables, wires, and equipment into place. By this point, so much inaccurate and inflammatory information had poisoned the airwaves that it felt impossible that the issues could be rationally and reasonably discussed. But having senior FBI staff on the congressional hot seat in front of the cameras is always good for a politician's image.

Representative Edwards walked over to greet Geer and Tom DuHadway with an outstretched hand and a huge smile. Both agents knew that a Congressional hearing exists in a kind of stage-show atmosphere that has its own dramatic rules of performance and posturing for the camera. Politicians want to make an impression on television, and that's what a congressional hearing is: staged for TV. As the lights went up, the cameras rolled, and the action began, the smile on Edwards' face vanished completely as he quickly took his seat and banged the gavel.

The subcommittee is very concerned about the chilling effect on the civil rights and civil liberties of Americans when a government agency can freely enter a public library and learn about the reading habits of our citizens. This Congress has provided the FBI huge increases in its budgets for national security work over the past few years and we have an obligation to ensure that the money we provided is being put to good use and not squandered on programs and ideas that fail to improve our national security and at the same time infringe upon our rights. This subcommittee will ask for answers from Misters Geer and DuHadway to those and other questions.

A Library Association executive spoke on behalf of its members. In the summer of 1987, the acting librarian at the Mathematics and Science Library at Columbia University declined to help two FBI agents from the New York Office when they asked about use of the library by foreign intelligence agents. The incident was reported to the association. After the story broke in the news, it was determined that FBI agents in a number of other states had made the same kinds of inquiries at libraries.

Assistant Director Geer noted that the FBI had a responsibility to identify the patterns, methods, and targets of hostile intelligence services in the United States. Over a period of time, he said, it had become clear that intelligence officers from Line X of the Soviet KGB were routinely visiting scientific and technical libraries.

He explained that the KGB officers were interested in unclassified scientific research that might offer some insight into future technological breakthroughs, classified military-and national-security-related applications, and identification of emerging technologies. Their work in the libraries helped identify companies, funding, and specific individuals that could later be targeted through operations and various scenarios. The FBI followed these known KGB officers into these libraries, because it was necessary to know what they were doing there.

Geer said that although the FBI in other cities had indeed made inquiries at libraries following KGB visits, they were not part of the Library Awareness Program recently launched by the New York office. Those agents were merely responding to the same patterns by conducting appropriate interviews when they also detected known Soviet intelligence officers visiting science and technical libraries. He added that the fact that KGB officers were pursuing the same activities at libraries around the country actually validated the original purpose of the New York initiative.[6]

As the hearings wore on, Edwards insistently championed the demands of the Library Association. The FBI should not be allowed in the library. The FBI should not be allowed to talk with librarians. Librarians present demanded that legislators recognize a special privileged relationship between the librarian and the library patron.

Attendees also heard an earful from a representative who charged into the meeting in the afternoon, took her chair near Edwards, and launched into a tirade using words like "chilling," "Gestapo tactics," and "spying on Americans." Red-faced and angry, Congresswoman Patricia Schroeder—whose ambition was nothing less than to be president of the United States—then stalked out as quickly as she'd entered and never returned to the hearing.

There were further meetings after the hearings between Geer, DuHadway, and the librarians, and although the FBI did not agree to immediately stop the Library Awareness Program, it was eventually ended. The Bureau never agreed to any proposals that it would forfeit the option to interview librarians or visit libraries, but did acknowledge that guidelines and protocols might have prevented the earlier incident. Finding the head librarian first and explaining in detail the predicate that brought FBI agents to a library was just one of them.

Six years later, Congress passed the Intellectual Property Act and Economic Espionage Act, legislation aimed at protecting America's competitive advantages throughout the world by making it a federal crime to steal unclassified information which was "company proprietary." The legislation was enacted after revelations of numerous examples of intelligence services plotting to steal corporate America's secrets to ensure their own competitive survival.

For years, FBI investigations had shown that these activities were rampant, and politicians were unresponsive to or even disparaging of the problem. The result was loss of American jobs to overseas markets and a loss in American competitive capability.

Edwards and his subcommittee had been unable to see the connection between KGB officers scouring libraries in New York and the eventual problems with competitive advantages that would later lead to this protective legislation. More pertinently, they were consistently eager for the media attention that intensification of accusations that the FBI had endangered the civil liberties of Americans had yielded for them ever since the 1970s.

In his testimony before the Senate Committee on the Judiciary on October 21, 2003, Assistant Attorney General Christopher Wray definitively explained the significance of spies, terrorists, and libraries for the record:

> . . . *Historically, terrorists and spies have used librar-*
> *ies to plan and carry out activities that threaten our*
> *national security. For example, Brian Patrick Regan,*
> *who was convicted last February of offering to sell U.S.*

*intelligence information to Iraq and China, used a com-
puter at a local public library to look up addresses for
Iraqi and Libyan embassies overseas. Similarly, in a
recent domestic terrorism criminal case, a grand jury
served a subpoena on a bookseller to obtain records showing that a suspect had bought a book giving instructions
on how to build . . . a detonator that had been used in several bombings. This was important evidence identifying
the suspect as the bomber. We should not allow libraries
or any other businesses to become safe havens for terrorist
planning, financing, or communication.*

When the Unabomber sent his manifesto to *The New York
Times* in 1995 and challenged the FBI to find him, it was clear
to the UNABOM Task Force that the manifesto's writer had to
be spending time in libraries doing research. As it turned out,
he had actually selected several of his victims using library edi-
tions of *Who's Who.*

We on the task force needed to contact select libraries that
might be relevant to the case and see what help was available.
We established strict criteria, to include contacting the head
librarian. One agent was designated to coordinate the effort,
and was responsible for ensuring that any agent contacting a
library did and said the same thing as every other agent
involved with reaching out. Instead of asking for specific help or
identifying any indicators of suspicious activity, we merely
briefed the librarians on UNABOM and requested any help they
felt they could provide. We left them with a contact number
should they see anything that they felt was relevant or bother-
some. Although we contacted numerous libraries, we never had
one complaint.

In late March 1996, just days before the search warrant was
served on Theodore Kaczynski's wilderness cabin, FBI agents

interviewed the librarian in Lincoln, Montana. She was well acquainted with Kaczynski and provided great detail of his endless afternoons in the corner of the small library, writing, researching, and asking for help in acquiring certain magazines and articles. He'd also shared information with her about cities and states he had visited during his 25 years in Montana. Some of this information provided the final pieces to the puzzle that corroborated information in the search warrant that was served on Kaczynski on April 3, 1996. During the search of his cabin, a fully assembled bomb, packaged and ready to mail, was found under Kaczynski's bed.

Librarians can assist in critical cases, and their voluntary cooperation and involvement can save lives. They, just as other citizens and U.S. persons, can be critical in fighting terrorism, whether foreign or homegrown.

On December 14, 2000, at the National Press Club in Washington, D.C., Don Edwards identified himself as a former FBI agent and challenged the FBI's opposition to clemency for Leonard Peltier, an American Indian convicted for the murder of two FBI agents. By letter, Edwards alleged that the Bureau "continues to deny its improper conduct on Pine Ridge in the 1970s," and said that Peltier had been used as a "scapegoat."

Former FBI Director Louis Freeh saw it differently:

> . . . *about Leonard Peltier I had, and still have, no confusion. He murdered those agents (Jack Coler and Ronald Williams) and he deserves to spend the rest of his life in jail. . . . Back in 1994, when we got word that the Peltier lobby was leaning hard on the president for his release, I prepared several memos for the attorney general to send over to the White House. I wanted to be sure that Janet [Reno] saw them, that she was familiar with our reasoning, that she knew why we opposed any kind of*

*leniency in Peltier's case. I took the argument public just
to be certain there was no confusion anywhere. . . . As for
myself, I was ready to submit my resignation as director
the moment Peltier was freed, whenever it happened.*[7]

President Clinton never pardoned Leonard Peltier.

In July 2003, the United States Congress bestowed upon
four of its former members the first Congressional Distinguished Service Award. One of the recipients was Don Edwards.
His successor, Zoe Lofgren, called him "a one-time FBI agent
who was willing to go after misconduct in the FBI."

To the FBI, Edwards was mistaken in his judgments. His
poor understanding of facts and relationships has been damag-
ing to the country's national security and economic well being.
He rose for reasons of publicity and pure politics to the defense
of convicted American terrorists like Leonard Peltier, who
planned, ambushed, and murdered two young FBI agents who
were driving on a Native American reservation. The tone and
methods Edwards used in Congress to accuse the Bureau of
malfeasance in order to glorify his image as a champion of civil
rights and civil liberties were passed to his successors.

In the years preceding 9/11, Congress conducted countless
public hearings condemning the FBI for alleged violations of
civil liberties of Americans, while paying little heed to the
assessment of the growing threat posed by homegrown and
domestic terrorism both within and outside the United States.

CHAPTER SIX

ALL REAGAN'S MEN

Iran Contra

What set Iran Contra apart from previous political scandals was the fact that a cover-up engineered in the White House of one president and completed by his successor prevented the rule of law . . . the cover-up likely could not have worked if the other institutions of Washington—Congress, the courts, and the press—had not helped.

Special Prosecutor Lawrence Walsh[1]

Marine Lt. Col. Oliver North rose from relative obscurity as a military aide to the National Security Council (NSC) to the ardent architect of a plan to trade arms for hostages that became known as the "Iran Contra Affair" during the presidency of Ronald Reagan.

Rambling on at congressional hearings, answering only questions he chose to address, invoking his Fifth Amendment right against self-incrimination and sometimes simply not telling the truth, North became a folk hero to the right, a political stalking horse to the left, and a symbol of the arrogance that often accompanies the exercise of political power.

Regardless of how people may have felt about North, he was an expert at handling Congress, giving them very little and at the same time protecting his legal rights and building an appeal process for a verdict that hadn't yet been delivered. His attorney, Brendan Sullivan, was just as effective in stonewalling Congress, reminding frustrated committee members, "I'm not a potted plant. I'm here as a lawyer. That's my job."

Sullivan did an exceptional job. North was indicted in 1988 on 16 felony counts connected with his role in the Iran Contra affair. A year later he was on trial in connection with 12 of the counts and convicted of three: accepting an illegal gratuity, obstructing a congressional inquiry, and destroying government documents.

By 1990, however, North's conviction had been vacated by a three judge appellate panel, and the trial judge dismissed the convictions after the case was made that his testimony in front of the congressional committee, with a grant of immunity, had had undue influence on witnesses in the trial.

The aftermath of the investigation of Iran Contra so startled and outraged its special prosecutor, Lawrence Walsh, that he wrote a bitter account of it years later.[2]

What was it that caused North as well as National Security Advisors Robert McFarlane and John Poindexter, Defense Secretary Caspar Weinberger, and others to illegally send weapons to the enemy state of Iran in order to illegally fund an army of rebels the CIA was building in Central America? And in the end, what were the real consequences of their actions to these Washington figures where their political and financial futures were concerned?

President Ronald Reagan entered the White House on the heels of the collapse of the pro-Western government of the Shah of Iran during the presidency of Jimmy Carter. Carter's foreign policy had stressed opposition to any leader of any nation who opposed true democracy and was involved in violations of human rights. In line with this philosophy, Carter largely withdrew long-established American support to the Shah of Iran's regime.

The subsequent collapse of the Shah's government, which had acted as a bulwark for Western political and economic influence in the Middle East, resulted in the growth of a radical Islamist Iran that in the present day is attempting to acquire the capacity for nuclear weapons. At the same time, Iran's anti-Western—and particularly anti-American—stances have focused its evolution into a state sponsor of terror.

When the American embassy population in Tehran was taken hostage in 1979 by a faction of Iranian students, the students were viewed in their own country as overthrowing a "den of spies" that was plotting to overthrow the new revolutionary government of the Ayatollah Khomeini. To Americans, they were terrorists who unlawfully imprisoned American diplomatic personnel for over a year, parading them in blindfolds before news cameras, as they demanded that the exiled Shah be handed over to them in exchange.

Weary of the spectacle and disheartened by the failure of the Carter Administration to resolve the crisis, Americans went to the polls in the fall of 1980 and voted overwhelmingly to send Carter and his administration packing.

With the election of Ronald Reagan, Republicans, frustrated by what they saw as the vacillations of the Democrats in dealing with the Middle East, set the stage for a new group of president's men who would work in secret to secure their political power in flagrant disregard for the law and at the expense of the security of their fellow Americans.

The manipulation and flagrant disregard for the law in the Iran Contra Affair led to a breakdown of leadership in both parties, as well as contributed to the growth of anti-Americanism and Islamic fundamentalism that drives the current international terror war.

On the day that Ronald Reagan was inaugurated as the 40th president of the United States, Iran announced the release of the remaining American Embassy hostages. The tactic of hostage taking, however, had proven all too effective in focusing world attention on events in the Middle East, and soon the terrorist group Hezbollah kidnapped a large group of foreigners in Lebanon. Among the hostages were six American Embassy workers.

With some help from Israel, a secret plan was developed whereby America would provide arms to Iran in exchange for Iran's help in securing the release of the hostages in Lebanon. The plan was coordinated by Reagan's National Security advisor Robert McFarlane, and the president signed a "finding" authorizing the arms for hostage deal and another authorizing CIA involvement in selling the arms to the Iranian government.

The fact that the plan was contrary to official Reagan Administration policy was eclipsed in its illegality by being in direct violation of the Boland Amendment, which was actually three legislative amendments between 1982 and 1984 that effectively limited U.S. government assistance to the rebel Contras in Nicaragua. The CIA had conducted clandestine acts of sabotage in Nicaragua without bothering to brief or even notify congressional intelligence committees, and the Democratic majority in Congress was adamant that this kind of independent international careering by the CIA in furtherance of the Reagan White House opposition to the Sandinista government in Nicaragua should be reigned in.[3]

Nevertheless, by late 1985, Oliver North, who worked for McFarlane and had an exceptionally bold manner as well as a creative mind, had refined the plan to use the millions of dollars received from the sale of arms to Iran to aid the Contra rebels fighting the anti-American Sandinistas in Nicaragua.

The scenario went forward, as then vice-president George H. W. Bush noted in an entry to his diary that has since become emblematic of his "non-involvement" in the affair:

> *Sometimes there are meetings over in the White House with Schultz, NSC guy, Casey and Weinberger, and they make some decisions that the president signs off on. . . . the Vice President is not in the decision-making loop.*

In October 1986, Nicaraguan forces shot down a cargo plane carrying supplies to anti-Sandinista rebels ("Contras") over an area in the south of the country. The only survivor, a 45-year-old former marine named Eugene Hasenfus, said in a press conference that two of the other passengers worked for the CIA.[4]

In November, a Lebanese magazine made the first public report of the weapons-for-hostages deal.[5]

Later that month, President Reagan declared on American television that although weapons had been provided to anti-Khomeini moderates in Iran, the U.S. had not traded those weapons for release of the hostages in Lebanon. The atmosphere in the backrooms of the White House as the conspirators watched the familiar and reassuring image of their commander in chief stating his ignorance of what had actually happened must have been thick with apprehension, and even panic. Knowing the FBI was on its way, North and Poindexter destroyed a large number of records that documented the deal before agents could arrive to take custody of them, including highly classified documents from the National Security Council. In the spring, Reagan again appeared on national television, where he took full responsibility for any actions in the matter he had been unaware of, and admitting that:

> *What began as a strategic opening to Iran deteriorated, in its implementation, into trading arms for hostages.*[6]

As the Iran Contra details began to leak out, FBI agents working with Special Prosecutor Lawrence E. Walsh tried to piece together the facts to determine whether the law had been broken by invisible people in America's shadow government. Subsequently, an American grand jury and trial juries across Washington confirmed that it had been.

Once again, television cameras crowded into hearing rooms on Capitol Hill. Although fashions and hairstyles had changed, the spectacle of White House and National Security personnel ducking and weaving allegations of wrongdoing looked much the same in the 1980s as they had during the Watergate era of the 1970s. The testimony of North's secretary, Fawn Hill, was camera-worthy not only because she was an attractive woman but because she was so obviously still convinced that she had done the right thing by helping North clog a shredder with hundreds of pages of incriminating documents. North himself testified that he watched John Poindexter destroy what may have been the only signed copy of a presidential covert-action finding that had authorized a shipment of Hawk missiles to Iran in November 1985.[7]

By the time the Special Prosecutor's investigation was complete, 14 people were indicted and 11 of those convicted for the role they played in the Iran Contra scandal. CIA official Clair George was convicted on two felony counts of making false statements and perjury. Reagan's National Security advisor Robert McFarlane pleaded guilty to four misdemeanor counts that involved withholding information from investigators. CIA official Duane Claridge was indicted on seven counts of perjury and making false statements; one of the charges involved the shipment of Hawk missiles to Iran. Defense Secretary Caspar Weinberger was indicted on five counts of obstruction of justice, perjury, and making false statements. In addition to North, his boss John Poindexter was convicted on five counts of obstructing justice, making false statements, and destroying documents.

Both North's and Poindexter's testimony before Congress led to their convictions being reversed because of the immunity they received during that testimony and its subsequent impact on trial witnesses.

And by the end of 1992, as his administration packed its bags in preparation to ceding the White House to a new Democratic regime, Republican President George H. W. Bush had issued pardons for six members of his administration who had been convicted for their involvement in Iran Contra: Clair George, Robert McFarlane, Caspar Weinberger, Duane Claridge, John Poindexter, and Elliott Abrams (a special assistant to the president and senior director for Near East and North African affairs on the NSC, who had pled guilty to two counts of unlawfully withholding information). None of the officials convicted had been incarcerated.

Given the actions of the first Bush White House in pardoning the principals of the Iran Contra scandal, it's not surprising that President George W. Bush, a little over two decades later, would commute the sentence of Lewis "Scooter" Libby, Vice President Dick Cheney's chief of staff, after his conviction for leaking the identity of a CIA officer to the media. Just as in the Iran Contra scandal, the White House had more interest in protecting members of its own, powerful elite than in seeing that justice was done. The similarities in technique (what is known in intelligence circles as "tradecraft") are astoundingly similar. Obstructing investigations by high-level political advisors, lying to the FBI and Congress, bribery, destruction of evidence, and hiding behind a wall of secrecy conveniently provided by the intelligence community as a cover to do whatever they want to do are aspects of political tradecraft that have proven unfailingly effective ever since Watergate.

As the administration of the second President Bush fades into history, it's instructive to take a brief look at the subsequent careers of several of the Iran Contra alumni.

Caspar Weinberger became publisher of *Forbes* magazine in 1989, and chairman of Forbes, Inc. in 1993. He wrote several books before his death in 2006.

Robert McFarlane, who had continued to act as an envoy for planeloads of weapons to Iran after his retirement as national security advisor, subsequently co-founded and served as CEO of Global Energy Investors. He currently serves on the Board of Directors for Aegis Defence Services, a London-based private military company with overseas offices and contracts with the UN and the U.S. government.

Elliott Abrams became president of the Ethics and Public Policy Center in Washington, as well as chairman of the U.S. Commission on International Religious Freedom. He was back on the National Security Council during George W. Bush's first term and in February 2005 was promoted to deputy national security advisor for global democracy strategy.

Oliver North ran unsuccessfully for the Senate in 1994 in Virginia. He became an author and a syndicated columnist, hosted radio and television shows, and is a frequent commentator for Fox News.

On August 2, 2002, an ambitious plan to collect information on hundreds of thousands of Americans in connection with the war on terror was outlined to an audience in Anaheim, California. Worked out of the Pentagon and called Total Information Awareness (or TIA), the plan was characterized as:

> . . . *a high-level, visionary, functional view of the world-wide system—somewhat over-simplified. One of the significant new data sources that needs to be mined to discover and track terrorists is the transaction space. . . . This is a list of transaction categories, and it is meant to be inclusive.*

The speaker was John M. Poindexter, who went on to become director of the DARPA Information Awareness Office for the administration of President George W. Bush from December 2002 to August 2003.

CHAPTER SEVEN

PATRICK LEAHY AND CHARLES GRASSLEY

A Hands-on Approach to the FBI

Congress sometimes has followed a hands-off approach about the FBI. Until the Bureau's problems are solved, we will need a hands-on approach for awhile.

Senator Patrick Leahy, July 30, 2001[1]

The senator from Iowa is comfortable as the agency's top inquisitor.

Des Moines Register, July 5, 2002[2]

On August 2, 2001, 39 days prior to the 9/11 terrorist attacks on the United States, Democratic Senator Patrick Leahy delivered 13 pages of remarks urging his colleagues to vote for former assistant attorney general Robert Mueller III to replace former FBI director Louis Freeh.

Seventy-four times during his remarks, Leahy, in his oversight role on the FBI as chairman of the Senate Committee on the Judiciary, focused on threats he said the Bureau posed to civil liberties in the United States. He characterized the power of the FBI as "extraordinary," and deplored the problematic nature of the "FBI culture." He reminded his colleagues about

FBI operations relative to the disasters at Waco and Ruby Ridge, allegations of incompetence at the FBI Laboratory, lack of performance and incompetence in the Wen Ho Lee espionage case, and the apparent ease with which FBI agent Robert Hanssen had operated for many years as a spy for the Soviets and then the Russians. He also cited issues about documentary evidence in the Oklahoma City bombing trial that surfaced prior to the execution of Timothy McVeigh.

Appearing to speak more in sorrow than in anger, Senator Leahy said that since the role played by the FBI in combating sophisticated cases of terrorism and espionage was so critical to the nation, Congress needed to "forge a constructive partnership with the Bureau's next director to get the FBI back on track." He made reference to the concerns of Senator Russ Feingold about the FBI's inability to distinguish between peaceful political dissent and criminal activity in the past and "possibly the targeting of Arab Americans today." Leahy repeated Feingold's worries that the FBI would infringe on fundamental First Amendment rights, and emphasized that FBI investigations within the U.S. should concentrate on criminal rather than intelligence activity.

On only two occasions did Senator Leahy use the word terrorism, and both times it was used only as a frame of reference to describe the FBI's many responsibilities. His characterization of the tragedies at Waco and Ruby Ridge referred primarily to operational errors by the FBI rather than as the expressions and harbingers of increased levels of violence in domestic terrorism that they actually were.

There was no acknowledgment that due to congressional actions for over two decades, the FBI had been dealing in the dark ever since the destruction of its domestic intelligence capability in the 1970s.

The appointment of Judge Louis Freeh as FBI director by President Clinton began in an atmosphere characterized by growing levels of both domestic and international terrorism, escalating political corruption, and continual efforts by Congress and the White House to exert partisan political influence over the Bureau. Freeh battled to maintain the Bureau's independence as deepening political divides put it in the middle of ongoing power struggles between the executive and legislative branches, and civil libertarians versus advocates of stronger centralized government.

In 1994, Senator Leahy joined with Representative Don Edwards in proposing a Digital Telephony bill that was designed to forestall the FBI's request for legislation deemed by some to be too intrusive to civil liberties. Adherence to privacy and a narrow focus on the criminal court process characterized the Leahy/Edwards approach.

For example, the Leahy bill required a court order and a showing of "specific and articulable facts" relevant to an ongoing criminal investigation in order for law enforcement authorities to access transactional records generated by telecommunications carriers. Law enforcement subpoenas would not be acceptable. "Pen registers" that identified the location of the caller, previously automatic when electronic surveillance was used, were no longer allowed, thereby preventing law enforcement from using the technique to preliminarily track people nationwide without first having to fully demonstrate appropriate cause.

Don Edwards summarized his and Leahy's approach in a letter saying that the bill "balances the interests of law enforcement, technological innovation and privacy."[3]

These 1994 political debates regarding law enforcement and privacy took on a new dimension in the wake of the terrorist attacks on America on September 11, 2001. In its report, the 9/11 Commission noted the critical need to balance security with civil liberties.

In a section titled "The Future Role of the FBI," in stunning contrast to previous exhortations to protect privacy above all, they concluded:

> . . . *The concern about the FBI is that it has long favored its criminal justice mission over its national security mission. . . . Under the structures we recommend, the FBI's role is focused, but still vital. The FBI does need to be able to direct its thousands of agents and other employees to collect intelligence in America's cities and towns—interviewing informants, conducting surveillances and searches, tracking individuals, working collaboratively with local authorities, and doing so with meticulous attention to detail and compliance with the law. The FBI's job in the streets would thus be a domestic equivalent, operating under the U.S. Constitution and quite different laws and rules, to the job of the CIA's operations officers abroad.*

After Watergate and the Church Committee hearings, the prevailing legend within both political parties was that the FBI had exceeded its limits and violated the civil rights of Americans through its domestic intelligence collection efforts. Two high-level FBI officials—one of whom, Mark Felt, had direct connections to the justice meted out to Watergate co-conspirators in the White House itself—were indicted and convicted for these "crimes."

In hearing after hearing by the Church Committee, and the Senate and House Intelligence and Judiciary Committees, the FBI's work was constantly evaluated with an emphasis on its adherence to civil liberties rather than its operational effectiveness. Whenever FBI performance was at issue, politicians decried it as an organization that was out of control, hopelessly mismanaged, and a potential danger to the civil liberties of Americans.

Nonetheless, after the international terrorist attacks on American soil in 2001, the 9/11 Commission concluded that the Bureau had not adequately developed its internal security capabilities. Essentially, according to the bipartisan commission, the Bureau had failed to "connect the dots" and prevent the attacks by adhering to the FISA law and the Wall that Congress itself had built to ensure protection of civil liberties.

The hypocrisy of congressional thinking prior to 9/11 was vividly demonstrated by their reaction to the revelation of the "Phoenix Memo" after 9/11.

In July 2001, FBI Headquarters received a pattern analysis developed by an FBI agent working terrorism in Phoenix, Arizona. The agent had discovered that a number of Arab Nationals were attending flight schools in the Phoenix area. He worried about a possible connection between the flight students and the placement of explosives aboard commercial aircraft.

The agent asked that FBIHQ consider compiling a list of and establishing liaison with flight schools, discussing the matter within the greater intelligence community, and acquiring information about visas held by students at the schools.

Given the general congressional stance towards the FBI with respect to the threat it supposedly posed to civil rights, the fact that FBI Headquarters declined to launch an intelligence initiative regarding students at U.S. flight schools was fully in compliance with the letter as well as the spirit of the FISA law and the inviolate "Wall" that Washington politicians had created after Watergate and the Church Committee. Had they launched such an initiative, politicians on both sides of the aisle would have howled the roof down and demanded the FBI's head in full view of national news cameras.

The true irony here is that should another successful terrorist attack occur on U.S. soil, misguided and hasty "analysis" of the intelligence failure that led to it will convince politicians that the FBI's national security mission should be given instead to a new organization that will closely resemble an internal Central Intelligence Agency.

In that event, if the law enforcement mission becomes separated from domestic intelligence, the constraint of law will be effectively removed, and intelligence professionals from the CIA and military intelligence agencies will be in charge of national security without either the transparency or the protection of law between them and the American public.

Senator Leahy has been a professional politician in the U.S. Congress for over 30 years, and with no evident presidential aspirations; at this writing, he is at the height of his power. Keenly intelligent, his long record shows that he is also a formidable political opponent.

A July 2001 article in *The National Review* characterized him this way:

> *By a consensus of Hill Republicans, Pat Leahy is the meanest, most partisan, most ruthless Democrat in the Senate . . . and following the ancient rule that a staff reflects the politician at its head, the consensus is that Leahy's staff is just as partisan, just as ruthless as the senator himself. Not even Democrats much trust or like that bunch . . . they play to win, whatever it takes. And they'll roll over Democrats just as fast.*[4]

For a Democratic senator to be feared by Republicans—and even his fellow Democrats—takes considerable power, and Leahy has shown no reluctance to use it. Leahy's long tenure in the Senate began in 1975, right after the Church Committee began its examination (and condemnation) of COINTELPRO, and his attitude towards and understanding of the FBI was shaped by those times.

By 2006, when the Senate Judiciary Committee held a hearing on the wartime powers of the executive branch and the surveillance authority of NSA, Senator Leahy reiterated the hypocritical stance that had put the FBI in the dark all those years ago with FISA and the 'Wall':

> . . . *now, a couple of generations of Americans are too young to know why we passed this law. It was enacted after decades of abuses by the executive, including the wiretapping of Dr. Martin Luther King and other political opponents of early government officials.*

For politicians to exert greater political influence and power over the management of the FBI, they need to demonstrate to the country that the FBI is seriously mismanaged and out of control.

Senator Charles Grassley, currently the ranking Republican on the Senate Finance Committee, has long criticized the FBI "culture" for being arrogant and unaccountable to Congress, and for valuing style over substance in its public image.

In May 2001, Grassley appeared on ABC's *This Week* and criticized the FBI's document discovery problems in the Oklahoma City bombing case:

> *I think there's a management culture here that's at fault. I call it a cowboy culture. . . . It's the kind of culture that puts image, public relations and headlines ahead of the fundamentals of the FBI.*

Two weeks later, he further explained his position during a PBS OnLine *News Hour* interview:

I'm talking more about arrogance. Obviously, the papers are a result of a management culture that, I think particularly in higher-profile cases, is conducted in a way to make people look good and to watch out for the image of the FBI, as opposed to the substance of the FBI.

Senator Grassley's eagerness to maintain his reputation as an exacting critic of FBI management has at times legitimized the allegations of conspiracy theorists, who provide him information that is not always adequately substantiated before it leads to serious interference and collection of the facts in sensitive investigations.

Following the tragic crash of Trans World Airlines Flight 800 into Long Island Sound in 1996, Grassley used a public senate subcommittee hearing to call into question the FBI's investigation into the accident. Acting on information he said came "from inside," he declared that the management team of the New York Office, in its handling of the incident, was a "disaster."

In February 2002, Grassley joined with Senator Leahy in the hands-on approach Leahy had mentioned at Director Mueller's confirmation hearings the previous year and co-sponsored the FBI Reform Act.

The FBI Reform Act of 2002 gives Congress the hands-on approach it has long desired in managing the FBI. Although he acknowledged that increased funding for FBI counterterrorism operations was an immediate necessity, Leahy made it clear that more money for the FBI meant more congressional involvement in management decisions:

. . . this bulking up of the FBI must be accompanied by increased congressional oversight. The 'hands off' approach to the FBI that Congress has taken in the past is no longer an option.

The FBI Reform Act expanded the authority of the Department of Justice inspector general to investigate allegations of FBI misconduct, required a GAO report on duplicative case statistics involving the FBI and other federal law enforcement agencies, strengthened "whistleblower" protections inside the FBI, ended a perceived "double standard" in meting out discipline, created improved security programs inside and outside the FBI to guard against intelligence and terrorist penetrations, and allowed Congress to participate in guiding strategies to prepare the FBI for the 21st Century, such as modernizing its information technology systems.

In early April 2002, two high-ranking FBI officials: Bob Dies, brought in from IBM as the FBI's chief information technology officer; and Robert Chiardio, the Bureau's executive assistant director for administration, praised the FBI Reform Act for its emphasis on modernizing the Bureau's information technology systems.

During a congressional hearing in front of Senator Leahy's Judiciary Committee, Chiardio attributed the technology problems to a "management and cultural issue which must be forthrightly confronted."

Shortly thereafter, both Dies and Chiardio left the FBI without fixing anything.

Leahy had called the continuation of Director Freeh's policy to reach outside the FBI and bring in leaders from America's corporations "promising." Another outside executive—this time brought in from the CIA to run the FBI's Counterterrorism Directorate after 9/11—told FBI employees that they would need to change their culture and worry less about civil liberties and more about protecting the country from terrorists.

The FBI Reform Act also supplied politicians with an ongoing information flow about FBI operations. Grassley and Leahy pointed directly to the "urgency" of 9/11 as the justification for more congressional oversight of the FBI, thereafter calling for the creation of a career security program to prevent cases like that of Robert Hanssen and the use of the polygraph, as well as the need to modernize the Bureau's computer efforts.

Ironically, the emphasis by Leahy and Grassley on reforming a supposedly intransigent FBI management "culture" has been followed instead by a wave of early retirements among highly experienced counterintelligence and counterterrorism agents in the Field and mid-level management positions. FBI Director Robert Mueller, under tremendous pressure from Congress and the White House, has chosen to discourage the voicing of differing opinions from all levels of the Bureau that point out the folly of some of the congressional mandates that are weakening the FBI and its overall credibility in the "war on terror."

One FBI agent who retired promptly after reaching his 50th birthday told us that although he'd loved the FBI and enjoyed every minute he worked in a major metropolitan FBI Field Office, he'd volunteered towards the end of his career to serve as a counselor to a new agents training class at the FBI Academy in Quantico, Virginia. He'd snared major drug dealers, had extensive experience in both counterintelligence and criminal investigations, and served as a high-profile member of the office SWAT team. Now, however, he wanted to get away from the operational atmosphere in the Field that had become so confused and politicized after 9/11.

Since he believed that the FBI since 9/11 was being browbeaten into doing whatever it was told to do by politicians, regardless of effectiveness and appropriate use of manpower, the agent thought a stint at Quantico as a mentor would be a morale boost for him.

At the graduation ceremony for his new agent class, he sat with them as they listened to FBI Director Robert Mueller carefully explain that the FBI in the current day has two kinds of employees: "collectors" and "analysts."

He was appalled to hear FBI agents described by the director of the FBI as "collectors." A seasoned investigator, he knew from experience that the use of the term was influenced by the ascendancy of the intelligence community in the "war on terror." For decades, the Bureau's mission had included responsibility for both law enforcement and intelligence. It was now evident that politicians had the mandate they'd clamored for after 9/11. The FBI he'd served for over 20 years, which was characterized by both its law enforcement and its intelligence mission, was now being primarily driven by post–9/11 politics to be primarily an extension of the intelligence community.

Like many of his fellow agents, he submitted his retirement papers earlier than he'd planned.

The financial "greenmailers" of the early 1980s bought controlling shares of weakened companies and then threatened takeovers to either force the target firm to buy its own shares back at inflated prices, or to break them up and sell the pieces to the highest bidders. Now politicians in Congress have seconded the Bureau's counterintelligence and counterterrorism divisions to the CIA, while leaving FBI criminal investigative responsibilities under-funded and under-prioritized. Included in the latter category are, of course, cases involving political corruption.

The "greenmailers" motive was profit. The motives of politicians, in the rarified and insular atmosphere that characterizes the nation's capitol, are dominated by the drive to enhance their own power.

But with the same myopic view of the "dangers" posed to civil rights that governed their view of the FBI after Watergate, the Church Committee, FISA, and the "Wall," politicians are allowing their satisfaction at the imposition of their power over the Bureau to blind them to the unforeseen consequences of their actions.

Although they view themselves as the champions of civil liberties, Senators Leahy and Grassley have contributed to setting in motion a trend towards less transparency and oversight of the conduct of the terror war by the rule of law. The primacy of intelligence community professionals and practices over the restraint that is built into the duality of the FBI's law enforcement and intelligence roles will be a disaster for the civil liberties of Americans, while at the same time it will provide no enhanced protection in this new age of terrorism.

Chapter Eight

INVESTIGATING FRIENDS OF POLITICIANS

The Archer Daniels Midland Case

WASHINGTON, D.C. A federal judge has dismissed with prejudice a civil damages suit a former Archer Daniels Midland Corporation executive filed against an FBI agent who was his primary contact in the government's antitrust investigation of ADM, the Department of Justice announced today.

The action by Magistrate Judge David G. Bernthal of U.S. District Court in Springfield, Illinois, bars Mark E. Whitacre, the executive, from ever again bringing the accusations against Brian Shepard, a special agent in the FBI's Decatur, Illinois, office.

U.S. Department of Justice Press Release
February 10, 1998

In the midst of Watergate and the exposure of its numerous examples of poor judgment and bad decisions, it came to light that President Nixon's once popular vice president, Spiro Agnew, took bribes from the construction industry while he was governor of Maryland. His bad conduct and criminality continued when he went to Washington, D.C. In October 1973, Agnew pleaded no contest to criminal tax evasion and money laundering. He resigned as vice president and ultimately paid close to $270,000 in fines, the amount he took in as bribes.

International Telephone and Telegraph gave $400,000 to the Republican Party in support of the party holding its 1972 national convention in San Diego. A subsequent trail of internal memos, especially the revelation of a memo by ITT lobbyist Dita Beard, confirmed that based on the contribution, the Department of Justice settled several pending lawsuits with ITT under favorable terms to the company. When the scheme came to light, the convention was moved from San Diego to Miami under the orders of President Nixon. Attorney General John Mitchell had already left his position amid the furor of the Watergate scandal. It was his successor, Attorney General Richard Kleindiest, who approved the ITT settlements.

The Watergate affair involved so many members of the Nixon administration and so greatly impacted the nation that many of the other scandals of Nixon's presidency get little attention. But the past actions of politicians, the political machines that are the backbone of each party, and the corporations that fund American politics repeat their behavior decade after decade, ignoring the law as somehow inapplicable to them. When they're caught, they're defended by heavyweight law firms, whose job it is to keep the machines and their main players out of trouble and out of jail. Sometimes they succeed, and sometimes they don't.

The 1990s price fixing case of Archer Daniels Midland (ADM) Corporation, whose former CEO Dwayne Andreas, along with his company, were indicted as a result of inquiries during the Watergate era, is a stark illustration of the gauntlet run by individual FBI case agents who dare to expose the corruption inherent in the unholy alliance of government with big business.

Andreas and ADM were alleged to have provided illegal campaign contributions to President Nixon's presidential run. They weren't alone, standing with a number of other American icons who were both indicted and convicted of the same charges. ADM and Andreas pleaded not guilty to the charges and were eventually exonerated.

Years later, during the administration of President Clinton, ADM and its management were up to a different sort of dirty business and had once again drawn the attention of the FBI. The story of their behavior and the FBI investigation that finally succeeded in nailing them illustrates that the FBI is the only government agency powerful enough—and independent enough—to take on billion dollar corporations, while it further explains the deep resentment of the Bureau by politicians in the pockets of those corporations.

Brian Shepard was the senior agent in the Decatur, Illinois, FBI office in the 1990s. He became the case agent in one of the most significant conspiracy and price-fixing investigations in the history of the federal government.

In 1992, Archer Daniels Midland Corporation was fixing the price of the animal food additive lysine with two Japanese companies as well as a Korean subsidiary who were ostensibly its competitors for the additive. Together, they raised lysine prices 70 percent within their first nine months of cooperation, resulting in higher prices paid for many products possessing the additives all down the distribution line.

ADM chairman and CEO Dwayne Andreas had long befriended numerous presidents, ambassadors, senators, members of Congress, and foreign leaders, and made political contributions to a long list of both Democrats and Republicans. ADM was a tightly run family operation that had grown into a worldwide powerhouse with major political clout, regardless of the political party in power. With legions of attorneys, millions of dollars at its disposal, and the ability to pick up the phone and call friends in high places, the company was accustomed to doing whatever it wanted in pursuing its business.

Usually corporations that plead guilty to a federal crime lose their government contracts. ADM has not. Attorney and author James B. Lieber also notes that during the course of his research for a book about the case,[1] many government documents were withheld. Not everyone's loyalties were with the company, however:

> 'In time, I came to understand that the simultaneous providing and withholding of information represented a government at odds with itself,' Lieber writes. 'One part wanted the law to run its course notwithstanding the power of the accused. Another sought to protect ADM and do its bidding.'[2]

Lieber's "understanding" is a critical point in illustrating the value of a politically independent FBI, which as an investigative agency was the "part" of the government that wanted the law to run its course, despite the political and economic power of ADM. The "part" of the government that has been accused of protecting the politically favored company is the politically influenced Department of Justice, whose attorney general is a political appointee of each sitting U.S. President.

The comfort that ADM officials apparently felt with their privileged status as players in the worlds of both business and government made it easy for Dwayne Andreas to call the FBI when he was made aware that there might be corporate espionage directed against the company by a foreign competitor. Andreas sent an up-and-coming company executive, Mark Whitacre, to meet with the Bureau and make the complaint.

It was a near certainty that Whitacre would be the company's next president, and he was assured of even more millions and perks than he was already accustomed to at ADM. He was a trusted insider, and prior to meeting with the Bureau, Whitacre met with company attorneys and Andreas' son, who briefed him on what to tell the FBI and what not to tell the FBI. Specifically, Whitacre was told to lie to the FBI about relevant facts connected to the industrial espionage allegations. The lies were necessary to cover the company's own price fixing conspiracy with the very companies it was alleging had sabotaged one of its factories. It seems clear that ADM officials were confident they could keep their price-fixing activities from the Department of Justice. Their mistake was in thinking they could keep it from a particularly diligent special agent of the FBI.

With an ADM attorney at his side, Whitacre met with Special Agent Brian Shepard, reporting only what he had been instructed to say. They scheduled a second meeting to delve further into more details concerning the industrial sabotage of ADM.

But before the second meeting with Shepard, at which the company attorney would not be present, Whiteacre started to feel bad about lying to the "nice" guy from the FBI. He also felt a sense of obligation that he needed to tell the agent the truth about illegal activity undertaken by the company that had his loyalty.

In an article in *Fortune* magazine, "My Life as a Mole for the FBI," Whitacre's discussion of his motivation for telling the truth is highly informative to today's debate on the effectiveness of a skillful interview versus a coercive interrogation in obtaining critical information:

> *I did not feel comfortable lying to the FBI . . . and when Brian Shepard showed up at my house I told him the truth . . . why did I decide to tell him the truth? Brian . . . was a very trustworthy guy. I really hit it off with him well . . . I don't know. I just really trusted the guy. If it*

were another kind of guy, I might not have told him. He was really trustworthy, and I found it a real relief to talk with him. . . . A week or so later, Brian came back with another guy, a colleague, and we talked further. We built more and more trust.

Several years later, Archer Daniels Midland Company was on trial for numerous counts of price fixing, obstruction of justice, and conspiracy. An army of high-priced attorneys from the formidable law firm Williams and Connolly mounted the only defense they had: they launched a merciless attack on both the informant, Mark Whitacre, and his FBI handler, Special Agent Brian Shepard.[3]

The jury didn't buy it. The company was found guilty and fined millions of dollars, and several of its officers, including Andreas' son, Michael, traded in their fancy cars and clothes for prison "pen" stripes and a short ride in a government inmate bus.

Brian Shepard learned how to be an FBI agent the hard way, assigned to the New York Office working Soviet foreign counterintelligence during the busy 1980s. Shepard had a reputation as one of the finest agents targeted at the Soviet KGB, and worked long days, nights, and weekends while commuting to his home in New Jersey. Born and raised in Illinois, Shepard finally got his "dream" transfer after long years in the Big Apple to the FBI Field Office in Springfield, Illinois, and was eventually assigned to the Decatur Resident Agency.

Friendly, sociable, and highly likeable, Shepard was a perfect fit in the community, and he represented the FBI in an admirable fashion, both on and off duty. He might have anticipated that his days of working big cases were over when he was assigned to this quiet town in the middle of Illinois, but that wasn't how it happened. Soon he'd be using everything he'd learned during his time in the Bureau as well as the rest of his experience in dealing with one of the biggest investigations the FBI had ever undertaken. Just as in his New York years, his ability to build strong connections and relationships with people relied on his own integrity. But because of that integrity, Shepard would become the target of attacks by an industry titan and its legion of attorneys as they tried to change his public reputation from dedicated FBI agent to that of a corrupt and manipulative criminal in his own right.

Shepard recalled his first meeting with Whitacre in 1992:

I feel very strongly that it was a personality issue, first and foremost. I related to him on a level that put him at ease. Whitacre was a very bright guy with a tremendous amount to lose, and I felt that his trust in me is what would make this thing work. I think I was the right guy at the right time. He and I talked in the car until the wee hours of the morning. I did it to gain his trust. I felt that he liked me. Because I was there and he felt safe— that he had a safe harbor with me. I told him the truth. It was my life, this case, developing the relationship and developing the trust. That's why it worked.[4]

Shepard's case hinged on Whitacre's ability to successfully tape record meetings he had with high-ranking executive officers inside the company to collect the necessary evidence to support the price fixing charges. Whitacre never knew ahead of time when a meeting might be scheduled or occur or who he was going to talk to. The ADM Corporation controlled the playing field. With 30 guards at the gates, it was up to Whitacre, the "insider," to work the tapes and get the evidence that he passed along to Shepard several hours later at various clandestine meetings in the Decatur area.

From 1992 to 1995, Whitacre delivered some 239 surveillance tapes to Shepard, who carefully amassed and protected the evidence that would lead to the ADM case being dubbed "the best documented corporate crime in American history."[5]

In a textbook illustration of the interpersonal skills and integrity that underpin the handling of a valuable but volatile informant, Brian Shepard constantly assessed and reassured Whitacre at the same time:

I tried to look into the guy's eyes and gain his trust. It was a constant.[6]

As the case developed and the company found out about the investigation, allegations surfaced that Whitacre himself had been involved in embezzling from ADM. Charges and counter-charges flew as ADM and several of its highest ranking executives were indicted for price fixing. Then Williams and Connolly, who ADM paid millions of dollars to defend the company, turned their attention and their heavy legal weapons on FBI Special Agent Brian Shepard.

Warily, the Department of Justice and the FBI itself considered the possibility that Shepard had known about Whitacre's embezzlement, and designated agents from the FBI's Chicago office to take over the ADM investigation as it proceeded further. Although no FBI Office of Professional Responsibility (OPR) inquiry—the equivalent of an internal affairs investigation in a police department—was ever opened, Shepard remained the subject of rumor and speculation as he readied himself to appear as a critical government witness in the trial of the main ADM case.

Decatur was—and still is—an ADM town. It was dominated by its major employer, which was unaccustomed to being challenged by anyone. Shepard remembers the chill:

The ADM case took an emotional and physical toll. Defense attorneys interviewed the father of my granddaughter.[7]

At the trial, the evidence against ADM—much of it in the form of many hours of tape recordings—was extensive. The only defense ADM had available was to impugn the character and reputation of Brian Shepard, whose testimony on the witness stand lasted for three days. During that time, Shepard was accused of destroying evidence and lying about aspects of the investigation and his handling of the informant Whitacre. Shepard knew the whole case hinged on convincing the jury that he wasn't the bad guy.

Coordinating the investigation, long hours of contentious examination on the witness stand, and weathering constant attacks against both his person and his profession was heavy enough going. In addition, Shepard endured a backroom fight with federal prosecutors even before he took the stand because they didn't believe he would make a good enough witness.

But in the end, ADM entered a plea of guilty and paid a record $100 million dollar fine to the U.S. government. Michael Andreas went to jail. Terry Wilson, another high-ranking ADM executive, went to jail. And Dwayne Andreas, who along with his company had beat the federal government's Watergate-era charges of providing illegal campaign contributions to the Nixon re-election, was removed from his position of CEO of ADM by its Board of Directors. As part of a plea agreement his Williams and Connolly lawyers struck with the U.S. Justice Department, however, Dwayne Andreas was never questioned about any criminal matter involving ADM or anything else.

In 2000, journalist Kurt Eichenwald wrote a book about the ADM case called *The Informant*. A movie based on the book is being filmed this year by Director Steven Soderburgh, starring actor Matt Damon as Mark Whitacre. The movie is scheduled for release in 2009.

Over the years, journalists and entertainment industry representatives have made repeated requests to Special Agent Brian Shepard, now retired, to contribute to the public record of the case. Shepard has consistently declined, and has relied on official court documents of his testimony to provide his account rather than having it interpreted by the media. He still lives in Decatur, Illinois.

CHAPTER NINE

BILL CLINTON

Too Little, Too Late

By the fall of 1998, I had been Bill Clinton's top cop for half a decade, but he hadn't spoken to me in two years.

Louis J. Freeh, *My FBI*

President Bill Clinton's uneasy relationship with the FBI began almost immediately following his election. He fired Judge William Steele Sessions, who served as the FBI's director for five years before author Robert Kessler exposed his unethical conduct in a book about the Bureau, replacing Sessions with another federal judge and former federal prosecutor, Louis J. Freeh.

Things looked rosy at first. Freeh had actually been an FBI agent, in the trenches in New York City, and had significant track records of success both in his agent career as well as his subsequent work as a federal prosecutor. The president had good reason to think he'd taken care of morale and performance problems in the FBI that had grown during Sessions' troubled tenure, and he must have assumed that Freeh would become a loyal Clintonite purely by joining the charismatic president's team.

But one of Louis Freeh's specific goals when he came into office was to keep the FBI independent of politics, and even the supremely adept politician that is Bill Clinton was unable to cajole him away from that goal. Both men had keen intellects, but their personal lives and values were so incompatible that Clinton soon began to view Freeh as disloyal, while Freeh became increasingly uncomfortable with the president's free-wheeling style when it came to legal and moral issues.

As FBI agents worked inside the country and around the world to collect minute fragments of evidence at one terrorist crime scene after another, Clinton's presidency and the Democratic Party machine were engulfed in a continuous wave of scandal and corruption. In an unprecedented move to avoid any appearance of conflict of interest and to prevent the Bureau itself from being dragged into the controversies that swirled around the White House, Attorney General Janet Reno and Director Freeh developed a policy to guide the FBI's interactions with the White House. The FBI would deal with the president indirectly through the attorney general and the Department of Justice. Director Freeh would maintain a policy of no direct contact with the president.

The tragedy of this incompatibility for the country was that the seeds for the terrorist attacks of 9/11 were planted during President Bill Clinton's White House years. The facts are undeniable. President Clinton took the oath of office in January 1993, and his education in the destructive power of terrorism was immediate.

On February 26, 1993, international terrorists drove a Ryder truck into the sub-basement of Tower One of the World Trade Center, carrying a bomb that was intended to topple both of the twin towers. Investigation led by the FBI after the blast resulted in the indictment and convictions of ten international terrorists, including the leader of the plot, Kuwaiti-born Ramzi

Ahmed Yousef. After the attacks, Yousef fled to Manila, the Philippines.

In July 1993, FBI agents prevented international terrorists from implementing a second plot to bomb New York City-related targets (the United Nations Building, the Holland and Lincoln Tunnels, the Jacob K. Javits Federal Building) and from murdering Egyptian President Hosni Mubarak. A federal court jury convicted ten conspirators of 48 of 50 terrorism-related charges, including an Egyptian cleric, Sheik Omar Abdel-Rahman. The FBI used an informant to penetrate the group, and a surveillance tape showed them plotting the attacks from the garage of a house they rented in Brooklyn.

On December 11, 1994, Ramzi Yousef used a fake name and identity to board a Philippine Airlines flight and, when he departed the plane, left a bomb underneath one of the seats. When the plane resumed its journey as Philippine Airlines Flight 434, the bomb exploded, killing one passenger. The plot to bomb airliners, referred to by Yousef as Operation Bojinka, was funded by al Qaeda. Yousef left the Philippines to seek sanctuary at an al Qaeda safe house in Pakistan. Early in February 1995, Pakistani authorities arrested Yousef in Islamabad and rendered him back to the United States for trial. Yousef was the nephew of Khalid Sheikh Mohammed, who would ultimately plan the 9/11 terrorist attacks against the United States.

In the largest and most destructive terrorist attack on American soil until 9/11, the Alfred P. Murrah Federal Building in Oklahoma City was destroyed by a fertilizer bomb carried in a Ryder truck on April 19, 1995. An hour after the attack, an alert state trooper stopped a car with no rear license plate and detained the driver, Timothy McVeigh, for carrying a firearm without a permit. McVeigh, Terry Nichols, and Michael Fortier were charged with murdering 168 people and injuring 800. All were convicted. In June 2001, McVeigh was executed for his crimes.

On March 20, 1995, ten members of the Japanese group Aum Shinrikyo released sarin gas in five simultaneous chemical attacks aimed at Tokyo subway lines. Twelve people were killed and a thousand suffered severe vision problems as a result. One of the individuals convicted in the attacks was a medical doctor. Several others were graduates with degrees in physics or artificial intelligence. Aum Shinrikyo, known today as "Aleph," is a religious group that still claims over 2,000 members.

During the celebratory atmosphere of the 1996 summer Olympics in Atlanta, Georgia, a bomb carried inside a backpack exploded at Centennial Olympic Park. Two people died. In 1997, two more bombing incidents, one at an Atlanta abortion clinic and another at a gay nightclub, preceded the January 1998 killing of an off-duty police officer at an abortion clinic in Birmingham, Alabama. Witnesses provided license plate information that resulted in the identity of the bomber, Eric Robert Rudolph. An extensive search focused on 500,000 acres of rugged mountains in western North Carolina. By the summer of 1998, two dozen local, state, and federal agencies led by the FBI were involved in the pursuit of Rudolph. The search was so intensive that Rudolph was forced to stay holed up in the forest, preventing him from ever committing another bombing attack. On May 31, 2003, a rookie police officer from the Murphy, North Carolina, Police Department apprehended Rudolph as he stumbled out of the woods looking for food. The case against Rudolph was so strong and the witnesses so credible that he pled guilty prior to trial and now serves a life sentence at the Super Max Prison in Florence, Colorado.

On June 25, 1996, 20 American servicemen were killed and 372 people representing a variety of countries were injured when a truck bomb packed with the equivalent of over 20,000 pounds of TNT was driven into the Khobar Towers military housing complex in Saudi Arabia. The FBI investigation that followed connected the bombing to military and government officials of Iran. The Clinton Administration ignored the Bureau's plea to secure indictments against those responsible.[1]

Following the election of President George W. Bush, indictments were returned on June 21, 2001, against those alleged to be responsible for the Khobar Towers attacks.

On August 7, 1998, over 200 people were killed and 4,000 injured when truck bombs rocked U.S. embassies in Kenya and Tanzania. An FBI investigation tied the bombings to Osama Bin Laden and al Qaeda. Before the terrorist attacks of 9/11, the ongoing investigation had led to 21 indictments, including Bin Laden and his deputy, Ayman al Zawahiri. Four of the conspirators have been convicted in federal court and are serving prison sentences of life without parole. Several have been killed in fighting since 9/11 and some are held at Guantanamo Bay or by the United Kingdom. Eleven are still being sought, including Bin Laden. President Clinton responded by launching cruise missiles at suspected al Qaeda training camps in the Sudan and Afghanistan.

Algerian-born Ahmed Ressam first entered Canada in 1994. After training at an al Qaeda camp in Afghanistan, he tried to enter the United States at Port Washington on December 14, 1999. Alert Customs agents were suspicious and asked him to step out of his car. Their suspicions were warranted and prevented Ressam from launching a terrorist attack at Los Angeles International Airport and other targets in California. Ressam's rental car concealed bomb components and explosives. Subsequent FBI investigation resulted in his indictment and conviction for attempted terrorist acts against America.

While docked in Aden Harbor, Yemen, on October 12, 2000, the *U.S.S. Cole* was attacked by terrorists piloting a small boat loaded with explosives. The policy of the American government at the time prohibited the sailors on board the *U.S.S. Cole* from taking any action since they were not being fired upon. Although they saw the boat coming directly towards the *Cole*, they stared helplessly as it rammed into the ship and its explosive cargo detonated. Seventeen sailors were killed and 39 injured in the blast, which the FBI tied to al Qaeda. Presidents Clinton and Bush never responded to the attack on the *U.S.S. Cole*. They, their advisors, and respective party loyalists debate today about what they knew and when they knew it. They continue to deny they were provided any conclusive evidence about the al Qaeda connection to the *Cole* attack in the days leading to 9/11.

Clinton's education in the reality of international terrorism was fortified by congressional hearings on the topic, draft legislation, and the work of special commissions led by former United States government officials and elected representatives. Seminars involving the intelligence community, Department of Defense, and assorted think tanks were already referring to the "defense of the homeland" and using terms like "homeland security" many months before the 9/11 attacks. The FBI was asking Congress and the White House for expanded resources and increased funding to address what it perceived as the growing threat to the country from terrorism. Politicians in both parties were continually provided with evidence of the growing menace of terrorism.

In 1998, Clinton and the Congress endorsed the creation of the U.S. Commission on National Security/21st Century, proposed by Secretary of Defense William Cohen, to foresee future national security threats to the United States. Co-chaired by former Senators Gary Hart and Warren Rudman, the commission included Newt Gingrich and Lee Hamilton (who later served as the co-chair of the 9/11 Commission).

In the first of three reports the commission released between September 15, 1999, and February 1, 2001, the commissioners reached 14 "key conclusions." Three in particular painted a portrait of America's not too-distant-future that looks almost prescient in retrospect:

America will become increasingly vulnerable to hostile attack on our homeland, and our military superiority will not entirely protect us. (Americans will likely die on American soil, possibly in large numbers.)

U.S. intelligence will face more challenging adversaries, and even excellent intelligence will not prevent all surprises. (. . . the United States will continue to confront strategic shocks, as intelligence analysis and human judgments will fail to detect all dangers in an ever-changing world.)

All borders will be more porous; some will bend and some will break. (Traditional bonds between states and their citizens can no longer be taken for granted, even in the United States.)

In November 1999, FBI Director Freeh issued his first press release concerning plans to restructure FBI Headquarters and establish a Counterterrorism Division within the FBI. He emphasized that "protecting America from terrorism and ensuring our national security are the FBI's highest priorities." Dale Watson, the first assistant director of the new Counterterrorism Division, declared in May 2000 that "our number one priority is the prevention of terrorism."

During the first week of March, 2000, Freeh testified before the Senate Appropriations Committee about the Bureau's fiscal year 2001 budget request. The FBI asked Congress for $13,100,000 to "improve and enhance existing counterterrorism initiatives including WMD preparedness, 2002 Winter Olympics preparation, Hazardous Devices School, and counterterrorism research and development."

In a follow-up hearing with then CIA Director George Tenet, the FBI director emphasized that future threats:

> . . . *would require that the intelligence, law enforcement, and security communities adopt a new ethos that embraces cooperation, coordination, collaboration, accountability, and specific strategic objectives for collecting, analyzing, and acting on information revealing intent to harm U.S. national security.*

Tenet emphasized the specific threat of al Qaeda, saying that Osama Bin Laden "wants to strike further blows," at America.

From $5.7 billion in 1995 to a proposed $11.1 billion in 2000, increases in funding were proof that the urgency in taking on terror and defending the nation from a terrorist attack had been strongly emphasized and brought to the attention of Congress. Initiatives, legislation, and government assessments confirmed the importance of being pro-active in the fight against terror. Republican Senator John Kyl and Democratic Senator Diane Feinstein co-sponsored legislation to improve technology, address use of pathogens, and go after terrorist fundraising activities.

Although the overall U.S. government budget to combat terrorism grew steadily during the Clinton years, it focused largely on the process rather than the product. Aspects of the bill proposed by Kyl and Feinstein that would have allowed the FBI to "share foreign intelligence information obtained from domestic wiretaps with the CIA and other intelligence agencies" were dropped after Senator Richard Shelby received a letter from the ACLU opposing the sharing because it breached "the well-established and constitutionally vital line between law enforcement and intelligence activities." Even the Department of Justice joined with the ACLU in opposing the sharing and in maintaining the Wall between intelligence and law enforcement.

Senator Kyl's impatience with the process of politics as usual showed:

> *Everybody talks about trying to do something about terrorism, but little action ever ends up occurring.*

There was considerable political opposition to stronger anti-terror strategies in the years prior to 9/11. After 9/11, however, many of those who had been part of that opposition began contradicting their former positions.

The Senate Appropriations Committee, quoting from a study by Syracuse University, blasted the FBI for securing only 45 terrorism convictions in 1998.

FBI Assistant Director of Public Affairs John Collingwood noted in response:

> *We're now working with the CIA and foreign agencies to disrupt terrorists before they can carry out their actions and preferably before they get inside the United States.*

In December 1999, when the FBI conducted an awareness outreach within Muslim communities in America in a pro-active effort to prevent terrorist acts during the Millennium, the Bureau's Office of Public and Congressional Affairs had to defend the practice to the media. When the FBI developed a computer system called "Carnivore" to covertly search email messages that would assist in counterintelligence and counter-terrorism investigations, *The Wall Street Journal* editorialized that:

The FBI has upset privacy advocates and some in the computer industry. Experts say the system opens a thicket of unresolved legal issues and privacy concerns.

As a result, Congress sputtered and fumed in hearings on "Carnivore" in 2000. Another *Wall Street Journal* editorial from June 2000 aroused concerns over government trends towards secrecy:

Officials . . . talk of winning the war against terrorists and spies. But it's worth stopping to ask what price the country wants to pay for victory. The terrorist and espionage threats are certainly real, but it would be a tragedy to burn down the American system in the name of saving it.

One newspaper editorial looked nervously in 2000 at the trend toward military involvement in domestic counterterrorism:

*. . . military involvement is a favored practice of dictators, such as Saddam Hussein . . . domestic crises have been the domain of police, the FBI, and the Federal Emergency Management Agency . . . it is possible to imagine a massively destructive attack that would force a president to call in the troops . . . **as long as that horror remains remote**, changing laws to make constitutional rights easier to violate risks tearing the American fabric more than a bomb ever could.*[2]

But the horror wasn't remote.

In the early spring of 2000, FBI Director Freeh journeyed to seven far eastern nations in as many days on an urgent trip to seek support locating and apprehending Osama Bin Laden for his role in the bombings of the United States embassies in Kenya and Tanzania in August 1998. Prior to embarking for Turkey, India, Pakistan, and several of the new Russian republics, the director discussed his trip with CIA Director George Tenet, Ambassador Madeline Albright, and others close to the president. The FBI had authority to share critical information with the president of Pakistan in order to convince him of the continuing dangers posed by Bin Laden and the need to find him sooner, not later.

It was midday in the dead of winter and the sun was shining high in the sky as the Gulf Stream with the seal of the government of the United States passed and then circled the small airfield over Lahore, Pakistan. The plane landed in front of a terminal guarded by unsmiling, heavily armed soldiers. Freeh's plane had been diverted from meeting with Pakistani President Pervez Mushareff in Islamabad because of terrorist threats to the city. After a short greeting by Pakistani officials in an eerily abandoned airport facility, the delegation was informed that only the FBI director and his chief of staff would be allowed to journey on to another location to meet the Pakistani leader. The rest of the FBI delegation stayed at the terminal, where Pakistani security guards posted outside the doors facing the airstrip kept the delegation sequestered.

Although it was winter, the air inside the small hangar-style room, upgraded with stylish and brightly colored carpet and matching furniture, was heavy and still. Director Freeh and his chief of staff Bob Bucknam sped away in a convoy of trucks and cars, driven by members of the Pakistani army. Thousands of miles away from home, bringing a message of the extreme danger Bin Laden and his confederates posed to America, Pakistan, and the world, the rest of the FBI team waited, protected only by a hand full of men they knew nothing about, any one of whom could have been a "mole" for the al Qaeda terrorist network.

Freeh and Bucknam returned after about 75 minutes. As soon as they entered the airport waiting room, the party was moved out the door and re-boarded on the American Air Force plane. Everyone was quiet as the plane took to the sky. They were off the ground, but for at least a few minutes were vulnerable to a hand-fired rocket launched by terrorists on a high-value American target.

As the plane banked and climbed steeply, everyone held his or her breath. A short time later, as rugged mountain peaks in the distance pointed to Afghanistan, Director Freeh looked out the window at the vast wilderness of snow-covered mountains with endless valleys in between and said:

Bin Laden is out there hiding, just like Eric Rudolph is hiding in the mountains in western North Carolina.

Freeh spoke thoughtfully about his meeting with Mushareff:

He's an interesting guy, and very astute. I think he understands the threat from Bin Laden and has his own concerns about the danger he poses, but I think he's reluctant at this point to completely sign up with the Americans in hunting Bin Laden down. Time will tell. He's more than ready to meet again. It'll be important for George [Tenet] and [Madeline] Albright and I to compare notes about the things he has told us and continue moving this effort along. For now, I believe he looks at it as just as much a local issue as one impacting us in America.

At 37,000 feet the plane was heading over Chinese airspace. Earlier after takeoff, they had anxiously awaited permission from the Chinese government to fly over rather than around their country as they headed for the former Soviet Republic of

Kazakhstan, which had become an ally in the fight against terror. It was ironic that the safety of a plane full of FBI agents was assured in the protected sanctuary of the People's Republic of China and the Russian Republic, old Cold War antagonists, but now seemingly friends and partners in a world confronted with the threat of terrorist bandits.[3]

In June, 2000, the National Commission on Terrorism, headed by former ambassador L. Paul Bremer III, released its Final Report. Mandated by the 105th Congress, "Countering the Changing Threat of International Terrorism" proposed sweeping changes in the approach to terrorism. Of special interest is a section of the report that addresses the ineffectiveness of the Clinton administration concerning Iran:

> *There are indications of Iranian involvement in the 1996 Khobar Towers bombing in Saudi Arabia, in which 19 citizens were killed and more than 500 were injured. In October 1999, President Clinton officially requested cooperation from Iran in the investigation. Thus far, Iran has not responded. . . . International pressure in the Pan Am 103 case ultimately succeeded in getting some degree of cooperation from Libya. The U.S. Government has not sought similar multilateral action to bring pressure on Iran to cooperate in the Khobar Towers bombing investigation. The president should not make further concessions toward Iran and should keep Iran on the list of state sponsors of terrorism until Tehran demonstrates it has stopped supporting terrorism and cooperates fully in the Khobar Towers investigation.*

On June 26, 2000, a workshop called "Defending the American Homeland Against Asymmetric Threats, Deterrence, and Preemption in the 21st Century" was held at the Wye River

Conference Center in Maryland. During three days of meetings and group discussions that included the CIA, FBI, State Department, Joint Chiefs of Staff representatives, NSA, National War College, and representatives of congressional committees and academia, America's national security was the sole topic. National security strategies, consequence management, retaliation for an attack on the "homeland" were all intensely reviewed and debated. Over all three days, there was one nagging question that no one could conclusively answer: Would a terrorist attack on America be considered a law enforcement matter, a military matter, or both?

One month later, CIA official Cofer Black and the FBI deputy assistant director for counterterrorism testified before the House Committee of Representative Christopher Shays on issues related to terrorism. While Cofer Black presented an overview of the CIA's assessment of the international terrorist threat (which the FBI shared), the FBI deputy assistant director used much of his time to discuss an additional growing concern of the FBI about a companion threat: the rise of domestic homegrown terrorism, especially the nature of the threat posed by "Lone Wolf" domestic terrorists like the Unabomber, Timothy McVeigh, and Eric Robert Rudolph, then still at large. These cases were time-intensive and extremely difficult to solve. A world where the Bureau simultaneously would be tracking down both domestic and international terrorists and working constantly to differentiate the two when a terrorist attack occurred would seriously confuse the issue as well as over-tasking investigative resources.

Nonetheless, the FBI agreed with the CIA, and told the committee:

Osama Bin Laden has emerged as the most urgent threat to U.S. interests internationally and in the United

States. In fact, threats to U.S. interests worldwide have increased to unprecedented levels in the aftermath of the August 1998 bombings of the U.S. embassies in East Africa and the subsequent U.S. missile strikes against suspected terrorist facilities in Afghanistan and Sudan. Bin Laden has been indicted for his role in masterminding the East African bombings, and in June 1999, was placed on the FBI's Top Ten Most Wanted Fugitives List.[4]

A few months after President Clinton left office in May, 2001, a congressional subcommittee held hearings to amend a bill on domestic terrorism preparedness. Its chairman, Steven LaTourette said:

. . . Two years ago, this committee began an examination of the federal programs designed to assist state and local emergency personnel to prepare for and respond to terrorist attacks . . . Throughout our review, the question we continue to ask is, who is in charge? . . . There is no single person to call . . . The federal government will spend more than $11 billion during fiscal year 2001 on counterterrorism, but there is no coordinated national strategy to guide this effort . . . The Department of Justice has made significant progress, but their efforts simply do not meet the requirements of a national strategy.

Congressman Shays, invited to attend the hearing because of his expertise in the counterterrorism area, added:

Our nation needs a comprehensive national anti-terrorism strategy. Congress and the Administration have an obligation and an opportunity to work together against terrorism. We should do so with a proper sense of

urgency, because one thing is certain, our terrorist adver-
saries will not wait for us to act on this very important
issue.

Although the FBI director was careful to keep clear of political entanglements with the White House, FBI agents still had
plenty of contact with the White House and Congress during the
Clinton years. This was mostly because they were serving an
unusually large volume of search warrants on the White House
staff and elected representatives. Even if international events
had been peaceful throughout Clinton's eight-year tenure, the
FBI would have been justified in asking for additional resources
and manpower, if only to keep up with the public corruption
cases that surfaced during the same time frame:

A four-year FBI investigation of the powerful Demo-
cratic House member Dan Rostenkowski and several
other Democrats in Congress in the Congressional Post
Office scandal ended in Rostenkowski's conviction and
imprisonment.

In 1993, the Clinton Administration was engulfed in
a scandal that became known as "Travel Gate." In the
same year, Vince Foster, White House attorney and close
friend of the Clintons committed suicide amid specula-
tion that documents from his office had disappeared.

In 1996, White House staff members got their hands
on FBI files which pertained to Republican Party mem-
bers. "File Gate" had all the earmarks of an attempt to
compile an "enemies list," just as President Nixon had
delighted in doing years earlier. Howard Shapiro, the
FBI's general counsel at the time, shared responsibility
for the files going to the White House and was forced to

resign from the Bureau. His departure was a blow to the institution, as his judgment and grace under fire had become significant attributes in addressing a myriad of investigative concerns and issues from the Field.

Five of the president's cabinet members came under investigation during his tenure. Housing Secretary Henry Cisneros pleaded guilty to lying to the FBI about money he had paid to a mistress. Clinton pardoned Cisneros in the final days of his presidency. Agriculture Secretary Michael Espy resigned but was later acquitted in his corruption trial. A lack of sufficient evidence resulted in no charges being brought against Interior Secretary Bruce Babbitt for allegedly lying to Congress. Labor Secretary Alexis Herman was cleared of any wrongdoing in an illegal fundraising case. Commerce Secretary Ron Brown was under investigation at the time he was killed in a plane crash.

Vice President Al Gore became wrapped up in accusations of illegal fundraising. "China Gate" drew attention to the fundraising activities of the entire administration, with allegations that American policies towards the People's Republic of China were unduly influenced.

"Whitewater" was the name attached to a six-year investigation of the president, his wife, Hillary, and some of their business associates in connection with land deals in Arkansas. Insufficient evidence resulted in no charges brought against the Clintons.

As he left the White House, President Clinton signed off on 177 pardons, with allegations that some were tied to political contributions to the Democratic Party or Clin-

ton's campaigns. When word began circulating that the president might pardon Leonard Peltier, convicted of murdering two FBI agents on the Pine Ridge Indian Reservation, Louis Freeh made it known to the Department of Justice that he would resign in protest if this happened. Peltier remained in prison.

All of these scandals took their toll. The FBI's relationship with the White House continued to deteriorate, and Director Freeh frequently faced tough questioning on Capitol Hill for the FBI's transgressions or mistakes in one area or another, in apparent retaliation for his relentless drive against corruption in politics and refusal to cede FBI independence from politics in general. Two things stand out. First, human nature and the nature of power politics in Washington mean no one ever forgets. Getting even and protecting the power base from any threat is the paramount concern of America's elected officials. The FBI became the real threat to both parties during the Clinton administration. Corruption was growing and unchecked. According to one analysis:

Forty-seven individuals and businesses associated with the Clinton machine were convicted of or pled guilty to crimes with 33 of these occurring during the Clinton administration itself. There were in addition 61 indictments or misdemeanor charges. Fourteen persons were imprisoned.[5]

Second, President Clinton's lack of any real progress in addressing the rising tide of terrorism with substantive and meaningful policies was understandable: he was too busy directing traffic at the intersection of his own personal scandals and those of the party he led.

During his years in the White House, President Clinton had ample opportunities to strike significant blows to the evolving terrorist threat overseas. He chose rhetoric each time there was a terrorist attack, ignoring the development of effective policies, laws, and potential combinations of military responses that might have prevented al Qaeda from having the capability of launching its surprise attack on the United States on 9/11. But Republicans in Congress can't claim any better record in dealing with this issue. The steady stream of international terrorist attacks since 1993 should have alerted both of America's major political parties that a new and emerging threat would require their undivided attention. The Bremer Commission Report had called for new and aggressive steps to prevent and combat the evolving terrorist menace. Senators Gary Hart and Warren Rudman presented a gloomy and foreboding forecast of the asymmetric threat to come in their year-2000 study on terrorism. Think tanks like the groups that convened at the Wye River Plantation to hear from the FBI and the CIA were already sounding the warning bells.

Still, the Clinton Administration and most of the politicians in Congress were preoccupied with other matters. The FBI responded by asking Congress to increase its counterterrorism resources. It expanded the placement of FBI legal attachés in foreign countries so that counterintelligence, counterterrorism, and global criminal enterprise issues could be more effectively handled through high-level liaison and information exchanges. The creation of Joint Terrorism Task Forces in many of its field offices improved information exchanges and established working relationships with local, state, and other federal agencies that became members.

Contrary to the conclusions of the 9/11 Commission and public statements of so many politicians, the Bureau (along with the CIA) was one of the very few federal agencies taking terrorism seriously in the years before 9/11.

Several years earlier, the FBI had refocused its overall counterintelligence role to address a combination of countries and issues that posed a national security threat to the United States. The resulting National Security Threat List identified 22 critical technologies and seven categories of issues that the Bureau's counterintelligence program regarded as paramount to any effective national security strategy. Included was the issue of the "proliferation of special weapons of mass destruction to include chemical, biological, nuclear, and delivery systems of those weapons of mass destruction."

Every politician in Washington was aware of the FBI's counterintelligence and counterterrorism mission and the constitutional and legal restraints that guided it. As noted earlier, many politicians spent considerable amounts of time and taxpayer money getting television time as they indignantly accused the Bureau of overstepping the line in its investigations prior to 9/11. Many of the same people criticized the FBI afterwards for not doing enough, condemning the FBI "culture" and calling for the Bureau's national security responsibilities to be vested in another agency.

Against this contradictory backdrop, President Clinton drew his advice and counsel in making decisions related to the emerging terrorist threat. Meanwhile, the Clinton White House was crippled by repeated scandals, unethical conduct, and immoral behavior. The president's decision to lie to the American public (and his own cabinet) about his romantic affairs with a female intern robbed him of integrity in his role as America's leader. President Clinton's personal conduct and his failure to accept responsibility for it caused a line to be drawn that prohibited even the most commonplace contact between the White House and the FBI, just blocks away from each other in actual distance. The president's conduct not only impacted on his relationship with the FBI, it distracted his decision-making capacity during the growth of one of the most critical threats to the nation during the 1990s: radical Islamist fundamentalist terrorism.

Just one day before the terrorist bombings of the American embassies in Kenya and Tanzania on August 7, 1998, Monica Lewinsky testified in front of a federal grand jury and provided detailed accounts of her relationship with the President. The Lewinsky/Clinton story continued to unravel through much of August and September, unfolding daily even as FBI Rapid Deployment Teams responded to bloody crime scenes in far-away lands. Working around the clock for months on end, they collected the pieces that would eventually tie al Qaeda to the murder of hundreds of innocent citizens of America and other countries. Their efforts to search for justice competed with the evolving scandal rocking Washington, D.C., as their FBI colleagues searched for the truth amid Clinton's attempts to obstruct it during the same time. On August 17, President Clinton finally reversed his repeated denials and admitted his affair to the grand jury and federal prosecution team.

Clinton defenders will no doubt resist and label as "nonsense" or worse the notion that a presidential administration can become so engaged with and distracted by scandal that the actual security of the country is affected. The hours of tapes and hundreds of transcripts from the Nixon years offer proof indeed that it happens. Presidents are human beings. Left to their own devices, presidents will attempt to control the FBI—especially when they are under stress and/or scrutiny—in the same way they control the Department of Justice by appointing their own attorneys general.

As President Clinton's time in office waned, Washington bureaucrats were far less concerned about terrorism than about preserving their legacy and getting into good graces with people who could give them jobs when Clinton left town. Some of the decisions that people made were completely lacking in common sense. For example, Washington, D.C., politicians were agitated that the barricades surrounding the White House prevented vehicular traffic from passing down the Pennsylvania Avenue side of the commander in chief's residence. They lobbied to have the barricades lifted despite the FBI and Secret Service opinions that doing so would pose an extreme threat to the safety of the president. After a storm of law enforcement protest, the barricades remained in place.

It is a certainty that President Bill Clinton was sufficiently informed during his time in office of the nature and ramifications of international and domestic terrorism. His disinterest in seriously addressing the threat could also have been influenced by three decades of Democratic Party sympathy for terrorist causes and anger at the FBI dating back to the days of the Church committee. But the past always catches up with the present. In the days before his time in office ended, and just as police in San Francisco, California, were making strides in connecting domestic terrorists from the radical Weather Underground to the unsolved murder of a San Francisco police officer in a 1970 bombing, President Clinton pardoned two convicted Weather Underground members serving time in prison.[6]

CHAPTER TEN

AL GORE

Waltzing with Chinese Intelligence

Some people and media in the United States specu-
lated . . . about so-called participation by Chinese indi-
viduals in political donations during the U.S. elections.
It is sheer fabrication and is intended to slander China.
China has never, nor will we ever, use money to influence
American politics.

PRC Foreign Ministry spokesman
May 1998

The "Republican Revolution" in the 1994 midterm congressional elections rocked the Democratic administration of Bill Clinton, then in the middle of his first term. According to a 1998 U.S. Senate report,[1] it also rocked another group of political leaders on the other side of the globe.

The People's Republic of China (PRC) was engaged in a steady increase of commercial negotiations with the United States, and a "New China Lobby," composed of big business interests (AT&T, General Motors, and Boeing), was joined by several former U.S. secretaries of state (Henry Kissinger and George Shultz, among others) in promoting an increase in economic relationships with China.

But there were several problems with this promising new political and business model. The first of these was the "old" China lobby that had pressured Washington for years on behalf of the disputed territory of Taiwan. The second was the negative image that had been created by the sensational crackdown by the Chinese government on student protesters in Tiananmen Square in 1989.

Chinese officials were well aware of the longstanding pro-Taiwan faction in the U.S. Congress, and they had been disturbed by the Clinton administration's acquiescence to the granting of a visa to Taiwanese President Lee Teng-Hui, despite Secretary of State Warren Christopher's assurance to his Chinese counterpart that this would be "inconsistent with" the unofficial nature of the U.S. relationship with Taiwan.[2]

If the U.S. president could be persuaded by Congress to continue to play ball with the Taiwanese, China's plans to enhance its relationship with the United States would have to be strengthened by also enhancing its understanding of and contacts with members of Congress. With the "Republican Revolution" of 1994, this new tactic would be more difficult, since their understanding was that a Republican Congress was also a "China bashing" Congress, and it appeared to them that as a result, there was an increase in anti-Chinese sentiment in Washington at the very time when establishing relations was critical to the new economic relationship between the PRC and the United States.

It's difficult to overestimate the expertise of the Chinese Intelligence Service (known in U.S. intelligence circles as the Ministry of State Security, or MSS) and its influence on the government of the PRC. Although we knew from our own experience in FBI counterintelligence that the MSS is a formidable and tireless foe, our primary expertise in this area was not related specifically to China. We recently spoke at length with a legendary former FBI agent who has had over three decades of experience countering Chinese intelligence efforts directed against Americans. What he had to say is not only relevant to Chinese intelligence activities but to the war on terror as well.

"Guanxi" is a Chinese word that is most closely translated in English as "connections." Its real meaning is more complex; it's all about the art and practice of taking advantage of connections to build reciprocal relationships. Most Americans have never encountered the concept, nor is its significance in Chinese tradition and culture readily understood by Westerners.

To FBI agents and analysts who have long "worked the China target" (Bureau language for countering the operations and intelligence efforts of the People's Republic of China), "Guanxi" describes how and why Chinese targeting of some of America's most sensitive and classified information has been so successful for so many years.

The MSS, whose counterpart is the American CIA, has learned over the years that it's unnecessary to take dangerous risks in mounting collection operations against the United States. The legendary tactics of espionage that are the subject of countless books and movies about the Cold War—clandestine meetings, "dead drops," signals, and encoded messages—are generally superfluous in the Chinese intelligence model.

Instead, relationships established through legitimate avenues of government or business activity are carefully developed and nurtured over time—often years—a long, long period by Western standards of intelligence work. These relationships are carefully analyzed for prospective usefulness by MSS headquarters staff in Beijing. When the time and necessity is right, the Western scientist, or student, or businessman, or politician is invited very cordially to be an official visitor to the PRC on behalf of the U.S. government.

Classically, the MSS targets Westerners of Chinese ancestry, who are shown a tremendous amount of regard and lavish hospitality during their "official" visit to China. They are introduced to dozens of people who apparently represent many levels of Chinese society and culture, and encouraged to value their Chinese origins as highly as they are apparently being regarded during their visit.

Of course, many of these new, admiring, and accommodating friends are MSS officers, who are usually quite familiar with an extensive amount of information on their visitors that has been collected throughout their evaluation period before their visit. Western scientists, engineers, or student interns who labor in the ranks of America's scientific and research centers, laboratories, and corporations are subjected to a torrential downpour of conferences, meetings, questions, and talks, and encircled by an admiring coterie that appears to value them far more highly than they are in their work routines at home. Being human, and subjected to this onslaught of favorable attention and admiration, some will inevitably say things they shouldn't say—or in a way they didn't intend to say it—to their new friends. It's easy to rationalize such a slip, especially since one incautious remark might not seem very revealing in and of itself.

But there are hundreds, even thousands, of these conversations going on at any one time, and each revelation is added to and increases the potential value of many others until another piece of information critical to American national security becomes another casualty of the careful and relentless performance of the Chinese intelligence service.

The genius of this approach is far beyond the capacity of most non-Chinese intelligence officers, who operate on an individual rather than group accomplishment basis that doesn't allow for many years of development that may extend over many careers. When a compromise of critical information is discovered, Western intelligence analysts, agents and officers (in the United States, the FBI, and the CIA) conduct a frenzied search for the specific time and place the information was lost. Hundreds of possible leads run dry, indicators and probabilities remain short of proof. The usual result is that more questions are asked than answered, and the few prosecutions eventually mustered fail to answer them.

On more than one occasion, investigations to discover how a particular piece of information came into the hands of the Chinese have turned into referendums and public debate on race, law enforcement "profiling," and prejudice directed at ethnic Chinese Americans. Defense attorneys thrive on the jury appeal that springs from the image of the big and all-encompassing American government landing with all fours on a poor unsuspecting Chinese American caught in the middle of apparently unsupported allegations of espionage tinged with the ugly taint of racism.

Dr. Paul D. Moore served as the FBI's chief chinese intelligence analyst for 20 years. In a *Washington Post* article on May 31, 1999, he said:

> *. . . The physical transfer of information typically takes place in China and as a byproduct of a legitimate trip there by someone from the United States. The usual collection mechanism is simple elicitation. The visitor may be asked to give a talk to his colleagues in China, who then pepper him with questions that might induce at least a small security breach on his part.*
>
> *China's general strategy is to collect a little information from a lot of people, in the certainty that the aggregate pile will be large. To collect the intelligence they need, the Chinese are willing to expend the manpower and effort needed to nurture relationships with a large*

number of people. They also pay what it takes to sustain exchange programs that provide opportunities to make friends for China.

The classic tradecraft techniques of espionage—dead drops, secret writing, etc.—leave forensic trails or are subject to some sort of observation. As a result, some spies have even been caught in the act. The Chinese model is absent most of these vulnerabilities, and for decades the MSS has defied America's best efforts to plug the leaks that have led, among other things, to repeated losses of the country's nuclear weapons secrets. Dr. Moore notes:

> *. . . The Chinese seek to develop significant relationships with as many people as possible, in particular those of ethnic Chinese ancestry, whose thinking and value systems China's intelligence officers understand best. This they do on a very large scale and are quite content to let their efforts directed toward a given individual continue for many years.*

Against this backdrop of espionage and influence-peddling, the administration of President Bill Clinton and Vice President Al Gore came into office with the goal of pursuing "constructive engagement" with the Chinese government.

Their motives then and now appear well-founded. China was growing as a mighty economic and military power of the 21st Century. It would compete with the United States for shrinking supplies of world commodities, including oil, food, and precious metals, as it took a more prominent place on the world stage. Preventing future military conflicts over differences of opinion on issues such as Taiwan; growing American jobs by allowing American corporations to tap into the China market of hundreds of millions of people wanting Nike shoes, American cars, and Mickey Mouse dolls; and securing cooperation inside the United Nations on dozens of matters that impacted both countries seemed good enough reason to cultivate improved "relationships" with the Chinese government.

Historically, China's enthusiasm for changing its political and human rights policies to conform to international standards has been far less apparent than its pursuit of economic parity with the West. Hundreds of Chinese activists were killed and thousands injured protesting the authoritarian government in Tiananmen Square in 1989. In 2000, PRC President Jiang Zemin said that Taiwan's attempts to declare independence from Mainland China would result in war; and China moved to seal Tibet, where PRC forces have killed more than 100 protesters.

As a result, Americans have been cautious, and the tone of the Chinese government has been guarded in playing out this new relationship with the West, both to protect its carefully cultivated image as the ultra modern host of the 2008 summer Olympics and to avoid a confrontation with America over what is regarded as an internal matter for China to solve. In 2005, *U.S. News and World Report* noted:

> *A communist rival with wealth is a new worry for Washington. . . The booty in this battle is jobs and prosperity. A recent report by the National Intelligence Council warns that by 2020, the rise of China could drive the world's most powerful companies to lean more toward the east than the west, cause more displacement of middleclass workers in the United States and Europe, and make Washington 'increasingly irrelevant.'*[3]

As the Clinton administration's "constructive engagement" policy took hold in Washington, D.C, few questioned its value, or worried about its wisdom. But in the PRC, Chinese intelligence immediately seized upon the golden opportunities presented by American eagerness to open up its markets to Chinese goods. After the careful cultivation of hundreds of connections they had developed over many years, the PRC was ready and willing to use those connections to gain access to the White House and further influence American policy towards China. The job was easy, and almost second nature. And the U.S. government was highly vulnerable.

Unlike the longstanding guidelines that define contacts between "cleared" employees of U.S. government agencies and individuals they may meet from countries whose interests are often hostile to America's, there are no rules or routines requiring higher-level government policy makers to report the exact nature of each of their meetings with officials who are targeting American technology, secrets, and scientists.

For example, the Counterintelligence Program established within the Department of Energy requires that scientists who are in contact with individuals from hostile countries report those contacts to the appropriate counterintelligence personnel. A record is maintained of the nature of the contact, and the relationship is monitored and continuously analyzed to ensure that Americans working in sensitive posts are not targeted for recruitment by foreign intelligence services.

Many U.S. government agencies employ similar guidelines that dictate the rules of engagement; and if they are broken or not followed, employees can lose their clearances and/or jobs. In some agencies, such as the FBI, counterintelligence polygraphs are now given on a routine basis. These specialized tools don't dive into "lifestyle" related issues. They focus on one basic question:

> *Have you had any contacts with intelligence officers from other governments that you have not reported or had permission to engage in?*

The entire process is both preventive and probative, and need not be contentious. At its base, it's designed to detect the indications of incipient recruitment operations by hostile intelligence services before any damage is done.

But this process is completely lacking within the White House, where discussions with representatives of the interests of hostile governments continually involve the president, vice president, high-level officials, or members of the cabinet and their staff. On Capitol Hill, elected representatives in the Senate and the House who participate in major decisions about the security of Americans can meet and greet anyone they wish. There are no special rules, and they have no obligation to report on whom they met and what was said.

U.S. politicians who are high-value recruitment targets of hostile intelligence services are allowed unfettered access to agents of foreign governments, without any requirement to discuss the nature of their contact with counterintelligence officers from their own government. In fact, they would be most likely to resist such a requirement.

The same Congress that passed legislation mandating polygraphs for select government employees from various agencies is exempt from any type of polygraph. On Capitol Hill, there is no method to communicate and/or instill awareness of the threat posed by hostile intelligence-service targeting, despite the sensitivity of thousands of assignments involving congressmen and their staffs.

Here's how a typical briefing might work on Capitol Hill, if in fact there was an opportunity to provide it:

A congressman, on a tight schedule to make a vote in the chamber and thereafter needing to speed off to the airport to fly to the PRC in connection with a committee assignment, is surrounded by his staff members as he rushes out the door and heads for the escalator. The counterintelligence briefer trails along trying to keep up, but has a difficult time penetrating the ring of staff around the congressman. Finally, as they climb onto the escalator, there is room for two people on one step. On the way from one floor of the building to the next, in the space of about 20 seconds, the counterintelligence brief is given to the congressman. He asks no questions and is hurried off to his next obligation.

Politicians are busy people. At any one time they have hundreds of issues on their minds and are wrestling with solving a myriad of problems that seem to have no solutions. And politicians—as much as they may have capable and eager staff members to support them—are only human. So it's not surprising that they usually have little appetite for counterintelligence briefings. They are certainly unworried that their failure to deal with this information makes them vulnerable to foreign intelligence officers. After all, they're experienced, mature, and intelligent professionals, savvy about personal relationships and manipulation. How could they be the target of an intelligence approach without being aware of it?

Once again, the addiction to power in the lives of politicians handicaps them. They view themselves as too smart to be had. Their intellectual abilities, coupled with the large egos that their positions both demand and expand, make them invulnerable in their own minds to unwitting manipulation.

In fact, however, a highly intelligent target in a high position is an intelligence officer's dream. No powerful individual sees himself or herself as vulnerable—until it becomes painfully obvious in the aftermath of some disastrous compromise. Their egos are up, their guards are down, and they dismiss the necessity for caution. If, they reason, there was cause for concern, they would certainly know it already, and they don't need a career federal employee to cramp their style in doing what they do best: politics.

It's in taking advantage of this key component of human nature that makes the Chinese so good at what they do. Accessing America's politicians through established and trusted connections gives them more power over America's leaders than the FBI would ever be allowed to have.

With this operational environment in play, the PRC launched the full force of its very accomplished intelligence community against the Clinton administration to gain access and influence for the future betterment of China.

By 1996, China's intelligence services were operating in full force against the U.S. government, prepared to use their relationships and their money in the form of political donations to influence the 1996 American elections. The subsequent widespread FBI and Department of Justice investigation found it difficult to trace countless allegations back to specific Chinese intelligence officers and agents, but the resulting convictions of 22 individuals for violations involving campaign funding laws and fraud confirm and validate the effectiveness of the Chinese operation.

The ease of China's access to the highest officials in Washington politics validates what most counterintelligence officers fear: politicians who have no time to waste on counterintelligence (CI) briefings, whose staffs circle the wagons to protect their time from being intruded upon, nevertheless have ample time for sumptuous dinners and golf games with their campaign contributors, even if those contributions come from foreign intelligence services.

Questions about unsavory characters and questionable campaign contributions swirled around the White House in the late 1990s. The Senate Governmental Affairs Committee held a hearing on September 11, 1997. President Clinton's National Security Advisor Sandy Berger was among those who testified.

Senator Fred Thompson asked about the White House process for screening visitors to the president and vice president. He included questions about a coffee the president held in February 1996 with Won June, chairman of the Chinese International Trust and Investment Company. The company was run by the People's Liberation Army, and it made and distributed arms; it had been connected to a plan to smuggle assault rifles into the United States.

President Clinton later remarked:

> *I can tell you for sure nothing inappropriate came from it in terms of any governmental action on my part. . . . We have to do a better job of screening people who come in and out of here.*[4]

Several days prior to June's visit to the White House, the U.S. government granted import permits to Poly Technologies (a front company for the Chinese military) to ship 100,000 semi-automatic weapons to a company in Detroit. That company, China Jiang An, also had connections to the military in the PRC.

In October 1993, Gregory LaShinsky, an international businessman with links to Russian organized crime, smuggling of both drugs and nuclear materials, and money laundering, attended a dinner with President Clinton.

Although Sandy Berger announced that the White House had instituted screening procedures to avoid such situations in the future, he hotly defended his own meeting, at the request of Democratic Party officials, with Eric Hotung, a Hong Kong businessman whose wife had pledged a $100,000 contribution to the Democratic Party:

> *But this was not—at least from my perspective— related in any way to a campaign contribution.*[5]

Senator Thad Cochran, Republican from Mississippi, objected:

> *Democratic National Committee officials were pre-pared to intercede in behalf of those who contributed large sums of money to the Democratic National Commit-tee to try to get special access, to get favorable consider-ation for projects . . . there were regular meetings that involved a lot of people from the Democratic National Committee on a regular basis at the White House, where money was talked about, fund-raising techniques and strategies discussed, including the use of the president and the vice president for making fund-raising calls per-sonally and having coffees and other uses of the White House itself to reward contributors.*[6]

Harold Ickes, the former White House deputy chief of staff, responded:

> *. . . To raise the funds to stay competitive, it was nec-essary and fully appropriate to involve the president and vice president in fund-raising activities. I so advised them and I have no regret.*

> *In that regard I did on occasion ask the president and the vice president to make a limited number of fund-rais-ing telephone calls. I advised the president that it was proper to do so. I confirmed my understanding of the law with the White House counsel's office before asking the president to make the calls and was told that he could make those calls from the White House, preferably from the residence.*[7]

Vice President Al Gore placed fund-raising-related phone calls from his White House office during 1996, prior to Clinton's re-election. In 1997, the FBI interviewed Gore in connection with an investigation of campaign finance law violations. He said he had believed that a massive Democratic media effort during the 1996 campaign was going to be financed entirely by "soft money" funds, which are not fully regulated under federal law.

This appears to be contradicted by notes taken at a White House meeting on November 21, 1995, by Gore's former deputy chief of staff, David Strauss, where a discussion ensued about financing the campaign "with both soft money and fully regulated 'hard money.'" Strauss' notation on a memo read, "65% soft/35% hard." The vice president was clearly a participant during the meeting. When it was outlined that Gore would do 10 phone calls and attend two fund-raising meetings compared to the president's 20 phone calls and two events each for him and the first lady, Gore volunteered to take more of the events and the calls.[8]

One of the more serious issues in the campaign financing morass was the vice president's attendance at an event held at the Hsi Lai Buddhist Temple in Los Angeles in 1996. It was much more than a gathering of old friends and new. It was a place where the Democratic National Committee was soliciting campaign funds. Coordinated by DNC fundraiser Johnny Huang, who had collected $3.4 million on behalf of the Democrats, the Temple event raised $140,000. Eventually, as investigations by the FBI, the media, and both political parties proliferated, over half of the money Huang obtained for the Democratic Party was returned after it was determined that the manner in which it was collected violated campaign funding laws, and that many of the donors were either unknown or were from overseas.

In December 1993, President Clinton appointed Huang as a deputy assistant secretary for international economic affairs at the Department of Commerce. His specialty was trade with Asia.

Huang had easy access to President Clinton, and occasionally attended classified briefings while he continued his ties with the Lippo Group, an Indonesian multinational corporation. He first met Bill Clinton in 1980 at a financial seminar held by the Lippo Group. Clinton was a featured speaker. Huang's future as a person with access began there. He had come a long way since he came to the United States from China in 1969.

Mochtar and James Riady, a father and son, owned the Lippo Group. Huang and the younger Riady eventually were convicted of violating campaign financing laws through a series of complex banking transactions that attempted to both conceal the true source of specific donations and unlawfully reimburse individuals who had contributed.

In 1998, an unclassified report of the U.S. Senate Committee on Governmental Affairs concluded that "James Riady and his father Mochtar had a long-term relationship with a Chinese intelligence agency."

Maria Hsia was a friend of both Huang and Riady, who sent a letter to Al Gore in 1988 when he was a senator, inviting him to visit Taiwan and promising:

If you decide to join this trip, I will persuade all my colleagues in the future to play a leader [sic] role in your presidential race.

Gore accepted the invitation, which initiated an eight-year friendship with Hsia. The subsequent FBI campaign finance investigation resulted in Hsia's conviction in March 2000 for violating campaign funding laws. When investigators attempted to secure records and documents from the Temple, the documents were destroyed before investigators gained access to them. A supposed video of the appearance of Vice President Gore at the Temple also disappeared. Two witnesses from the Temple admitted to destroying documents and donor lists.

Gore told the media:

> *I did not know that it was a fund raiser. But I knew it was a political event, and I knew there were finance people that were going to be present, and so that alone should have told me, 'This is inappropriate and this is a mistake; don't do this.' And I take responsibility for that. It was a mistake.*[9]

The Campaign Financing Task Force was initiated toward the end of 1996 to examine the web of charges, suspicions, and allegations related to possible illegal political donations.

In a letter to President Clinton dated June 22, 2000, Senator Jeff Sessions (Subcommittee of the Judiciary Committee) criticized Attorney General Janet Reno's decision not to appoint a special prosecutor to look at vice president Gore's culpability with respect to any criminal intent related to the event at the Temple. He stressed that FBI Director Louis Freeh and the head of the Justice Department task force had recommended that a special prosecutor be appointed.

Sessions' letter also describes Gore's reaction to federal investigators as they tried to interview him about the campaign funding allegations:

> *News accounts in the New York Post recently reported that at the interview, the vice president 'blew his top . . . because they asked about his illegal Buddhist temple fundraiser for the first time.' Further, the vice president*

'seemed stunned' and 'fumed' when confronted with these allegations, and the interview 'ended in a yelling match between Gore and federal investigators.'

In 1999, four FBI agents involved in the campaign financing investigation testified before Congress. They said that Justice Department prosecutor Laura Ingersoll had directed them "not to pursue any matter related to solicitation of funds for access to the president." One of the agents, I. C. Smith, wrote in a letter to FBI Director Freeh:

I am convinced the team at . . . [the Department of Justice] leading this investigation is, at best, simply not up to the task.

Although there were numerous convictions after the campaign finance investigation, the prevailing theory within the FBI was that not enough had been done to further pursue the connections between Chinese intelligence and the fundraising connections.

At almost every turn, it seemed someone connected to the fundraising and the Democratic Party had at least a "third degree of separation" from someone in the Chinese military or intelligence services. Johnny Chung, who raised $366,000 for the DNC during a two-year period from 1994 to 1996, visited the Clinton White House 49 times and made 12 personal or corporate donations. He was subsequently convicted on charges of illegal campaign contributions, and told FBI agents that he was provided with $300,000 by a lieutenant colonel in the Chinese Army, Liu Chaoying.

Chaoying was the daughter of a high-ranking Chinese military official and vice president of the state-owned China Aerospace Corporation, which boasted large corporate American clients. In 1996, Chaoying and President Clinton were photographed together at a fund raiser in Los Angeles. During Clinton's presidency, export waivers were granted to Loral Space and Communications so that the company could send satellite technology to China Aerospace.

In a report to Congress dated September 5, 2001, titled "China: Possible Missile Technology Transfers from U.S. Satellite Export Policy—Actions and Chronology," the opening statement read:

> *Congress has been concerned about whether U.S. firms, in exporting satellites, provided expertise to China for use in its ballistic missile and space programs and whether the administration's policies might facilitate transfers of military-related technology to China.*

In 2007, the Chinese military successfully tested laser weapons over the Taiwan Straits that had the capability to blind American military satellites that supported the American navy in the region. During a time of war, such a capability as China now possesses would threaten the safety and security of U.S. military personnel in the region.

Whether or not they would like to see it as such, the addiction to power in politicians who live both their personal and professional lives for years on end in the rarified atmosphere of Washington is a situation tailor made for exploitation by some of the craftiest practitioners of the art: the Chinese Intelligence Service.

CHAPTER ELEVEN

RICHARD SHELBY

Leaking with Impunity

A two-year investigation into how the news media obtained classified intercepted messages has found that Senator Richard C. Shelby, the Alabama Republican and former chairman of the Senate Intelligence Committee, was almost certainly a source.

The New York Times
August 6, 2004

On September 10, 2001, the National Security Agency (NSA) intercepted at least two conversations in Arabic where people in Afghanistan were talking with people in Saudi Arabia:

'The match begins tomorrow,' said one caller.
'Tomorrow is zero hour,' said another.

NSA analyzed and translated the intercepts on September 12, one day after the devastating terrorist attacks on the World Trade Center and Pentagon left more than 3,000 people dead and many more wounded.

On June 19, 2002, as the United States refined its counterterrorism strategy, the CIA provided a highly classified terrorism briefing to the Senate Intelligence Committee that included the details of the September NSA intercepts. NSA analysts noted that the intercepted conversations had come from sources—either a location or a phone number—that put them in a high-priority category that mandated their translation within two days.

On the same day as the Committee briefing, CNN broadcast a story about the intercepted communications. *The Washington Post* noted the next day that, as a result, a congressional investigation on intelligence failures "which has been dominated by concerns about the performance of the FBI and the CIA," was likely to widen to NSA's handling of the intercepts.[1]

By the spring of 2002, the way to get headlines in Washington was to hurl accusations of incompetence and outright malfeasance at the intelligence agencies that hadn't connected the dots in time to prevent the 9/11 terrorist attacks. Politicians from both parties took full advantage of it.

In August 2001, the FBI in Minnesota had arrested a French National born in Morocco. Zacarias Moussaoui was being held on immigration charges while FBI agents explored his possible connection to a terrorist organization. Their concern: Moussaoui had paid $8,000 to a flight school so that he could learn to fly a commercial jetliner. During his training, Moussaoui had expressed little interest in learning how to take off and land. FBI agents in Minnesota were unaware that a fellow agent working in the Phoenix FBI office had become so concerned about Arabs taking lessons at flight schools in Arizona that he had written a memo to FBI Headquarters asking that a canvass of all U.S. flight schools occur to see whether a pattern indicating possible operational targeting by Middle East terrorists existed.

On May 18, 2002, Senator Richard Shelby was interviewed on CNN by Robert Novak and co-host Mark Shields. Asked about the revelation of the Phoenix flight school memo, Shelby said:

Well, I believe that it is the FBI that's the responsible party. And I believe that the FBI has failed the American people in that regard. That is, the information they got out on, I believe it's the July the 10th memo at the head-quarters dealing with the flight schools, basically saying they should act on it. Nothing was done. The FBI was either asleep or inept or both.

Two days later, Shelby repeated his charges about FBI incompetence in an interview with CNN's Paula Zahn:

I believe myself it wasn't what the president knew, it's what he didn't know and why he didn't know it. And I believe why he didn't know it was because we've had some great failures of intelligence—CIA, NSA, and especially the FBI. The Phoenix memo, we've talked about, and also the situation August the 17th in Minneapolis.

Essentially, Shelby claimed that the FBI had failed to communicate properly with the CIA, NSA, and other agencies within the intelligence community and that it was this failure to share information that prohibited any opportunity to thwart the 9/11 attacks.

He deflected any notion that the two political parties shared any responsibility for intelligence failures that led to attacks, and declared that had President Bush known of the information in the FBI's possession, he would have taken appropriate steps to protect the country.

Interestingly, Bush's own vice president and secretary of defense didn't reach the same conclusion. Vice President Cheney said:

What would the notification look like? If you're going out, if you're trying not to panic people, you don't have anything very specific. You've got, you know, an increased level of noise in the system that you're picking up on you're going to go through the relevant agencies, law enforcement when that's appropriate, transportation systems when that's appropriate, try to put those people on alert. You can also only sustain an alert for so long.[2]

Speaking on NBC's *Today* show, Defense Secretary Rumsfeld said:

Well, I wasn't aware of the FBI information that you mentioned until it showed up in the press very recently. . . But it seems to me that the information is collected, it is collated, and judgments are made and warnings are issued. . . . The advantage a terrorist has is a terrorist can attack at any time at any place using any conceivable technique.[3]

Now, a month later, in a highly classified CIA briefing to the House and Senate Intelligence Committees, it looked like another member of the U.S. intelligence community, NSA, had failed to connect its own dots prior to the 9/11 attacks. The rush to provide the media with more headlines that featured the indomitable members of Congress taking intelligence agencies to task proved irresistible to someone in attendance at the briefing.

The next day, CNN ran a story that NSA had neglected to translate intercepts that appeared to be related to 9/11 until the day after the attacks. But the story took a different twist when it became obvious that, in their zeal to add NSA to the congressional whipping post, the source of the story had leaked highly classified information to the media.

Furious, Vice President Cheney called then Senate Intelligence Committee chairman Bob Graham on the morning of

June 20th and told him the Bush administration would end all cooperation with the joint inquiry by the Senate and House Intelligence Committees unless they took action to discover who had leaked the information about the intercepts.[4]

The idea that NSA could have prevented the 9/11 attacks by translating two ambiguous phone calls hours beforehand was obviously absurd when looked at logically, and Cheney further told Graham that unless they pinpointed the leak from inside their own ranks, President Bush would make the case directly to the American people that Congress "could not be trusted with vital national security secrets."[5]

Graham and Porter Goss, then chairman of the House Intelligence Committee, sent a letter to the Department of Justice asking for an investigation of the leak. Members of both committees signed the letter, but Senator Richard Shelby gave a curious statement relative to it:

> *I do believe that the American people need to know a lot about the shortcomings of our intelligence community, but they also need to know the good things that are going on, and what we are going to do in this investigation, I believe, is bring out the best of both.*[6]

The first and most important step in investigating a leak to the news media is the identification of the "universe" of individuals who had access to the information. Most of the time, hundreds of people in multiple agencies have access to information that is leaked to the press. It is not uncommon for the "universe" to be so large that the Department of Justice decides against pursuing the matter because of the resources that would be required. If a decision is made to move ahead with a leak investigation, interviews are undertaken of everyone composing the "universe."

Until the conviction in March 2007 of former Cheney chief of staff Lewis "Scooter" Libby in the case involving the outing of CIA officer Valerie Plame, no modern-day investigations into leaks of classified information to the press have resulted in a successful prosecution. Even in Libby's case, the conviction centered on furnishing false information to the FBI, and it was never conclusively determined in a court of law who was responsible for the original leak of the identity of a CIA officer.

After the leak of NSA intercept information, the FBI wasted no time swooping down on the lawmakers who made up the House and Senate Intelligence Committees. The "universe" for this leak was relatively small, and the time that elapsed between the CIA's briefing to the committees and the leak to the press was only a matter of hours. The Bureau asked for evidence from the lawmakers of contacts with reporters; calendars, schedules, emails, appointment books, telephone calls, and personal meetings were all of interest in tracing the trail from the classified briefing room to the door of the CNN newsroom.

The media cried foul, alleging that the FBI leak investigation would have "a chilling effect on the flow of information" (*Cleveland Plain Dealer*) and that FBI agents swarming all over Capitol Hill "creates a mood of fear and dread" (*Associated Press*). Senator Richard Shelby, who had initially said the investigation would bring to the public evidence of the "good things" the intelligence community had done in addition to its failings, began to denounce it publicly.

According to an article in the August 29, 2002, *Houston Chronicle*, Shelby said the FBI investigation:

> . . . *breaches the separation of powers between the executive and legislative branches—particularly while the committee is examining intelligence shortcomings at the FBI and other agencies.*

That month, the FBI had asked members of Congress and their staffs to take polygraph examinations relative to the information they'd provided on the matter. Many refused, but it was Shelby who told the press:

> *I don't know who among us would take a lie detector test. First of all, they're not even admissible in court, and second of all, the leadership [of both parties] has told us not to do that.*

More broadly, he complained:

> *Here we are investigating the FBI for huge failures, and now we're asking them to investigate us.*[7]

Doggedly, FBI agents pieced together the timeline that ultimately pointed to Senator Richard Shelby himself as the source of the media leak of classified information on the NSA intercepts.

In an August 5, 2004, article, *The Washington Post* reported:

> *Federal investigators concluded that Sen. Richard C. Shelby (R. Ala) divulged classified intercepted messages to the media when he was on the Senate Select Committee on Intelligence, according to sources familiar with the probe. . . .*
>
> *Specifically, Fox News Chief Political Correspondent Carl Cameron confirmed to FBI investigators that Shelby verbally divulged the information to him during a June 19, 2002, interview, minutes after Shelby's committee had been given the information in a classified briefing.*

Fox decided not to run the story, the *Post* reported, and Shelby met with CNN reporter Dana Bash after speaking with Cameron. CNN then ran the story.

Whenever the FBI completes a criminal investigation of a leak of classified information, the results are forwarded to the Department of Justice for a decision about whether a prosecution is warranted.

By the summer of 2004, the Department had evaluated the investigation and referred the matter of Shelby's disclosure of classified information to the press to the Senate Ethics Committee. From the time the investigation was initiated to the referral, Shelby commented on the matter only through statements released by his staff, which consistently maintained that he had "never knowingly compromised" classified information.

In November 2005, Senate Ethics Committee Chairman George Voinovich, a Republican, and Vice Chairman Tim Johnson, a Democrat, sent Shelby a letter saying the Ethics Committee had ended its leak investigation.

The committee provided no accounting to the American public of the facts on which it based its decision, nor did the Department of Justice ever offer any public statements about the merits of the leak investigation and the evidence against Shelby. Shelby issued a statement responding to the Ethics Committee decision:

> *I have been confident that the committee would dismiss this matter, and I was pleased to learn of their decision to do just that.*

What is the cost of a leak investigation that goes nowhere? More to the point, what is the cost to national security if Americans cannot have faith in their elected representatives to use good judgment in protecting sensitive information they receive in the public trust, and not to exploit it in the interests of their own political ambition?

Ironically, Senator Shelby spoke on this matter two years before his own leak, when he became the sponsor of legislation that would make it a crime to leak sensitive government information. During a June 29, 2000, *Online News Hour* interview, Shelby said:

> *Leaks, I believe, basically we've found out come from the executive branch–about 80 percent. I think they undermine national security. I think they do damage to this country. I certainly do not ever want . . . something to be classified to protect the wrongdoings of politicians. I think that would be wrong. But I do want to do everything I can to protect the integrity of the nation and the security of the nation.*

Why is it that Senator Richard Shelby, a senior member of Congress and a high-ranking member of the Senate Intelligence Community, leaked highly classified information involving intelligence community sources and methods to the press in violation of both his oath of office and his own personal conviction that leaks "undermine national security [and] do damage to this country"?

Being the source of new, apparently derogatory information about NSA would have appeared to add strength to his public position as a key player in the supposedly critical restructuring of U.S. intelligence agencies after 9/11. It would also secure his level of importance and influence with the news media.

Protecting classified information became secondary to enhancing Shelby's own power and reputation, and to guaranteeing that he would continue to garner media attention. In other words, Shelby's addiction to the heady drug of power was the core reason for his impulsive bid for media attention. Although it was classified, the information also was sensational, and Shelby couldn't resist the opportunity to be involved in the rush to use the media in heaping scorn on U.S. intelligence agencies after 9/11.

Senator Shelby has long been adept at using the power available to him by virtue of his position. As the FBI leak investigations were swirling about him in the middle of 2002, he was preparing his views of intelligence community reform in a manner that particularly singled out the FBI.

In a report dated December 10, 2002, titled "September 11 and the Imperative of Reform in the U.S. Intelligence Community, Additional Views of Senator Richard C. Shelby, vice chairman, Senate Select Committee on Intelligence," Shelby wrote:

> . . . *I believe that a very strong argument can be made for removing the CI and CT portfolios from the FBI. Despite repeated reorganizations, the FBI has simply performed too poorly for the American people to have much faith in its ability to meet current and future challenges no matter how many aggressive 'reform' plans are announced by FBI management.*
>
> . . . *a freestanding 'domestic spy agency' might offer advantages over our current structure even in terms of civil liberties. . . . I suspect that most Americans, however, would feel safer having such collection performed by intelligence officers who do not possess coercive powers— and who can only actually take action against someone through a process of formal coordination with law enforcement officials.*

By "coercive powers," Shelby appears to refer to the law enforcement role of the FBI, which includes, of course, investigations of leaks of classified information.

Ultimately, the most critical setback for the professionals who fight the war on terror on the world's most dangerous battlefields and in uncovering terrorist hideaways within U.S. borders is the inability to protect sources of information (electronic or human). Where the source is a human being, it is necessary to provide him or her the protection of confidentiality as complete as is ever possible.

Without this major ingredient in the war on terror, none of the other tools available will work as effectively, be as timely, or offer a convincing look inside the terrorist mind. Without these vital and protected human assets, the war on terror will not succeed.

The case of Senator Richard Shelby demonstrates that the biggest challenge of all may be protecting these sources from the politicians who sit in oversight of America's intelligence agencies, and who use information hard won by those agencies as a vehicle to enhance their own personal and political power.

Chapter Twelve

GEORGE W. BUSH

"Groupthink"

The United States of America will not permit the world's most dangerous regimes to threaten us with the world's most destructive weapons . . . Our war on terror is well begun, but it is only begun. This campaign may not be finished on our watch—yet it must be and it will be waged on our watch.

President George W. Bush
State of the Union Address
January 29, 2002

With those words, President George W. Bush prepared the way for a new era of large-scale military invasions, the deployment of hundreds of thousands of American troops in locations worldwide, and massive increases in defense spending levels. He also staked the future security of the United States on a massive reorganization of the nation's intelligence services.

Unfortunately, these changes only strengthened a virulent form of "groupthink" that characterizes the Bush II administration, resulted in a consequent, critical loss of valuable counterintelligence experience in government, and dangerously rocked the delicate balance between civil liberties and definitive strategies to protect the country from terrorists.

In fact, the reorganization of the U.S. counterterrorism (and counterintelligence) apparatus that has been ongoing since the events of 9/11 has seriously undermined the ability of the FBI to combat the real, present threats of both international and domestic terrorism in the 21st century, at a time when those threats have never been greater.

The reason for this primarily has to do with the utter abandonment under the Bush administration of the notion that the independence of the FBI from political alliance with either party—or any administration—is key to its functioning.

In an interview during his book tour to promote his 2004 autobiography, former president Bill Clinton said of the FBI director appointed by George W. Bush:

Bob Mueller is doing a great job. He's at the White House every day, and that's got to improve things.

In his enthusiasm, Clinton noted that during his own administration, former FBI director Louis Freeh "never came to the White House," and then remarked that the only reason he hadn't fired Freeh was that he (Clinton) would have been accused of political maneuvering because he (Clinton) was under investigation by the FBI.

George W. Bush and Bill Clinton appeared to disagree on almost every issue imaginable. Yet, here was something they could agree on: having the FBI under daily supervision is a good thing for a sitting U.S. president.

Historically, the intelligence community, headed until recently by the director of the CIA, has been firmly linked in every administration with the party—and president—in power. Every U.S. attorney general is also a close political ally of the president.

The attorney general is the "Top Cop," representing and upholding the rule of U.S. law. The director of the CIA is responsible for ensuring that the country is protected from nasty surprises from foreign entities that represent potential military, economic, political, or health and safety threats.

One might think that the two would be in natural opposition to each other: the attorney general depending on transparency and the rule of law, the CIA director relying on valuable intelligence from highly vulnerable—and therefore classified— sources of information from around the world.

In reality, both of these big guns are political allies, whose service is characterized by intense loyalty to the president. They may—and frequently do—bicker, but because of their partisan allegiances as well as their own addictions to political power, their behavior has been historically tainted as a result by lying, obstruction of justice, conflicts of interest, and even criminal conspiracy.

This puts the FBI—which is technically overseen by the attorney general and which shares responsibility for obtaining critical intelligence with the CIA—under enormous pressure to act on behalf of administrations that may be already seriously compromised by irregular and even illegal actions based on their political agendas.

In 1969, President Nixon appointed John N. Mitchell as his first attorney general. Nixon first met Mitchell when he entered the law practice of Nixon, Mudge, Rose, Guthrie and Alexander in 1967. By 1968, Mitchell was appointed as Nixon's presidential campaign manager. In 1972, Mitchell left the Department of Justice to assume the leadership role in President Nixon's re-election campaign. Mitchell was involved in planning the Watergate break-in and attempts to cover up the role of the White House. He was convicted and sentenced to prison on perjury, obstructing justice, and conspiracy charges.[1]

Richard G. Kleindienst served as the deputy attorney general to John Mitchell and was appointed to succeed him in 1972. Kleindienst had served in the Arizona House of Representatives and worked for Barry Goldwater during his 1964 run for president. A *New York Times* obituary for Mr. Kleindienst discussed his loyalty to the president and the influence it had on his role as attorney general:

> *... Mr. Kleindienst was asked during his Senate confirmation hearings whether the White House had interfered with a Justice Department antitrust action against the International Telephone and Telegraph Corporation.*
>
> *'I was not interfered with by anybody at the White House,' the nominee replied.*
>
> *On April 19, 1971, a year prior to Kleindienst's congressional testimony, Nixon called him and ordered that he drop the ITT case, adding, 'Is that clear?' Kleindienst responded, 'Yeah, I understand that.' The entire conversation was caught on a White House tape. In 1974 Kleindienst pleaded guilty to a single misdemeanor of refusing to testify accurately before the Senate and given a $100 fine. The judge who sentenced him called him a man of the 'highest integrity' with 'a heart that is too loyal.'* [2]

Edwin Meese was the second attorney general to serve under President Ronald Reagan. Meese joined the staff of then California governor Reagan in 1967 and served as his chief of staff from 1969 until 1974. Meese worked on Reagan's presidential transition and then served as counselor to the president, a member of the cabinet, and on the National Security Council until his appointment as attorney general in 1985 to succeed William French Smith.

During his tenure at the helm of the Department of Justice, Meese was repeatedly dogged by corruption allegations, prompting several investigations by an independent counsel or special prosecutor. He was never indicted for any crimes. But it is undeniable that Meese was directly involved in the Iran Contra scandal, playing the role of presidential protector and loyalist, not the defender of the rule of law. Meese conducted his own investigation of the Iran Contra matter, which Special Prosecutor Lawrence Walsh found seriously lacking:

> . . . In the course of the weekend inquiry, Meese and his aides discovered in the National Security Council Office of Lt. Col. Oliver L. North a politically explosive document: An undated memorandum, apparently drafted in early April 1986, that outlined a planned diversion of $12 million in proceeds from the Iran arms sales to the Nicaraguan contras. This discovery caused the Meese inquiry to veer off onto two tracks—while facts about the 1985 HAWK shipment were still being gathered, there was a second effort to determine who knew about and who approved the diversion. After receiving confirmation from North that an Iran Contra diversion had occurred, Meese quietly imparted the news to the president, White House Chief of Staff Donald T. Regan, and Vice President Bush on November 24, sounding them out privately on their personal knowledge of it. He did not inform a senior advisers' meeting that afternoon. He informed the cabinet the next day.
>
> Meese attempted to resolve the separate but continuing problem of the HAWK shipment—particularly the president's contemporaneous knowledge—at the senior advisers' meeting on Monday, November 24, attended by President Reagan, Vice President Bush, Regan, National Security Adviser John M. Poindexter, Shultz, Secretary of Defense Caspar W. Weinberger, and CIA Director William J. Casey. In response to a question about the November 1985 HAWK shipment, Poindexter falsely claimed

*that before December 1985, McFarlane handled the Iran
arms sales 'all alone' with 'no documentation.' Meese then
added that the November 1985 HAWK shipment '[m]ay
be a violation of law if arms were shipped w/o a finding.
But the president did not know.' At least Meese, President
Reagan, Regan, Shultz, Weinberger, Bush, and Poindexter knew that Meese's version was false, but no one spoke
up to correct him. After the meeting, Shultz told his aide,
M. Charles Hill, 'They may lay all this off on Bud
[McFarlane] . . . They're rearranging the record.'* [3]

Perhaps no prior attorney general in recent U.S. history has
been as unabashedly complicit in undermining the balance of
the rule of law than Alberto "Fredo" Gonzales and his Office of
Legal Counsel (OLC) staff. Gonzalez may have moved in 2005
from his White House office to the Department of Justice building across from the FBI, but despite his assurances during his
confirmation hearings, he never relinquished his role as counsel
to the president. During his tenure, he played a key role in
developing the legal strategy to justify unprecedented actions in
the "war on terror," such as placing interrogations of "detainees" into the hands of the CIA, condoning torture, and authorizing NSA to conduct massive numbers of wiretaps without
warrants.

During Gonzales' tenure, OLC attorney John C. Yoo drafted
the March 2003 memorandum titled "Military Interrogation of
Alien Unlawful Combatants Held Outside the United States," a
document which, for a time, provided legal justification for some
of the Bush administration's most controversial tactics in
detaining and interrogating terrorism suspects.

Law Professor Jack Goldsmith became part of the OLC staff
with his "friend and fellow conservative" John Yoo, and was
expected to agree with the party line on giving the administration what it said it needed to wage the "war on terror" both at

home and abroad. But Goldsmith proved to be unwilling to join Bush and Cheney loyalists in the groupthink that characterized the Department of Justice in the years immediately after 9/11. In his 2007 book, *The Terror Presidency*, Goldsmith wrote:

> *I was astonished, and immensely worried, to discover that some of our most important counterterrorism policies rested on severely damaged foundations . . . After 9/11 [Vice President Cheney's legal counsel and later chief of staff David Addington] and other top officials in the administration dealt with FISA [Foreign Intelligence Surveillance Act] the way they dealt with other laws they didn't like: they blew through them in secret based on flimsy legal opinions that they guarded closely so no one could question the legal basis for the operations.*

Goldsmith emphasizes that although he clashed repeatedly with the volatile David Addington and other Bush and Cheney staffers, he never questioned the fact that they sincerely believed that in pushing for higher and more clandestine levels of presidential power, they were upholding the best interests of the country in both the "war on terror" and in general.

Whichever political allegiance provides the lens for viewing this situation, it seems clear that whatever malignancy attached to the groupthink of the power elite during George W. Bush's presidency, it was not because these were "bad" people with malevolent motives. This was a group of highly intelligent people with a high degree of conviction that what they were doing was right. Once again, they were staunch warriors in the service of a dauntless commander in chief during a critically dangerous war that their political opponents were either unable or unwilling to fight.

In a now famous incident that occurred prior to his appointment as attorney general, Gonzales and then White House chief of staff Andrew "Andy" Card rushed to the bedside of seriously ill Attorney General John Ashcroft to get his signature on a document authorizing domestic spying activities. This was an attempt to circumvent the dissent of Acting Attorney General James Comey, who later described his concerns to Senator Charles Schumer in a congressional hearing and provided a vivid picture of the scene at the hospital on March 10, 2004:

> . . . *We had concerns as to our ability to certify its legality, which was our obligation for the program to be renewed. . . . We communicated to the relevant parties at the White House and elsewhere our decision that, as acting attorney general, I would not certify that program as to its legality. . . . That was Tuesday.*

After he received a call from the White House telling him that Gonzalez and Card were on their way to Ashcroft's hospital bed, Comey contacted FBI Director Robert Mueller the next evening (Wednesday). Mueller told Comey he would meet him at the hospital and instructed FBI agents on Mr. Ashcroft's security detail that Comey was to stay at the bedside when Card and Gonzalez arrived regardless of what they might order. Comey told Schumer:

> *And it was only a matter of minutes before the door opened and in walked Mr. Gonzales, carrying an envelope, and Mr. Card. They came over and stood by the bed. They greeted the attorney general very briefly. And then Mr. Gonzales began to discuss why they were there—to seek his approval for a matter, and explained what that matter was—which I would not do.*[4]

Within days of telling his version of events to the Senate committee, Gonzales resigned as attorney general when his story didn't match the version on the handwritten notes of Director Mueller. He was succeeded by the Bush appointment of Michael B. Mukasey as attorney general on September 17, 2007. Although approved by the Senate, Mukasey to this day still has been unable to define torture or provide a public opinion on whether a technique such as "water boarding" constitutes torture. And the beatings go on.

Traditionally, American presidents have expected complete loyalty from the director of the CIA, with consequences to the rule of law that have been no less critical than those detailed above relating to the Justice Department. The price of disloyalty has been steep for those who dared defy a sitting president and chose instead to do the right thing. The career of Richard Helms provides a good example of the perils of both.

A career intelligence officer from his early thirties, Helms was the CIA director for Lyndon Johnson, staying in place after President Nixon took office. Following Nixon's orders, Helms directed the CIA's role in an attempt to derail the election of Salvador Allende as Chile's president in 1973. When Allende took office, the CIA worked continuously to destabilize his government by funding opposing groups.

When asked about the CIA's role in the matter by a Senate committee holding his confirmation hearings, Helms denied any CIA involvement. But in the aftermath of the Church committee hearings, it became apparent that Helms had provided false information to the Senate, and he was indicted and convicted in 1977. The sentence: two years (suspended), and a $2,000 fine.

Helms "self-destructed" in Nixon's eyes when he and his deputy, Lt. General Vernon Walters, worked a little too hard to try to maintain the CIA's independence from the White House during Watergate. In 1973, President Nixon fired him, but not before Helms oversaw the destruction of records representing

150 CIA research projects related to mind control. The extent of these projects and their conclusions has never been known.

To succeed Helms, President Nixon appointed another career CIA intelligence officer, William Colby, as director. Caught in a vise with the Church committee moving in on one side and his critics (who viewed him as too liberal) on another, Colby expressed open disapproval of some of the CIA's tactics and prohibited assassinations in furtherance of U.S. foreign policy. Unlike his predecessors, Colby also believed that the CIA had a moral obligation to cooperate with Congress, therefore demonstrating that the CIA was accountable to constitutional law. Morale plummeted at the agency when its traditional close relationship with the White House was replaced by Colby's openness with Congress.

President Gerald Ford remedied this problem when he replaced Colby with George H. W. Bush in 1976. Unlike Helms and Colby, Bush was not a veteran intelligence officer. He was a World War II hero, oil millionaire by age 40, and Texas Republican congressman from 1967 until 1971. In 1971, President Nixon appointed Bush the 10th United States ambassador to the United Nations. He served in the position until 1973, when Nixon wanted him to become the Republican Party chairman. He became America's main liaison representative to the Peoples Repubic of China until his CIA appointment in 1976. Always the loyal Republican, Bush became Ronald Reagan's vice president in 1980 and eventually was elected president in 1989.

The Iran Contra prosecutor, Lawrence Walsh, had strong words for Vice President Bush in his final report on the matter and in his book *Firewall*, claiming that the vice president had lied about the extent of his knowledge of Iran Contra. Of course, as president, Bush pardoned several of those convicted of Iran Contra-related offenses, completing the cover-up/conspiracy that had begun during the presidency of Ronald Reagan.

Involved in the election campaigns for both Richard Nixon and Ronald Reagan, William Casey was no stranger to either Republican politics or the secret and inner workings of American intelligence. After receiving a commission in the U.S. Naval Reserve during World War II, Casey joined the Office of Strategic Services, following Richard Helms and William Colby down the same road that would eventually lead to their appointments as director of the modern-day CIA. President Reagan thought so highly of Casey that he made him a cabinet member as well as CIA director. Casey was a major architect of the arms for hostage scenario that engulfed President Reagan's White House during the Iran Contra scandal. He was hospitalized just hours before he was to testify before Congress about his role and died in 1987 without ever having to explain the reckless manner in which he and the CIA behaved during the episode.

Robert Gates served as director of the CIA during the presidency of George H. W. Bush. Gates, who had been Bush's deputy when the latter was CIA director, was a high-level analyst within the agency. After leaving government service, Gates went on to become dean of the Bush School and president of Texas A&M, the location of the George H. W. Bush presidential library.

Gates did not escape entirely from the Iran Contra scandal. So many questions surrounded his relationship with and loyalty to William Casey and his possible acts of omission about Iran Contra that he resigned from consideration as CIA director when first nominated by President Reagan. In Gates' own memoirs, he said:

A thousand times I would go over the 'might-have-beens': if I had raised more hell than I did with Casey about non-notification of Congress, if I had demanded that NSC get out of covert action, if I had insisted that CIA not play by NSC rules, if I had been more aggressive with the DO in my first months as DCCI, if I had gone to the attorney general.

In the end, Gates resisted his instincts to do the right thing in favor of maintaining his political allegiances. At the end of 2006, President George W. Bush appointed Gates to succeed Donald Rumsfeld as secretary of defense.

From 1993-1995, James Woolsey served as CIA director during the Clinton administration. After the 9/11 terrorist attacks, it was immediately apparent that Woolsey advocated striking at Iraq in response. Appearing on *Nightline* on 9/16/01, Woolsey hinted to Ted Koppel that such a move would be retaliation for Iraq sponsoring terrorism. Koppel pointed out that there was no proof that Iraq was involved with 9/11. Woolsey's response:

I don't think that it matters. I don't think that it matters.

CIA Director George Tenet enjoyed, for a time, the unusual favor of two very different presidents. He was appointed by Bill Clinton in 1997 and retained in the position by George W. Bush until his departure in 2004. This fact alone would be evidence of Tenet's masterful abilities as a politician. An ability to accommodate the politics of two opposing political philosophies as well as two radically different presidents characterized his long tenure at the top of the intelligence community (the only CIA director who served longer was Allen Dulles).

Tenet was the last director of central intelligence (DCI). In response to a 9/11 Commission that called for unifying the intelligence community under a new national intelligence director, the director of the CIA—who previously also wore a bigger hat as the overall U.S. director of central intelligence (DCI)—was forced to hand that bigger hat over to a new director of national intelligence (DNI). The DNI has taken on the role of daily adviser to the president on intelligence matters across government agencies that was once the purview of the CIA director as DCI.

In August 2005, with great fanfare, President Bush appointed U.S. Ambassador to Iraq and long-time Republican loyalist John Negroponte as the first DNI. His job was to bring greater coordination and unity to the 20-plus agencies involved in the business of intelligence for the United States. Negroponte said:

> Our intelligence effort has to generate better results— that is my mandate, plain and simple . . . the things that need to be done differently will be done differently.

Less than two years later he was gone, replaced by Michael McConnell from NSA. McConnell is a protégé of General Michael Hayden, the Bush choice as CIA director to succeed Porter Goss, who resigned abruptly, and without fanfare after only a year, amid investigations of the CIA's role in defense contracting that resulted in the indictment of a top CIA official. General Hayden came from a stint at NSA, where, under the direction of President Bush himself, he misled Congress about warrantless wiretapping.

Within the CIA, the president created a National Clandestine Service (NCS) whose mission is to set standards for the operation and development of all human intelligence sources. The director of NCS answers to Hayden.

In September 2007, Hayden established a Board of Governors to oversee the development of human sources in all of the agencies that comprised the intelligence community in order to oversee "collaborative efforts to de-conflict and coordinate operations, synchronize capabilities, and standardize trade craft and training." The change gives the CIA a significant voice in the operation of intelligence and terrorism sources by domestic law enforcement agencies inside the United States, especially the FBI.

Several months earlier, McConnell had issued a decree requiring that 95 percent of the top ranks within the overall intelligence community complete "joint duty" assignments by the year 2010. Although "strictly voluntary," the duty exchanges among agencies of the intelligence community for a period of one-to-three years would be necessary if employees wished to pursue promotions within their departments.

This change gives political loyalists greater control over the careers of FBI agents who wish to pursue counterintelligence community leadership positions within the Bureau itself. It reduces the ability of the FBI to use its employees in a flexible manner, the value of which has been demonstrated time and again over its first 100 years. Worse, it sets the FBI up for conflicts of interest when pursuing allegations of criminal or other activities made against those within the intelligence community, where everything is colored by clandestine behavior and shrouded by secrecy.

Present at the announcement of this significant change was a phalanx of Bush administration loyalists: Secretary of Defense (and former CIA director) Robert M. Gates; former attorney general Alberto Gonzalez; Secretary of Homeland Security Michael Chertoff; Deputy Secretary of Energy Clay Sell; General Peter Pace, former chairman of the Joint Chiefs of Staff; and John Negroponte.

Responding to another recommendation from the commission on intelligence reform headed by former judge Lawrence H. Silberman and former senator Charles Robb, President Bush created a National Security Branch (NSB) within the FBI.

NSB combines the FBI's counterintelligence and counterterrorism divisions into one entity, with dual reporting to the FBI director and DNI. The reorganization effectively places control of the FBI's once independent domestic intelligence investigations—guided by and accountable to the rule of law—as well as its capabilities into the hands of political appointees from the CIA.

CIA official Philip Mudd was appointed to be the deputy head of NSB. He made clear that his goal was the remaking of the FBI into a domestic intelligence agency similar to Britain's MI-5.[5]

Democrats and Republicans alike claim that these changes will enhance communications and analysis within the intelligence community, making America safer. In an interview with *Meet the Press*, 9/11 Commission co-chairs Lee Hamilton and Thomas Keane bemoaned:

> . . . *The vulcanized and stovepipe structure of the intelligence community today, where they do not share information, where everything has been groupthink . . . The status quo is unacceptable. We've got to put someone in charge who can put it together, manage it, and you'll have more effective intelligence for the nation. The American people will be more secure.*[6]

These changes may sound reasonable to people who have never been exposed to the operational realities of the intelligence community—or who have never had a disagreement with their boss. But the picture that Keane, Hamilton, and other politicians paint of the relationship between the CIA and the FBI before 9/11 is inaccurate. Both agencies were interacting and working inside a necessarily intricate web of formal and informal relationships to further sharing of critical intelligence. Neither was perfect, but the changes made in the aftermath of the 9/11 report have not made the American people more secure.

Instead, they have created a military/intelligence/industrial complex that is assuming a more significant, while less visible, role in American society. Public corruption is more easily concealed and civil liberties more easily eroded. The changes subsume the FBI's counterintelligence role and potentially invade its law enforcement mission as well. At some point, both political parties will finally enjoy the prize they have wanted for 36 years: an FBI under their control and an intelligence "insurance policy" to keep it that way

Throughout this book, we have emphasized the importance of relationships in effectively combating the evils of society— crime, corruption, and terrorism. Unfortunately, there's another side to this coin.

Longstanding relationships combined with positions of power can turn open government into an insular, secret society. The result will be more public corruption, questionable policies, lack of transparency in government, manipulation of the media, prolonged political divisiveness, and more deceit perpetrated against America's justice system and the public.

The groupthink throughout government agencies began on the first day of the Bush presidency. A Bush family friend and former Republican senator, John Ashcroft, became the attorney general. Donald Rumsfeld, a long-time Republican Party stalwart, was appointed secretary of defense. Vice President Dick Cheney, whose political mentoring began in the midst of the Watergate scandal, became the most influential VP in recent history. Graduating from secretary of defense for the first President Bush, Cheney has constructed the role of the vice president on a foundation of secrecy, intelligence, intrigue, and seething hostility towards the Democratic opposition.

The only wild card in the mix was former chairman of the joint chiefs of staff for the first President Bush, Colin Powell. With a favorable reputation in his own right, Powell could have just as easily run for the Republican nomination for president and won. Instead, he returned to government service as the secretary of state for the Bush/Cheney team.[7]

Several months later, Powell found himself making the administration's case before the United Nations Secretariat that Saddam Hussein and Iraq possessed weapons of mass destruction.

First, administration surrogates tried to justify the war by hinting at a connection between Iraq and the anthrax attacks that had begun the week of September 18, 2001. Former CIA director James Woolsey loudly declared that Iraq was behind the anthrax attacks, despite the congressional testimony of Deputy FBI Assistant Director James Timothy Caruso that there was no indication of international terrorism in the attacks.

Woolsey then tried to connect 9/11 to a conspiracy between al Qaeda and Saddam Hussein. In an interview on November 24, 2001, he provided his "evidence":

Much of intelligence is hearsay, and would not be admissible, for example, in a court. There's some very suggestive evidence. For example, there are at least five individual witnesses—two American inspectors and three Iraqi defectors—who tell us about Iraqi government training of non-Iraqi Arabs at Salman Pak, on the southern edge of Baghdad, on an old Boeing 707 (aircraft), in hijacking techniques, including hijacking with knives. Now is that direct evidence? It strikes me that it's pretty darn suggestive evidence.[8]

Woolsey wasn't persuasive. But the message of weapons of mass destruction being in Iraqi hands delivered by someone with unquestioned integrity and honesty—Colin Powell—did the trick. The U.S.-led invasion of Iraq began, and so did the eventual, quiet disappearance of General Colin Powell from government service.

While Powell left the government, the man sitting behind him during the United Nations briefing, John Negroponte, continued to grow in influence. The former U.S. ambassador to the United Nations went on to become the American ambassador to Iraq before being appointed the first director of national intelligence. During Ronald Reagan's presidency, Negroponte was the ambassador to Honduras. Despite the substantial evidence of "hit squads" working in Honduras at the time, Negroponte recently told the media that he still does not believe they ever existed. Negroponte's involvement in the case for war in Iraq combined with his belief about Honduras should cause every American to be concerned about the soundness of his judgment in the DNI position. And even though he left the DNI in 2007 for a spot at the State Department, it's clear that his role was born of loyalty and in the service of groupthink rather than in defiance of it.

In fact, today's lineup in the country's intelligence structure serves more as a "lock down" on dissenting opinions than in encouragement of them. Retired Navy Vice Admiral John "M." (Mike) McConnell was a safe political choice to be Negroponte's replacement at DNI. After he left the Navy, McConnell was a senior vice president with Booz Allen Hamilton (Woolsey also did a stint there), a major Washington, D.C. consulting firm and think tank that goes after and consistently wins hundreds of government contracts each year with the very agencies from which it recruits its talent in the first place.

At DNI, McConnell now presides over the post–9/11 reorganization of the intelligence community, which gives him substantial power over the lives of every American citizen. General Michael V. Hayden, formerly Negroponte's principal deputy at DNI and, before that, NSA director, is now director of the CIA. Hayden replaced Porter Goss, the Republican congressman from the House Intelligence Committee, who lasted less than a year as CIA director, submitting a hasty resignation just days before the CIA's third in command, Kyle "Dusty" Foggo stepped aside, the subject of a growing FBI public corruption probe. With former CIA director Robert Gates taking over at the Department of Defense and Phillip Mudd, a former high-ranking CIA analyst assuming the role of second in command at the FBI's new National Security Branch, the intelligence community transition is complete: devoid of any domestic law enforcement officials in leadership positions and in a "lock down" situation with CIA and NSA officials who are solid political loyalists completely in charge.

It's unlikely that such a lineup is going to give "intelligence" to the president that is inconsistent with providing support for whatever political positions he's inclined to take. Former CIA director George Tenet is widely recognized as the one man who might have been in a position to dissuade President Bush from going to war with Iraq based on the premise that the country possessed weapons of mass destruction. Instead, he is widely quoted as having told President Bush that such a scenario was a "slam dunk."[9]

This political groupthink dominated the government after 9/11 and was just as responsible for the road to Iraq as the president's decision to mount the invasion. The sabers were rattling the minute after the terrorist attacks, and at every opportunity the so-called "experts" and dozens of analysts looked for justification that wasn't there.

The FBI provided no intelligence based on its own sources to the White House that Hussein and al Qaeda might have conspired to commit 9/11 or the anthrax attacks the following week, because there was no evidence to indicate that and there never had been.

In a press conference before the invasion of Iraq, President Bush reminded the American public of why such action was necessary. The world was a dangerous place where terrorist-sponsoring states such as Iraq—who possessed nuclear weapons—could use them against America. The possible connections between Iraq and al Qaeda might indicate complicity in the surprise attack on the country on 9/11. Saddam Hussein's financing of other terrorist organizations threatened American security. And as his entourage quickly pulled him from the microphone, he finished with, "He tried to kill my daddy."

The drama continues, and hanging on for the ride in a kind of "soap opera" virtual reality is taking its toll on the people and on the government agencies that are supposed to be protecting us from terrorists. Seven years after 9/11 and the expenditure of billions of dollars for homeland security, the American military is tied down in Iraq, although it is universally acknowledged that Osama Bin Laden and al Qaeda are in the border region of Afghanistan and Pakistan, just where they were before 9/11.[10]

Bush administration officials were unconcerned about awarding contracts to run the Port Authority of New York/New Jersey to the country of Dubai, although it's natural to assume that its banks are vulnerable to money laundering by al Qaeda and similar terrorist entities.

Meanwhile, we all wait patiently in line at the airport so that a staff of highly trained specialists can determine whether our carry-on deodorant is safe or might be an explosive, while fully half the cargo loaded underneath the commercial airliner we are boarding is still not checked for bombs.

CHAPTER THIRTEEN

DICK CHENEY

Absolute Power

*It will be necessary for us to be a nation of men, and
not laws.*

Vice President Dick Cheney[1]

Vice President Dick Cheney could be the "Godfather" for secrecy
in government. Imagine him as a character in a sequel to the
movie *Skulls*, assembling all of the loyal operatives he has stra-
tegically placed throughout the bureaucracy. At a deserted
warehouse in a secluded point on the Potomac River, this band
of true believers in the Cheney doctrine of absolute power
cements its strategy for declaration of martial law—and the
ultimate authority of the presidency—when, and not if, the next
terrorist attack hits America.

Cheney's obsession with secrecy is as native to his unique
personality as is his addiction to power. In his case, his absolute
conviction that his own judgment is flawless and that his opponents are grievously—dangerously—wrong, bolsters his determination to protect the country from heedlessly destroying
itself. He has dedicated himself to secrecy in order to circumvent what he sees as unreasonable intrusions on strong executive power by lesser, irresponsible bureaucrats in Congress and
by counterproductive organizations like the FBI, which might

interfere with him in conducting the current "war on terror" by insisting on the enforcement of laws he sees as an obstruction to his rightful power.

Consider the famous quail-hunting trip he took in Texas in 2006. He had just had lunch and was ready to resume the hunt. Although we weren't there, we can well imagine the knots in the stomachs of Cheney's Secret Service detail when they heard the blast, saw his wounded companion fall, and saw smoke pouring from the barrel of the vice president's shotgun.

President Bush was not informed of the accident for an hour and a half. It was a full day before the public heard about it. Four days later, the vice president finally spoke publicly about what had happened. In the meantime, Cheney deferred to his host, the owner of the Texas ranch where he was hunting, to inform the Corpus Christi media about the accident. Katherine Armstrong was a long-time friend of Cheney and a loyal member of the GOP. Her mother, Anne Armstrong, had been U.S. Ambassador to Great Britain during the Ford administration. She was also a former board member for Halliburton. The day after the incident, according to a CNN report, Armstrong suggested that the media be informed. It is typical of Cheney that he did not see the need to even engage in a discussion of the matter until then.

Dick Cheney began his government service in 1969 as an economic advisor to the Nixon administration, working for Donald Rumsfeld. By 1975, Rumsfeld had gone on to become secretary of defense for President Ford, and Cheney became the president's chief of staff. By that point he'd seen dozens of Nixon administration staffers indicted or convicted and imprisoned. But Ford pardoned Nixon, and the final chapter about what happened in Watergate was never written. Cheney must have been convinced early on that nothing good came of public disclosure of private, presidential actions in the service of an unappreciative Congress as well as the media and the public.

Only those who acquire and masterfully use power have the option of secrecy to protect them from being accountable to the police, the public, and the truth. It's an option unavailable to the regular guy.

The hunting event becomes important to the rest of us only as an illustration of the fact that Cheney never seriously considered that he had anything to explain to anyone. Surrounded by the Secret Service, longstanding friends, and political contributors, he assumed his friends and the Secret Service detail would deal with the issue as they saw fit. Without a word spoken, the vice president could count on their support to buy him time to gauge public reaction. He could then decide whether he should say anything at all. His position automatically exempted him from the agony the rest of us would face in a similar situation.

Cheney's persistent and characteristic view of the private nature of power has sheltered him from the most solemn of his obligations: public accountability. This element of his personality dominates the way he exercises the power of his elected office and colors every decision he makes.

It was Cheney's experience during Watergate that shaped his ambition to return power to the presidency. The bitter divisiveness that has characterized the relationship between both of America's major political parties since Watergate provided his sense of urgency. It hasn't hurt that President Bush has given Cheney unprecedented authority to manage the affairs of government as he sees fit. Cheney's quest for power started before he and the president won the election. In August 2000, he told the GOP convention:

When I look at the administration now in Washington, I am dismayed by opportunities squandered. Saddened by what might have been, but never was. These have been years of prosperity in our land, but little purpose in the White House. Bill Clinton vowed not long ago

*to hold onto power 'until the last hour of the last day.'
That is his right. But, my friends, that last hour is coming. That last day is near. The wheel has turned. And it
is time. It is time for them to go.*

After the Republican victory, Cheney wasted little time
building his power and exercising it. In an appearance on ABC's
Nightline, John Hulsman, a research fellow at the conservative
Heritage Foundation, remarked:

*His power is unparalleled in the history of the repub-
lic, frankly, for that position. Everybody knows that the
vice president is going to fundamentally affect the foreign
policy of the country. [When his office calls] you better get
down there and you better wipe your hands on the side of
your jacket on the way in the door.*

Cheney has a long history of helping presidents defy Congress and ignore its laws. When Congress passed the Boland
Amendment that prevented President Reagan from providing
assistance to anti-Marxist militias in Nicaragua in 1982, then
congressman Cheney declared that the Boland Amendment did
not apply to the president, or to his immediate staff. When *New
York Times* reporter Seymour Hersh wrote a 1975 article about
the Cold War cat and mouse game played by Soviet and American submarines, Cheney wanted him indicted under the 1917
Espionage Act so that Congress and the media would learn the
price of making formerly secret information public. In 1975,
Cheney joined with then secretary of defense Rumsfeld and
then CIA director George H. W. Bush in opposing a draft of the
Foreign Intelligence Surveillance Act (FISA) that would require
warrants for domestic surveillance.

In a 2006 *Boston Globe* article, Cheney is quoted as telling
ABC News:

In 34 years I have repeatedly seen an erosion of the powers and the ability of the president of the United States to do his job. I feel an obligation . . . to pass on our offices in better shape than we found them to our successors.

In effect, Cheney's desire to reclaim what he sees as lost presidential power by undoing or disobeying the laws that emerged from the intelligence scandals of the 1970s effectively returns the nation to that era. His relish of—and the way he wields—his power has served to reopen unhealed wounds stemming from the pardon of President Nixon by President Ford. Decades of suppressed political rage have burst onto the national stage, threatening to undermine the law of the land and longstanding American institutions, placing them in the hands of politicians with their own power as the real agenda.

Former White House counsel John Dean, a young powerhouse in his own right when he worked for President Nixon to undermine the same institutions, should be regarded as an expert in the quest for power at any cost. In his book *Worse Than Watergate: The Secret Presidency of George Bush,* Dean calls the Bush-Cheney administration, "truly scary and . . . frighteningly dangerous."

The trails leading back to Cheney's office that illustrate his involvement in subverting the law of the land seem to validate Mr. Dean's worry.

Vice President Cheney is the leading architect of America's strategy to fight the "war on terror." In the early stages of the war, Cheney advised President Bush in his decision to bypass the FISA laws and approve NSA to conduct wiretapping and surveillance of international terrorists without warrants as the law required. Although the president briefed some members of Congress on the program, most had no knowledge of it. After the Senate Select Committee on Intelligence was briefed on

July 17, 2003, Senator John Rockefeller, vice chairman, sent Cheney a handwritten letter expressing his concern about the inability of the committee to perform any meaningful oversight role:

> *As I reflected on the meeting today, and the future we face, John Poindexter's TIA [Total Information Awareness] project sprung to mind, exacerbating my concern regarding the direction the administration is moving with regard to security, technology, and surveillance.*

When the news of the wiretapping without warrants was broken by *The New York Times* in December 2005, Rockefeller issued a statement to the press that the administration had prohibited members of the Senate Select Committee on Intelligence to share any information even with its own members on warrantless wire tapping by NSA, and that meaningful oversight by the committee on legal and operation aspects of the program was therefore impossible.

Cheney was quoted in the *Boston Globe* as saying rather matter-of-factly that bypassing the warrant law was consistent with the constitutional authority of the president.

The administration's decision to bypass FISA laws began a divisive political debate that raged privately from 2003 until the information was leaked to *The New York Times* in 2005. It illustrates a critical piece of the complex psychological puzzle that is Dick Cheney, and it connects human behavior and political calculation to the decision-making process that has taken America to war.

Cheney never forgot the humiliation visited on the Republican Party during Watergate and its aftermath. Determined to use his power to reverse that course years later, he and many of the same Republicans scarred by Watergate resorted to the tactics and ruthlessness of power that characterized the Republican Party machine in the Nixon years. Obsessed with secrecy, "justified" by the attacks on America on 9/11, and having the CIA and NSA available to do the administration's bidding, Cheney believes the president's authority—particularly in "wartime"—to be almost unlimited. And he is not inclined to forget when other government officials thwart his efforts in establishing that authority.

In 2007, Attorney General Alberto Gonzales testified before Congress that when he and presidential aide Andrew Card had visited the then hospitalized Attorney General John Ashcroft to get his signature on the warrantless wiretapping order Acting AG Comey had refused to sign, Ashcroft was alert and fully competent to do so.

Obviously uncomfortable during the hearing, FBI Director Robert Mueller disputed Gonzales' congressional testimony with the notes he'd written contemporaneous with the events of March 10, 2004:

> *@1920: Called by DAG while at restaurant with wife and daughter. He is at AG's hospital with Goldsmith and Philbin. Tells me Card and A. Gonzalez are on the way to see AG, but that AG is in no condition to see them, much less make decision to authorize continuation of the program. Asks me to come to hospital to witness condition of AG.*

> *@1940: At hospital. Card and A. Gonzalez have come and gone. Comey tells me that they saw the AG and were told by the AG that he was in no condition to decide issues. . .*

Just as Deputy FBI Director Mark Felt played a major role in exposing Watergate in 1974, FBI Director Robert Mueller was the key to exposing lies and illegal activity that went all the way to the door of the White House. But his discomfort was visible. Mueller knows that history repeats itself. No one in the White House or any of its loyal allies within the Republican machine and the greater intelligence community will forget that Mueller's testimony marked the end of Alberto Gonzalez' term as attorney general. To Dick Cheney, it was a clear sign that the establishment of his vision of an imperial presidency was still unfinished: the FBI hadn't passed the loyalty test. Mueller knew that he and the FBI would pay a price for being disloyal.

Former United States ambassador James Wilson and his wife, Valerie Plame Wilson, found out the hard way that disloyalty was a felony offense within the Bush administration. Vice President Cheney served as judge, jury, and executioner.

As members of the administration developed its Iraq war plans in 2002, they were having a difficult time coming up with a plausible excuse to gain the support of the American people. There was no evidence that Iraq was behind the 9/11 terrorist attack on the United States, and even less that showed any connection between Saddam Hussein and al Qaeda. They needed intelligence that showed Saddam Hussein had weapons of mass destruction that were poised and ready to use against America.

Cheney and his staff went to work, sifting, sorting, and selecting intelligence that filled that need and supported his version of the threat. Any information to the contrary was ignored. A November 2003 *Newsweek* story, "How Cheney Sold the War," provides a vivid portrait of the process:

> *. . . Cheney was the one to make the case to the president that war against Iraq was an urgent necessity. Beginning in the late summer of 2002, he persistently warned that Saddam was stocking up on chemical and biological weapons, and last March, on the eve of the invasion, he declared that, 'we believe that he (Saddam Hussein) has in fact reconstituted nuclear weapons.'*

. . . It appears that Cheney has been susceptible to 'cherry-picking,' embracing those snippets of intelligence that support his dark prognosis while discarding others that don't. . . Top intelligence officials describe the Office of the Vice President, with its large and assertive staff, as a kind of free-floating power base that at times brushes aside the normal policymaking machinery. . . On the road to war, Cheney in effect created a parallel government that became the real power center.

A crucial step in connecting Saddam to weapons of mass destruction was a report that Iraq had tried to procure uranium from the African nation of Niger. Former ambassador Wilson was dispatched to validate the information, but instead wrote a report that concluded the story was inaccurate and shouldn't be included as "evidence" that there were nuclear materials in Iraq. Despite this, Secretary of State Colin Powell dutifully made the case to the United Nations that the Niger uranium connection was confirmed. After Wilson went public with his findings to the contrary, his wife's identity as a CIA officer was leaked to the media, ending her career.

In the Bush administration, secrecy is sacred. When the identity of a CIA employee was leaked to the media, the president's immediate response was predictable. After all, lives could be at stake. America's ability to wage the war on terror could be jeopardized. There was a solid principle to uphold. So the president went public and said he would fire anyone who was determined to have leaked the information.

When it became apparent that the president's own deputy chief of staff, Karl Rove, had given a *Time* magazine reporter the same information, however, Bush quickly declared that a firing would only occur if it could be shown that a crime had been committed.

Accordingly, a massive FBI investigation of the leak was led by Chicago U.S. Attorney Patrick Fitzgerald. It was quickly established that at more than one place in the Bush/Cheney administration, Valerie Plame's name had been leaked to the media after her husband had disagreed in public with the administration's use of the Niger information. The FBI interviewed highly placed politicians, including Vice President Cheney's national security adviser, Lewis "Scooter" Libby. Libby denied any involvement in leaking the name, or even having heard the name during the relevant time frame.

He was contradicted by more than one witness, including a former spokeswoman for the Vice President, Cathie Martin. Martin recalled telling Cheney and Libby about Plame several days before Libby said he heard the name from a reporter. Martin said that Cheney and Libby were intensely interested in what she had to say.

A federal grand jury indicted Libby on charges of lying to the FBI, perjury, and obstruction of justice. He went to trial in the federal courthouse in Chicago, backed by a heavyweight defense team and pleading not guilty to the charges. In early March 2007, a jury saw otherwise and convicted Libby of obstructing justice, making false statements to the FBI, and perjury. One juror, Denis Collins, was quoted after the verdict:

> There was a tremendous amount of sympathy for Mr. Libby on the jury. It was said a number of times: What are we doing with this guy? Where's [top White House political aide Karl] Rove? Where are these other guys?

President Bush soon commuted Libby's sentence, ending any possibility that he would spend a single day in prison. It's a good bet that the president will grant Libby a full pardon by the time he leaves office. After all, to the end, "Scooter" Libby was a loyal and silent soldier to the cause. The FBI, on the other hand, conducted hundreds of interviews during the leak investigation, and this administration appears more intent than any in recent memory to remember and punish any perceived disloyalty.

In 2006, President Bush sealed the search warrant the FBI served on the congressional office of Representative William Jefferson in connection with a political corruption case that involved taped evidence of Jefferson taking bribe money. Republicans and Democrats alike agreed that the FBI was out of line and had interfered with Congress and the legislative process by conducting the search.

A crisis built as FBI Director Mueller, Attorney General Gonzalez, and his aide, Paul McNulty, warned of resignations if they were forced to turn over the evidence seized from Jefferson's office. Cheney offered a proposal that would seal the files for 45 days, prohibiting FBI agents from looking through them. The president saw to it, and over half of the files are still under seal today despite Jefferson's indictment on multiple counts of bribery, money laundering, racketeering, and obstruction of justice.

Cheney has been able to subvert the law because during most of the Bush presidency, Congress has been run by Republicans or a typically disunited Democratic Party. Wherever the veil of secrecy has—if only briefly—parted, there have been bold statements of outrage from Congress that are never followed by any significant action in response. Hands have been slapped, but the Bush/Cheney team has been for the most part remarkably successful in relying on the specter of 9/11 to intimidate their opponents in Congress and the media, accusing them of encouraging America's enemies and endangering national security. As the administration enters its final months, however, it's instructive to remember one of Cheney's first acts as vice president.

In the spring of 2001, before the September terrorist attack on America, Cheney created an energy task force to develop policy recommendations that would encourage tax breaks and other incentives for companies involved in the energy business. In keeping with his penchant for secrecy, he refused to release the names of the individuals or companies that met with him or his task force. A federal court sided with the vice president when the government was sued by environmental and other groups that wanted the information disclosed to the public.

But *The Washington Post* obtained a detailed listing of close to 300 individuals and companies that met with task force members or with Cheney personally. Thirty-nine of the companies were involved in energy production, including seven from Canada. Twenty-seven organizations were concerned with the environment or energy efficiency. Twenty-two were independent energy, and five were academic think tanks. Twenty-seven represented state or regional interests, and 75 the interests of specific companies or trade associations. Forty-four congressmen or their staffs were involved in meetings, including 14 who identified themselves as Democrats. The remainder identified themselves as Republicans. The 14 Democrats included 11 elected representatives from Oregon or Washington and one each from Texas, Virginia, and West Virginia.

Two national laboratories run by the Department of Energy were invited to meetings of the task force: the Sandia Nuclear Weapons Lab in New Mexico and Princeton Plasma Physics, a science lab. Cheney met with the Sandia Nuclear Weapons Lab on April 20, Representatives Tauzin and Barton on March 27, and the Northwest Energy Caucus and Ken Lay of Enron Corporation on February 22 and April 17.[2]

Americans need to consider the prospects of a country where military and intelligence policy makers from inside government become titans of private industry the day after they leave government service. With elaborate relationships built over years of working together and ongoing connections inside government agencies, they have the potential to continue enriching each other's companies long after they vacate elective office.

Dick Cheney's involvement with Halliburton and his designated leadership role in energy policy have resulted in a current wave of privatization of the nation's weapons laboratories. The influence of current and former intelligence officers inside and outside the United States government is superceding the ability and influence of law enforcement in countering both the counterintelligence and counterterrorism threats to those laboratories. This could have consequences that most Americans— including congressional politicians—simply don't see coming, because the requirements for regulation and transparency under the law are far weaker for private corporations than for public institutions.

Vice President Cheney was secretary of defense for President George H. W. Bush from 1989 to January 1993. As the U.S. prepared to lead a worldwide military alliance to oust Saddam Hussein from Kuwait in early 1991, Cheney's DOD was evaluating the outsourcing of some Defense Department work to private contractors.

Halliburton was given a contract to study the matter and on the completion of the report, the department began outsourcing to private firms. In 1995, Cheney became the CEO for Halliburton. In that role, Cheney gave a speech in 1999 to the London Institute of Petroleum. Covering a wide variety of themes related to oil policies, gas exploration, and political instability, his economic assessment of the Middle East was a harbinger of America's future:

> . . . let me say at the outset that I am unreasonably optimistic about our industry. . . Oil remains fundamentally a government business. While many regions of the world offer great oil opportunities, the Middle East, with two thirds of the world's oil and the lowest cost, is still

where the prize ultimately lies. Even though countries are anxious for greater access there, progress continues to be slow. It is true that technology, privatization, and the opening up of a number of countries have created many new opportunities in areas around the world for various oil companies . . . but dealing with above-ground political risk and commercial and environmental risk are increasing challenges.

When Cheney returned to government as the vice president in January 2001, partisan debate swirled around the nature of his contacts with Halliburton. By 2001 Halliburton had extensive contracts with the U.S. government, and Cheney had stock options with the company totaling 433,333 shares and a deferred compensation account of between $500,000 and $1,000,000. Cheney's total assets were between $19.1 million and $86.4 million.

Cheney took steps to legally sever his involvement with Halliburton, and to separate his personal interests from those of the company. He declared that there was no conflict of interest in his role as vice president and his past service to Halliburton.

The company has raked in over $18 billion in contracts in Iraq since the war began, including one no-bid contract that was valued at about $7 billion. With 85,000 employees in 100 countries around the world, Halliburton was comprised of two "wholly owned" subsidiaries: the Energy Services Group of Halliburton, which provides products and services to oil business customers; and until 2007, KBR Engineering and Construction, which builds a variety of plants and infrastructures in support of the oil and gas industry.

Halliburton is the subject of dozens of ongoing investigations involving agencies of the U.S. government. Although the vice president claims he has no conflict of interest with his current role and past role as Halliburton's CEO, a 2003 email written within the Department of Defense regarding a Halliburton no-bid contract included the statement that it was "coordinated" with Cheney's office. Other investigations of Halliburton and some of its employees range from allegations of kickbacks related to military contracts, questionable activities concerning the company's business dealings with Iran, payment of bribes to foreign government officials, and a variety of audits by the Department of Defense surrounding the execution of Halliburton's contracts with the government.

Halliburton is being pursued by a group of "whistleblowers" alleging significant government contractor fraud. However, the Department of Justice has expressed little interest in assisting with the suit to recover billions of dollars of the taxpayer's money and has placed restrictions on the ability of FBI agents to pursue the trail as they normally would. An article in the November 2007 issue of *Vanity Fair* offers a possible explanation:

> *. . . the Bush administration has special sensitivities to claims concerning KBR and its former parent company, Halliburton. Dick Cheney's deep connection with the firm is well established. It is less widely known that former Attorney General Alberto Gonzalez, the Cabinet member who headed the Justice Department until August, when he was forced to resign, also has long-standing links with both Halliburton and its legal counsel, the venerable Texas firm of Vinson & Elkins.*

> *. . . In 1982 it was V&E that gave Gonzalez his first job as a lawyer. . . In 2000, Gonzalez amassed a record $843,680 war chest to finance a race for the Texas Supreme Court . . . V&E . . . was the source of his biggest donation—almost $30,000. Halliburton executives also stepped up, with a gift of $3,000.*

With all of the allegations swirling around Halliburton and the volume of investigations under way to look at the company's government contracts, it would be natural to assume that the company and some of its executives might be a little nervous these days. Nothing could be further from the truth. During the past year, Halliburton's CEO, Dave Lesar, announced the movement of the corporation's headquarters from Houston, Texas, to Dubai with these words:

> *The eastern hemisphere is a market that is more heavily weighted toward oil exploration and production opportunities, and growing our business here will bring more balance to Halliburton's overall portfolio.*

Lesar didn't mention that since there is no extradition treaty between Dubai and the United States, the Department of Justice cannot compel Lesar to return to testify in any of the ongoing investigations of Halliburton.

The U.S. government's relationship with Halliburton continues to grow. Halliburton and its subsidiaries continue to profit from the decision by the Bush administration to go to war with Iraq. Cheney was and continues to be the main advocate for that war. The basic assumptions that led to war in Iraq, which were pushed forcefully by the vice president, are a matter of fierce debate. Regardless of Cheney's attempts to deny any current interest in Halliburton, these facts give rise to the perception that decisions in the terror war by the nation's highest political leaders have been made for personal enrichment of friends, associates, and business contacts rather than in the best interests of America. The habitual secrecy that characterizes his office, along with the partisan misuse of government agencies and placement of loyal political allies in significant positions that seem to characterize all administrations, strengthen this perception.

The vice president brings a long and profitable business background to government, and it's clear that he is more comfortable with his friends and associates in the business world than with government bureaucrats, regardless of their level. Cheney treasures the secrecy with which decisions and judgments can be made in the business world. The only parallel within government is the intelligence community.

As he left office in 1961, President Dwight Eisenhower gave a speech that may have surprised those who regarded him as first a military, then a civilian leader:

This conjunction of an immense military establishment and a large arms industry is new in the American experience. The total influence—economic, political, even spiritual—is felt in every city, every Statehouse, every office of the federal government. We recognize the imperative need for this development. Yet we must not fail to comprehend its grave implications. Our toil, resources and livelihood are all involved; so is the very structure of our society.

In the councils of government, we must guard against the acquisition of unwarranted influence, whether sought or unsought, by the military-industrial complex. The potential for the disastrous rise of misplaced power exists and will persist.

We must never let the weight of this combination endanger our liberties or democratic processes. We should take nothing for granted. Only an alert and knowledgeable citizenry can compel the proper meshing of the huge industrial and military machinery of defense with our peaceful methods and goals, so that security and liberty may prosper together.

As a former secretary of defense who helped bring military contracts to Halliburton, as a businessman and as a personality who protects his privacy above all else, Dick Cheney is the primary advocate of the military-industrial-intelligence perspective. It colors his advice to President Bush. It is the reason for eight years of policy moves within the administration that favor the primacy of intelligence agencies and the military rather than law enforcement solutions to issues of national security.

Transparency in government and the primacy of the rule of law are the only way American citizens can be both alert and knowledgeable. The consistent emphasis on secrecy and manipulation of the law in the Bush/Cheney administration has endangered both these elements to a near catastrophic degree.

The compelling need to prevent another terrorist attack has long given weight to the Bush/Cheney view that a military response is more effective than a law enforcement response in deterring future acts of terrorism. Most Americans are willing to accept some perceived loss of freedom if that is the price they must pay to be safe in their daily lives. As a consequence, politicians who endorse and cover up the use of warrantless wiretaps, who advocate torture as an interrogation technique, and attempt to coerce a bedridden attorney general into signing an illegal order have bet on the notion that Americans will look the other way.

At the same time, there has been a menacing addition—a third tier—to the equation of military and industrial power President Eisenhower foresaw: the rise and steady intrusion of the intelligence community into the lives of everyday Americans.

Chapter Fourteen

DENNIS HASTERT AND NANCY PELOSI

The House Protects its Own

Rep. William J. Jefferson (D. La.), the target of a 14-month public corruption probe, was videotaped accepting $100,000 in $100 bills from a Northern Virginia investor who was wearing an FBI wire, according to a search warrant affidavit released yesterday.

A few days later, on Aug. 3, 2005, FBI agents raided Jefferson's home in Northeast Washington and found $90,000 of the cash in the freezer, in $10,000 increments wrapped in aluminum foil and stuffed inside frozen-food containers.

Washington Post
May 22, 2006

Large numbers of Americans have low opinions of their elected leaders. A CNN/*USA Today*/Gallup poll in December 2005 found that 49 percent of those interviewed believed that "most members of Congress are corrupt." A May 2006 Gallup poll, referenced by Citizens for Ethics and Responsibility in Washington (CREW), placed the number of Americans feeling that corruption is a serious issue at 83 percent of those polled, while 64 percent believed that addressing corruption in its own ranks "should be a high priority for Congress."

It's disturbing to realize that an urgent and effective response to the real and growing threat of terrorism in the early 21st century depends on action from elected officials who, under the influence of their addiction to power, have consistently demonstrated track records of poor judgment, unethical, and even criminal conduct during their public service.

Corruption thrives when there is a lack of transparency in government. As government leaders from both parties endorse steps to fight today's terror war that depend more on secrecy and intelligence than on law enforcement and public support, the actions of the government become more and more opaque to its citizens. This is supposedly for the public good, and we are the first to acknowledge that there is an undeniable need to protect sensitive sources of information in conducting the war on terror.

But less transparency also allows politicians to act for their own reasons, and in their own interests, behind a protective curtain of secrecy. Recall the desperate ploy resorted to by the Nixon White House in attempting to conceal its activities from FBI investigators by having the CIA throw a cloak of "national security" over its activities during Watergate.

Adding the promise of financial gain to a politician addicted to power creates an allure that proves irresistible to many. Whenever power and money collide, corruption—followed by a pattern of deceit and cover-up—is often the result. These dynamics are so endemic to human existence that they've been depicted in theater for millennia—from ancient Greece to the Elizabethan England of Shakespeare. Greed and a sense of entitlement lead to actions that compromise the public trust by heads of state as well as bureaucrats at the lowest levels of government.

FBI Director Robert S. Mueller III, testifying before the Senate Intelligence Committee on February 16, 2005, had this to say about public corruption and its impact on the fight against terror:

> *Public corruption continues to pose the greatest threat to the integrity of all levels of government. Recent investigative efforts have been intensified to identify and convict Immigration, Department of State, and DMV officials of illegally selling visas or other citizenship documents and drivers licenses to anyone with enough money. Their illegal activities potentially conceal the identity and purpose of terrorists . . . facilitating their entry, travel, and operation without detection in the U.S. . . . Many major metropolitan areas in the U.S. have witnessed the indictment and conviction of corrupt public officials who betrayed the public trust for profit or personal gain. Over the last two years alone, the FBI has convicted more than 1,050 corrupt government employees, including 177 federal officials, 158 state officials, 360 local officials . . . .*

Nearly 200 government officials have been indicted for misappropriation of billions of recovery dollars sent to New Orleans in the wake of Hurricane Katrina. Over 80 percent already have been convicted on charges of fraud and bribery.

The case of Democratic Congressman William Jefferson from Louisiana presents a stunning example of the fierce opposition by politicians of both parties to FBI investigations of their own actions.

Jefferson currently faces a 16-count indictment alleging he received hundreds of thousands of dollars in bribes and was involved in racketeering, conspiracy, and money laundering. He and some members of his staff allegedly solicited millions of dollars from African business deals negotiated through his congressional office. FBI agents serving a search warrant on Jefferson's New Orleans' home found $90,000 in cash in his freezer, days after he received $100,000 in cash from an FBI undercover agent posing as an intermediary for African business interests.

The public revelation in 2006 of Jefferson's indictment on charges of bribery was overshadowed almost immediately by condemnation from Republicans and Democrats alike that the court-authorized "raid" on Jefferson's congressional office by the FBI threatened the Constitution itself.

United in their outrage, then Speaker of the House J. Dennis Hastert and Democratic Party Leader Nancy Pelosi issued a joint statement:

> *The Justice Department was wrong to seize records from Congressman Jefferson's office in violation of the constitutional principle of Separation of Powers, the Speech or Debate Clause of the Constitution, and the practice of the last 219 years. These constitutional principles were not designed by the Founding Fathers to place anyone above the law. Rather, they were designed to protect the Congress and the American people from abuses of power, and those principles deserve to be vigorously defended.*

The invasion of the seat of congressional power by the FBI—for whatever reason—was seen as intolerable and a violation of the separation of powers doctrine. Although he acknowledged that the raid was unprecedented, Chief Judge Thomas F. Hogan, U.S. District Court for the District of Columbia, rejected the bipartisan House of Representatives claim that it violated the Constitution:

> *. . . the Speech or Debate Clause [of the Constitution]*
> *does not shield members of Congress from the execution*
> *of valid search warrants. Congressman Jefferson's inter-*
> *pretation . . . would have the effect of converting every*
> *congressional office into a taxpayer-subsidized sanctuary*
> *for crime.*

Hogan's decision was immediately overruled by an appellate court that directed him to consider individual seized documents in the case that Jefferson claimed were covered under legislative privilege. President George W. Bush played along, freezing the search warrant pending further review by the Justice Department Solicitor General. Although they have a difficult time agreeing on the most simple of concepts, the leadership of both parties agreed without prior consultation or debate that invasion of their congressional offices was a threat to the real balance of power in Washington: the "safe harbor" they allege the Constitution has awarded them in return for their selfless labors as government servants.

Although he was under indictment, Jefferson was returned to the Congress by Louisiana voters in a 2006 re-election bid. It didn't seem to surprise his constituents that Jefferson had blatantly taken bribe money in exchange for his influence and ability to act in his official capacity as a U.S. congressman, and they expressed little outrage either on their own or on his behalf. They had seen it all before.

When their power is challenged, politicians know from the experiences of their colleagues that the best defense is to immediately use the media to counterattack the investigating agency—usually the FBI. It's all theater, brought on by a mutual concern that investigations of congressmen like Jefferson will spill over into the Democratic and Republican machines themselves, and will expose "the way business is done in Washington" to be the remarkably corrupt process it is.

In fact, corruption probes don't work the way Speaker Hastert and Democratic Leader Pelosi described. However much they believe that the president of the United States and the attorney general can choose who will be subjected to an investigation by the FBI and who will not, investigations begin when FBI agents do the basics of the job they're sworn to do: talk to people. Across the FBI's 56 field divisions and from within its headquarters divisions, FBI agents work daily to develop relationships with a variety of American citizens representing all walks of life. They talk to thousands of people who report suspicious and criminal behavior, and then knock on doors, conduct interviews, gain trust, and consider the likelihood that the information they gather is either true or untrue based on what they hear and what they are able to develop. Every case develops a different way, but they all come together based on direct contact with people who contribute information that demonstrates a clear probability of the violation of federal law. If that probable violation is demonstrated to be by an official charged with the public trust, a public corruption case is opened.

As specific evidence is developed to indicate a crime has occurred or is occurring, any FBI agent in one of the Bureau's offices can bring to bear unlimited resources, diverse talents, and highly specialized skill sets to address the issue. When solving a crime hinges on forensic evidence, agents can call on the real "CSI." Every FBI field office has its own Evidence Response Teams (ERT), whose members have extensive and continuous training in identifying, collecting, and preserving evidence at the most complex of crime scenes. From sifting through the charred rubble at the site of the first al Qaeda attack on the World Trade Center in 1993 to the millions of financial records at companies like Enron, Bureau specialists—often working with other federal, state, and local law enforcement evidence technicians—routinely pull the most difficult elements together for analysis and presentation in a court of law as evidence of a crime.

Whether the forensic evidence involves fingerprints, DNA, hair, fibers, tire treads, or a hundred other possibilities, investigators bring cases together by combining the use of physical evidence with witness and expert interviews. While the average investigation may involve limited numbers of these and wrap up quickly, there are others that may take years and involve interviews of thousands of people. Forensic evidence, as vital as it is, must be accompanied by explanations about why the evidence was found at a certain place or location, and in many types of crimes, must fit hand-in-hand with evidence of the intent of the accused. Evidence of intent is found by knocking on doors, building relationships, and "connecting the dots," which is the FBI's stock in trade, despite the hypocritical howling politicians engaged in for public display as they criticized the Bureau for its alleged failure to do so after the tragedy of 9/11.

When the dots lead to the doors of Congress, as they did in William Jefferson's case, politicians appear to be far less happy with the FBI's ability to connect them.

The political corruption case involving William Jefferson developed like all FBI cases before it. Through a combination of people reporting information and developing evidence to validate the allegations, the case picked up steam and pointed in his direction. The collection of facts led to indictments by an impartial federal grand jury and issuance of a search warrant by a federal judge.

The Jefferson investigation wasn't suggested by the executive branch or driven by the Department of Justice; it was conducted by FBI personnel doing their jobs and enforcing the law. Although corrupt officials—as well as other criminals—may not like it, the Bureau receives a continual stream of information from the public—which includes political insiders with a whole variety of motivations—that must be evaluated during the investigative process. This isn't done on behalf of the administration—although presidents and their staffs have often attempted to influence investigations (as in Watergate), it's done rather as a matter of procedure, and according to indications that violations of specific federal law may have occurred.

When ABC News aired a story portraying Dennis Hastert as "in the mix" of a political corruption investigation involving Republican lobbyist Jack Abramoff, the former Speaker went on the offensive. He labeled the leak of the information as a reprisal for his condemning of the FBI's raid on the congressional office of Congressman Jefferson. "We're just not going to be intimidated." Hastert fumed, and he went on to state the leak was an attempt to "smokescreen some of the separation of powers stuff that we're doing."

Separation of powers was a hot topic at the time on Capitol Hill. As an aggressive FBI conducted a leak investigation to identify who might have leaked classified information to the press about the NSA domestic surveillance program, Democratic Congresswoman Jane Harman questioned the tactics of the FBI and the Justice Department. Harman was quoted as saying:

There is no credible claim that anyone in Congress leaked anything. I urge the Justice Department to carefully consider the separation of powers issue and the appearance of intimidation before proceeding any further.[1]

There was, in the end, considerable evidence supporting the identification of Senator Richard Shelby as the member of Congress who leaked the information. However, neither the Senate Ethics Committee nor the Justice Department saw to it that he suffered any consequences for his actions.

Scandals involving the Washington, D.C., political elite are nothing new, and they don't necessarily shock the public. There have been massive corruption probes before, and there will be corruption probes in the future. But the threat corruption poses to American democracy and clean government in an age of state and organization-sponsored terror has deadly ramifications that threaten American national security itself.

Politicians who either engage in corruption or refuse to deal with it apply the same poor judgment in evaluating avenues to war, debating the effectiveness of torture, and charting the nation's future strategies in fighting terror. The pattern of failure by top congressional leaders to set the proper standards for all who come through the doors of Congress allows corruption to flourish, diffuses responsibility, and endangers national security by a tacit acceptance of bad behavior and corruption in their own ranks.

Illinois Congressman Dennis Hastert was elected to the House of Representatives in 1987. He became the Speaker of the House in January 1999, and served in the position until the Democrats regained the majority during the November 2006 elections. Replaced by Nancy Pelosi, Hastert announced that he would leave Congress at the end of 2007.

Hastert leaves behind a range of ethical issues and confrontations with the FBI. In response, he repeatedly blasted the Bureau and the Department of Justice for allegedly singling him out for special scrutiny.

Hastert's own actions, however, were the reason for public questioning of both his motives and actions respective to his own political power as Speaker.

Hastert was in charge when allegations erupted in 2006 that Representative Mark Foley, a Republican from Florida, had been sending inappropriate emails to teenage boys serving as House pages. Foley resigned suddenly from his position and Hastert himself called for a Department of Justice investigation.

Although that investigation is ongoing, a House panel released its own findings on the matter in December 2006. The panel concluded that Republicans had ignored several instances of similar behavior by Foley over a ten-year period and that two of Hastert's aides, Chief of Staff Scott Palmer and Chief Counsel Ted Van Der Meid, were repeatedly warned about Foley's improper behavior towards House pages. Two Republican congressmen, John Boehner of Ohio and Thomas Reynolds of New York, contradicted Hastert's account that he knew nothing about the conduct until Foley's resignation. Both Boehner and Reynolds told the panel they had advised Hastert of Foley's conduct early in 2006.

Despite this, the House panel concluded that none of its rules were broken, and that there had been no systemic cover-up of the facts. In a telling phrase, they announced that "there is some evidence that political considerations played a role."

In an article in the *Baltimore Sun* dated January 7, 2005, "Enabling Corruption," Gary Ruskin cites yet another example of the complacent attitude and flawed decision-making process that is endemic in the political apparatus of the United States:

> *. . . Speaker Dennis Hastert wants to replace the current chairman of the House ethics committee, Colorado Republican Joel Hefley, with Lamar Smith of Texas, who is notoriously soft on corruption. Mr. Smith is famous in ethics circles for being chairman of the only ethics committee ever to have asked a federal judge to grant limited immunity to the target of an investigation, GOP Rep. Bud Shuster of Pennsylvania, who was chairman of the House Committee on Transportation Infrastructure. In 1997, Mr. Smith also was the only ethics panel member to vote against reprimanding Speaker Newt Gingrich and fining the Georgia Republican $300,000.*

Speakers of the House have long been notorious for getting themselves into ethical and legal issues, so it's important to note that Dennis Hastert is only following the examples of his predecessors. Speaker Carl Albert retired in the middle of the Koreagate scandal brought on by South Korean political fundraiser Tongsun Park. Tip O'Neill came to the rescue of his friend and colleague John Murtha during the FBI's ABSCAM probe, securing Murtha's seat in Congress even though he had failed to advise the FBI that he had been approached by Arab businessmen offering bribes. Jim Wright resigned as the House Ethics Committee explored ethics violations charges against him. The charges against Wright were brought by Newt Gingrich, who left Congress in 1998, himself the subject of 84 ethics charges. Bob Livingston of Louisiana was slated to replace Gingrich until *Hustler* magazine exposed Livingston's sexual dalliances. Tom DeLay resigned from Congress in June 2006 as investigations of massive influence peddling swirled around his Republican Party. And Dennis Hastert left Congress at the end of 2007—after joining forces with Nancy Pelosi to make a stand against FBI agents "raiding" congressional offices (executing a federal search warrant) looking for evidence of political corruption.

The Speaker of the House of Representatives is second in the line of presidential succession. The position involves tremendous power and an equal amount of responsibility to the public trust. The fact that so many Speakers have sorely abused that trust is itself an indication of the corrupting influence of power, as well as the fact that the higher one's position, the greater the temptation to abuse one's power becomes.[2]

As the first woman to become Speaker of the House, Nancy Pelosi pledged to return the image of the U.S. Congress to a public service rather than public corruption. Her actions on behalf of William Jefferson, however, are not the only indications that she is as much a politician of the old school as her predecessors.

President Jimmy Carter appointed Alcee Hastings as a United States federal court judge in 1979. By 1981, a federal Grand Jury had indicted Hastings for accepting a $150,000 bribe to protect two convicted mobsters from receiving a prolonged prison sentence. A key witness at Hastings' trial was his friend who had participated in the conspiracy surrounding the bribery. A Florida jury convicted Hastings' friend, but acquitted the judge. Subsequent federal appellate court reviews of the case forced it into the United States Congress for consideration of impeachment. In 1989, Hastings stood impeached by the House of Representatives and was convicted by the Senate on charges of perjury and obstruction of justice.

The investigation of Hastings' bribery was conducted by the FBI, which had him under surveillance at critical times, and the Bureau developed the sources, evidence, and the court case that resulted in Hastings' eventual impeachment and conviction. Congressman John Conyers gave this statement to the Congress after he independently reviewed the evidence and weighed the case against Hastings:

> As a lawyer who occasionally got into courtrooms, I have been before my share of hostile judges, racist judges, in the North and in the South. I found nothing more satisfying, in the course of my congressional career, than to help the development of a capable and vigorous bar of African-American lawyers, men and women, and the elevation of some of its more outstanding practitioners to the prestigious position of federal judge where they can serve, not merely as dispensers of equal justice under the law, but as models for their community and for the nation.
>
> So, I am saddened to come before you today to urge the removal of one of the handful of black judges who

presently occupy the federal bench. I am not happy to come here to argue that Alcee L. Hastings has forfeited his right to one of the most honored places in this American political system. But we did not wage the civil rights struggle in order to substitute one form of judicial corruption for another.

. . . It is precisely because he betrayed his trust and betrayed those who looked to him for leadership, the possibility of a fairer, better system, that our obligation to face the truth as we see it in this matter is so great.

In 1992, Hastings was elected to represent the 23rd Congressional District in Florida. In 2006, after the Democratic Party recaptured the House, Nancy Pelosi began considering Hastings for the chairmanship of the House Intelligence Committee. In doing so, Pelosi overlooked an obviously qualified candidate, Jane Harman, who had substantial experience in national security matters and the respect of other members of congress. But Pelosi did not like Harman or her lobbying for the post.

Public outcry at Pelosi's choice of Alcee Hastings forced her to retreat, nominating instead Congressman Silvestri Reyes, who today serves in the important post. But Alcee Hastings remains a member of the committee, passing judgment on the FBI and some of the nation's most sensitive intelligence operations. In a bid to become the chairman of the House Committee on Intelligence, Hastings had this to say about the agency he would oversee:

. . . the FBI tampered with the evidence to trump up their charge that I lied. It was FBI whistleblower Frederic Whitehurst of the FBI who came forward with the revelation that Fred Malone in the FBI laboratory cut the strap of a man-purse of mine (they were popular in the

'70s) and then testified that the lab determined that I had cut the strap to provide myself an alibi. That and additional revelations about improper FBI conduct in my case caused Judge Sporkin of the Federal District Court of the District of Columbia to state that if he had the constitutional authority, he would reverse the impeachment.

Hastings' election to Congress and placement on the House Intelligence Committee gives him the green light to see and hear the nation's most sensitive investigative efforts by the agency he so detests. Years after his impeachment, Hastings paints a "common man" picture of his past:

I don't know anybody who has had their life gone over for nine years and they didn't find anything. . . There were no Swiss bank accounts. What they found was I drank liquor and I had some girl friends. That's not a crime.

At the very least. Alcee Hastings' past behavior seems to be at odds with the qualities of character necessary for serving on one of the most sensitive committees in Congress. It's clear that in considering him for chairman of the House Intelligence Committee, Pelosi was motivated by political relationships more than careful consideration of national security.

Placing politics before national security has become the hallmark of Nancy Pelosi's judgment. Consider the thinking behind her decision to support Democratic Congressman John Murtha for House majority leader. In a letter to Murtha she wrote:

Your strong voice for national security, the war on terror and Iraq provides genuine leadership for our party, and I count on you to lead on these vital issues . . . for this and all you have done for Democrats in the past and espe-

cially this last year, I am pleased to support your candidacy for majority leader for the 110ᵗʰ Congress.

During the late 1970s, FBI agents posed as business representatives from a Middle Eastern country and sought to bribe United States congressmen who thought they were currying potentially lucrative deals with a fictitious Arab sheik. By the time the cases were exposed and came to trial, 31 politicians were implicated in the scandal. As a result of the ABSCAM investigation, a United States senator and five United States congressmen were convicted of bribery and conspiracy.

Although never charged with any crime, Congressman John Murtha was videotaped during a meeting with one of the supposed Middle Eastern businessmen, where he said the following:

> *Now . . . I want to deal with you guys a while before I make any transactions at all, period. I want to say, 'Look put some money in these guys.' And I, just let me know, so I can say, you know, these guys are going to—they want to do business in our district. Then there's a couple businesses that I'm not personally involved in but would be very helpful for the district, that I could make a big play of, be very helpful to me.*

> *After we've done some business, then I might change my mind. But right now, that's all I'm interested in . . . And I'm going to tell you this. If anybody can do it, and I'm not bull (expletive deleted) you fellows, I can get it done my way.*

The undercover agents offered Murtha a $50,000 bribe, which he didn't accept, although his wording appeared to preserve the possibility that he would reconsider after further evaluation of his suitors. Murtha and Pelosi, in his defense, have repeatedly emphasized that he didn't accept any bribes and didn't commit any crime. Once again, it is his faulty judgment and the dubious nature of his conduct that are at issue, and these issues are unresolved.

Why didn't Murtha report this incident to the FBI? He'd been offered a bribe, which is clearly a crime. He might logically have concluded that other politicians were being offered bribes by foreign nationals, which would also pose a serious potential threat to national security. Why not report the event to the appropriate law enforcement authorities?

Murtha has never been forced to answer the question, and has never provided a satisfactory explanation. Pelosi should have insisted on one. But her judgment now is just as questionable as his judgment then. In considering Murtha for House majority leader, Pelosi again placed relationships and loyalties over national security. She has continued to use her powerful position as House Speaker to maintain the status quo. Despite all the fanfare accompanying her ascendancy to the position, she has failed to establish an oversight panel to aggressively pursue and emphasize ethics and honesty in the House of Representatives. It simply would not be the politically correct thing to do.

Significantly, the number of her fellow Democrats who decided not to support her selection of Murtha resulted in the election instead of Congressman Steny Hoyer as majority leader (by a vote of 149-86).

In reaction to this development, Murtha said:

I am disconcerted that some are making headlines by resorting to unfounded allegations that occurred 26 years ago. I thought we were above this type of swift-boating attack. This is not how we restore integrity and civility to the United States Congress.

For his part, Murtha has resisted a variety of ideas that would have made "the People's House" a more honest one. A *Wall Street Journal* article from November 15, 2006, reported positions Murtha has taken on important ethics issues:

> *In 1997 Mr. Murtha joined with Rep. Billy Tauzin, a Louisiana Republican, in blocking outside groups and private citizens from filing complaints directly with the House Ethics Committee.*

> *Mr. Murtha also pushed for a law that would require the Justice Department reimburse the legal bills of any member of Congress it investigated if it was shown the probe was not 'substantially justified'—a privilege no other American enjoyed.*

Integrity and civility will be restored to the United States Congress and to politics in America when American citizens use their votes to clean the place up, since Republicans and Democrats alike refuse to do it themselves.

Whether they're called political scandals, cover-ups, conflicts of interest, ethical violations, or violations of the federal criminal statues related to obstructing justice and lying, the result is the same. Americans lose faith and trust in their government and become cynical about the long history of betrayal of the public trust by elected officials. The sad truth is that no one expects politicians to behave or perform any better than they historically have.

But since these politicians are also the same people who are charged with insuring the safety of Americans in this latest age of terror, it is more important than ever to carefully monitor their "business as usual."

CHAPTER FIFTEEN

THE FRIENDS OF JACK ABRAMOFF

The Money Fix

I didn't create the system. This is the system that we have. . . Eventually, money wins in politics.

Jack Abramoff, March 2005[1]

In 1981, six U.S. congressmen—Democrats and Republicans—were convicted of bribery and conspiracy charges in the public corruption probe called ABSCAM. FBI agents, posing as wealthy businessmen from the Middle East, met with the congressmen in motel rooms and engaged in business deals with them, offering bribes and gifts. Democrats John Jenrette, Raymond Lederer, Michael Myers, Frank Thompson, and John Murphy were eventually convicted, along with Republican Richard Kelly. A Senate Democrat, Harrison Williams, was also convicted.

Although it was highly successful, the ABSCAM investigation, under the stewardship of then FBI director Judge William Webster, met with such anger from Congress that the FBI discontinued the pro-active "sting" tactic in government corruption cases, deferring thereafter to the investigation of political corruption complaints after the fact.

The Savings and Loan scandal of the late 1980s implicated five U.S. Senators in efforts to get the Department of Justice to back off on its investigation of Charles Keating, who was subsequently convicted of charges related to the affair. Two of the senators, Democrats Dennis DeConcini of Arizona and Donald Riegle of Michigan, did not run for re-election.

Following closely on the heels of the Savings and Loan debacle, 355 current and former members of the House of Representatives were identified as having over-drafted their personal accounts, taking advantage of a weakness in the House banking system and brazenly abusing their positions for financial gain.

In the late 1980s, some 20 local, state, and federal government officials were convicted on an assortment of charges related to a scandal called "Wedtech." Wedtech was a company in the Bronx, New York, that grew to have over $250 million in federal government no-bid contracts, mostly from the Department of Defense, based on the notion that it was a minority-owned business. It was not minority-owned, and the company went to great lengths to hide the fact, committing mail fraud, perjury, and obstruction of justice. The FBI Wedtech investigation reached the politically powerful Bronx Congressman Mario Biaggi, who was convicted on 15 counts of obstruction of justice and accepting illegal gratuities. President Ronald Reagan's attorney general, Edwin Meese, resigned following the disclosure of information that he had worked as a lobbyist for Wedtech prior to his appointment as the highest law enforcement officer in the land.

The 1990s saw its share of investigations of public corruption, as well as continued unethical behavior of highly influential and powerful members of Congress. Democrat Tony Coelho spent six terms in the House of Representatives and was elected as the Majority Whip in 1986. Four years later, Coelho resigned amid allegations that he purchased junk bonds with a loan from a savings and loan executive.

Former Republican senator from Minnesota, David Duren-berger, chairman of the Senate Select Committee on Intelligence, was denounced by the Senate in 1990 for accepting outside income. Facing severe criticism, he didn't stand for re-election in 1994 and by 1995 pled guilty to misusing public funds while serving as a U.S. senator.

Cook County, Illinois, Democrat Dan Rostenkowski was forced from the House of Representatives in 1994, after his indictment as a result of the infamous House Post Office scandal. Rostenkowski had served in Congress for an amazing 36 years, but he ended his career with a plea bargain on mail fraud charges that sent him to prison for 17 months, until he was pardoned by President Clinton in December 2000. The post office scandal had been simmering for some time because Democrats, including then House Speaker Thomas Foley, ignored evidence submitted to them that the House post office was being used to launder money. After Congressional Postmaster Robert Rota pled guilty to charges implicating Rostenkowski, the matter finally came to light.

In his book, *Rostenkowski: The Pursuit of Power and the End of the Old Politics*, Richard Cohen concludes:

> *The rise and fall of Dan Rostenkowski tracks the rise and fall of Democrats in the House. It is a story of power, accomplishments, and, ultimately, failure and humiliation.*

This was during the "Republican Revolution" in the House, spearheaded by Speaker Newt Gingrich, himself later run out of office on a raft of ethics charges.

In 1996, attorney and ordained minister Walter R. Tucker III, who represented the Compton area of California in Congress for over three years, resigned and was sentenced to

27 months in prison for demanding bribes and for extortion and tax evasion while he served as the mayor of Compton.

President Clinton's Secretary of Housing and Urban Development Henry Cisneros lied to FBI agents about "hush money" payments he made to a former lover, Linda Medlar. Medlar used the money to buy a house and committed fraud to cover up the origin of the money. She ended up pleading guilty to 28 charges of bank fraud, conspiracy, and obstruction of justice. In the fall of 1999, Cisneros entered into a plea agreement, which allowed him to pay a fine and avoid prosecution on an 18-count indictment that alleged he had committed conspiracy as well as obstructing justice by lying to the FBI. In January 2001, shortly before he left office, President Clinton pardoned Cisneros.

The 1990s ended as they began, with a continuous stream of corruption-based indictments of politicians for a variety of crimes. They all shared a common element: they all involved money.

There is a "second tier" of politicians addicted to power for which the acquisition of money becomes the embodiment of the power they hold instead of power itself. These are not presidents or the primary leaders in Congress as a rule; politicians at the highest levels generally become wealthy as a direct consequence of the power they hold in the far less regulated and more legally comfortable avenues like endowments to libraries, lucrative speaking engagements, and multimillion dollar book advances.

But the vast majority of politicians never reach the political stratosphere, and the levels of power and influence they reach aren't high enough to either satisfy their addiction to power itself or end up making them wealthy as a result.

It's a heady thing to stand at the head of a hall and wave to a cheering crowd that has just elected you to public office on their behalf. There is simply no way to retain a sense of humility when the next step is joining an exclusive club of fellow luminaries who enjoy perks and privileges beyond those of ordinary citizens.

Even politicians who feel a sincere duty to serve their constituencies, who believe they can go to Washington and make a positive difference in their own communities and for America in general, are subjected when they arrive to an extremely complex and evolved system of reciprocal relationships and lobbyists that immediately tests their resolve. Too many times, they succumb to the rarefied "business as usual" atmosphere that characterizes the seat of power of any government. Their principles are compromised when they join the club, and for those who will never reach the top of their party leadership—or the presidency or presidential cabinet level—the primary rewards of political power become identified instead with financial power that they can take advantage of whether they're in office or not.

If the 1990s were characterized by repeated scandals and personal enrichment schemes touching on America's politicians, the 21st century began with a bang. The public corruption scandals that next exploded onto the scene dwarfed anything that had preceded them in recent history.

In 2002, the Department of Justice and the FBI initiated an investigation of the massive energy company, Enron. The company's involvement with politicians had enormous reach. President George W. Bush considered Enron's president, Kenneth Lay, a top candidate to become secretary of the treasury. Enron made political donations to well over 250 Democrats and Republicans in the House and Senate.

The Enron criminal investigation soon touched on some of the most powerful companies and individuals in America, inside and outside of government. The reputable accounting firm

Arthur Anderson admitted it had destroyed documents that concerned the company's finances after the investigation began. An Enron executive named J. Clifford Baxter committed suicide as the investigation unfolded. Merrill Lynch settled a securities fraud case with the SEC involving the activities of four of its executives who were conspiring with Enron.

As Enron collapsed under the weight of its own fraud and corruption, nearly a dozen major executives were either found or pleaded guilty to charges that they had committed repeated frauds with the motive of personal enrichment. In the midst of it all, Enron executives remained at the table when Vice President Dick Cheney held "secret" policy discussions related to America's energy future.

The highly aggressive and now-convicted Republican lobbyist Jack Abramoff symbolizes Washington's latest corruption scandals and their ramifications for homeland security. The FBI's effectiveness in the Abramoff investigation will not win it many friends within the Republican Party establishment. It remains to be seen how much of a price the Bureau will pay for its diligence in rooting out corruption tied to Abramoff and his Republican friends. Today, the once-powerful Abramoff, who counted among his allies some of America's most influential citizens, sits in a federal prison doing his time. With his guilty pleas in federal courts in Washington, D.C., and Miami, his access to the White House and Congress is over—at least for now.

Jack Abramoff was born in New Jersey of influential parents. Spending his undergraduate years at Brandeis University and earning a JD at Georgetown University Law Center, Abramoff became involved with the College Republican National Committee (CRNC). Early on, he developed friendships that would eventually play an important role in the FBI corruption investigation years later. One of those friends was Ralph Reed. Abramoff and Reed went on to form a powerful team that exerted substantial control over the positions, policies, and operation of the CRNC, solidifying Abramoff's connection with the Christian Coalition and Republican leadership.

In the mid-1990s, Abramoff became a lobbyist for a Seattle law firm, establishing close personal relationships with Newt Gingrich, Dick Armey, and former House Speaker Tom DeLay. In 2001, Abramoff joined the Washington, D.C., law firm of Greenberg Traurig. The firm was heavily involved in political lobbying, and Abramoff recruited a team of well-connected people to help him that included a number of congressional staffers. One of those was Tony Rudy, DeLay's deputy chief of staff.

In April 2006, Rudy pled guilty to a single count of conspiracy, admitting he had accepted $86,000 in cash and tickets to sporting events to ensure that the Internet Gambling Prohibition Act would be stalled in Congress. Prior to Rudy, DeLay's former press secretary, Michael Scanlon, pled guilty in the same influence-peddling scandal.

By the end of 2006, Representative Bob Ney, a Republican from Ohio known as the "Mayor of Capitol Hill," resigned from the House after pleading guilty to conspiracy, corruption, and false statement charges that arose from the Abramoff investigation. Two former chiefs of staff for Ney pled guilty to charges that they had conspired with Abramoff in facilitating golf trips to Scotland, meals, and gifts in return for helping Abramoff clients. Found guilty by a federal court jury of lying about his involvement with Abramoff was David Safavian, the head of the General Services Administration (GSA). Safavian accompanied Ralph Reed and Congressman Ney on one of the golf trips to Scotland, while Abramoff was trying to secure a business deal with the government through GSA.

After the election of President George W. Bush in 2001, Abramoff secured a coveted spot on the Department of Interior transition team. Soon after, he became acquainted with Deputy Secretary for the Interior Steven Griles. The Department of the

Interior is responsible for millions of acres of federal land and plays a major role in the management of Indian affairs on that land. The department was made to order for Abramoff, who had built up a clientele of at least nine different Indian tribes while working at the two prestigious law firms. With regulations, policies, and decisions impacting on Indian gaming casinos on reservation land in several states, Abramoff took advantage of his contacts in the Congress and Interior Department to secure favorable decisions for Indian gambling. Griles was ultimately charged in the Abramoff corruption probe, after he lied to a congressional committee probing the nature of his connections with the lobbyist. He pled guilty to obstructing justice. Another Interior Department employee, Roger Stillwell, pled guilty to misdemeanor charges concerning his receipt of numerous "gifts" from Abramoff.

The trail of Indian casino gambling led the FBI to Congressman John T. Doolittle. Doolittle's wife, Julie, had a consulting business that received money from Abramoff's lobbying firm. FBI agents searched the Doolittle California residence in April 2007, and the congressman surrendered his seat on the House Appropriations Committee. Doolittle had received campaign contributions from Abramoff amid a growing corruption investigation into whether members of the Appropriations Committee were accepting bribes in exchange for their decisions as to which projects would be allocated federal funding. As the Abramoff trail took the FBI to Doolittle and his wife, they discovered that he had directed approximately $37 million in federal money to a military contractor in San Diego, Brent Wilkes. While he was earmarking millions of dollars into the House spending bills that benefited Wilkes' company, Doolittle and his political action committee were receiving thousands of dollars in contributions from Wilkes.

By late 2006, one of Doolittle's colleagues in the House of Representatives, Randy "Duke" Cunningham, pled guilty to receiving millions of dollars in bribes from Wilkes in exchange for sending $70 million in government contracts in his direction. Cunningham was a member of the House Intelligence Committee, which has oversight over the FBI's highly sensitive counterintelligence program. The Intelligence Committee makes recommendations on the spending and priorities of numerous agencies within the intelligence community. The House Appropriations Committee approves the actual allocations. Hiding behind the secrecy inherent with intelligence authorizations, Cunningham, who was also a member of the Appropriations Committee, used his position in Congress to steer funding to companies operated by Wilkes and Mitchell Wade. Wade later pled guilty to providing a variety of free gifts to Cunningham.

The continuing trail of guilty pleas took the Bureau to Wilkes' doorstep. He was indicted in early 2007 along with the former number three official at the CIA, Executive Director Kyle "Dusty" Foggo. Foggo had access to and knowledge of some of the CIA's deepest secrets. Appointed as executive director of the agency by former CIA director and former United States congressman Porter Goss, Foggo was in a position to steer highly classified CIA contracts to companies run by Wilkes. Wilkes and Foggo had been friends since high school, "served as best men in each other's weddings and named their sons after each other."[2]

While in their respective positions, Doolittle and Cunningham made spending decisions related to the war in Iraq. Foggo, as the top official responsible for administrative matters within the CIA, made decisions tied to the agency's operational spending there as well. The trials for Wilkes and Foggo are pending. Porter Goss left the CIA abruptly, Tom DeLay is under indictment for money laundering, and at least 78 politicians in both parties are donating or returning campaign contributions they received from Abramoff. The list is impressively nonpartisan, and it includes people from President George W. Bush to Senator Hillary Clinton, Representative Charles Rangel of New York to former House Speaker Dennis Hastert of Illinois.

At a time when the future security of the country depends even more critically than ever on responsible and principled public service, FBI investigations focus more than ever on a web of corrupt business dealings and conflicts of interest, while questionable ethics raise serious doubts about the credibility of specific politicians and the collective judgment of Congress itself. Congressional anger directed at every mistake the FBI makes in the implementation of its mission and congressional meddling in the day-to-day management of the FBI appear more reactive to this scrutiny than careful and well-reasoned. Both the Democratic and Republican Party machines are continually concerned that the Bureau is hot on the trail of massive and complicated schemes involving bribery, conspiracy, obstruction, and the overall selling out of American interests.

The tremendous authority vested in congressional committees allows them to literally decide the fate of the Bureau and even specific Bureau agents. During a time when decisions are being made that restructure the American intelligence community, the role of the FBI and its supremacy in conducting both criminal and national security investigations within and under the rule of law is threatened by politicians of both parties who wish to remove some responsibilities from the Bureau with the motive of weakening it in the eyes of the public and in its ability to perform this important mission.

The fact that politicians have placed military and CIA officials in more and more positions of power and authority within the FBI itself eliminates transparency, enhances the opportunity for secrecy to cover the government's mistakes, and interferes with the pursuit of justice. Poor judgment and unethical behavior in one area inevitably finds itself repeated in others. As a result, despite the grandstanding politicians continually do on the national media concerning their displeasure with the performance of the Bureau, the country is left less secure. A look at the FBI investigations under way at this writing is illustrative of the wide reach of these very powerful people.

Senator Pete Domenici, a Republican from New Mexico, placed a call to the U.S. Attorney for New Mexico, David Iglesias, asking questions about an ongoing investigation. Within weeks, Iglesias was among eight United States Attorneys across the nation fired by the Bush White House. All were spearheading major public corruption investigations at the time of their firing.

Domenici is the ranking member of the Senate Committee on Energy and Natural Resources and a member of the Appropriations and Budget Committees, with great potential power over issues impacting the FBI, a major player in some of the same corruption probes. Caught in the spotlight as a result of his highly improper phone call, Domenici is not running for reelection in 2008.

Senator Bob Menendez, a Democrat from New Jersey, received $300,000 in rent money from the North Hudson Action Corp, which he helped designate as a qualified federal health care center in Newark. Subsequently, North Hudson acquired $9.6 million in federal grants. Menendez says he sought and received a clearance from the House Ethics Committee for his actions.

In July 2007, the FBI and IRS served a search warrant on the home of Senator Ted Stevens, Republican from Alaska. Executives of the oil company VECO helped coordinate the remodeling of Stevens' home and asked contractors involved to send them copies of the bills. A former VECO CEO, Bill Allen, has pled guilty to federal charges of bribing Alaskan politicians.

No fewer than 21 United States congressman have been the subjects of FBI investigations in the recent past, involving a variety of allegations. Republicans John Doolittle, Tom Feeney,

Conrad Burns, Tom DeLay, and Bob Ney have all been implicated in the Jack Abramoff scandal. Ney has been sentenced to
30 months in federal prison for taking gifts from Abramoff.
Republicans Duke Cunningham, Tom DeLay, Jerry Lewis, and
Katherine Harris (who gained fame as the Florida secretary of
state who confirmed that President George W. Bush won the
close presidential race in Florida) have all been implicated in
the bribery probe involving defense and intelligence contracts
given to Brent Wilkes and Mitchell Wade. Cunningham has
been convicted and DeLay is under indictment. Democrat Alan
Mollohan of West Virginia resigned from his position on the
House Ethics Committee after his alleged involvement in steer-
ing $179 million in U.S. government contracts to nonprofit
groups who contributed to the Mollohan Family Charitable
Foundation, during a time when his personal wealth substantially increased. Republican Curt Weldon of Pennsylvania,
defeated in his 2006 re-election effort, allegedly used his position of influence in Congress to encourage American companies
to do business with a Russian company, Itera, when his daughter, Karen Weldon, was being paid $1 million a year to act as a
lobbyist for the firm in Washington.

The money that follows and amplifies a political career in
Washington serves both to elevate and confirm a politician's
addiction to power. There are continual expressions of shock
and dismay in the media—and in the public statements of outrage from whichever political party is not immediately implicated—at each revelation of the consequences of this addiction.

It would be far more useful to recognize this process and to
foster, instead, an awareness of this vulnerability. No form of
addiction is treated by ignoring the fact that it exists, and serious consequences for the security of the United States are not
mitigated when those in charge who are afflicted by it remain
undiagnosed.

CHAPTER SIXTEEN

OUTSOURCING THE WAR ON TERROR

The Business of Security

SAIC's approximately 44,000 employees serve customers in the Department of Defense, the intelligence community, the U.S. Department of Homeland Security, other U.S. Government civil agencies and selected commercial markets. SAIC had annual revenues of $8.9 billion for its fiscal year ended January 31, 2008.

www.saic.com/about

SAIC currently holds some 9,000 active federal contracts. . . . More than a hundred of them are worth upwards of $10 million apiece. Two of them are worth more than $1 billion. . . . No Washington contractor seems to exploit conflicts of interest with more zeal, or operates in greater secrecy.

Vanity Fair, March 2007[1]

Science Applications International Corporation (SAIC) has been famously described by one of its own executives as a "stealth company."[2]

Where Halliburton and Bechtel have public reputations as the go-to companies for government outsourcing, SAIC—which sells brainpower rather than the brawn employed by Halliburton—may be the most successful contributor to the privatization of government in the current "war on terror" that you've never heard of.

Where do former Washington public servants go after—or in between—periods of government service? They go where they can be compensated handsomely for their knowledge, experience, and connections: to private industry. While there, they are no longer subject to the scrutiny of their financial dealings that is the situation while they are actual government employees, and they make much more money at the same time.

In this way, the appetite for money that accompanies the addiction to power of Washington politicians is assuaged at the same time their positions in the power corridors continue to be acknowledged and rewarded whether they're in or out of office.

SAIC has had as part of its management and on its board of directors Melvin Laird, secretary of defense in the Nixon administration; William Perry, secretary of defense for Bill Clinton; John Deutsch, President Clinton's CIA director; Admiral Bobby Ray Inman, who served in various capacities in NSA and CIA for the Ford, Carter, and Reagan administrations; and David Kay, who led the search for weapons of mass destruction for the U.N. following the 1991 Gulf War and for the Bush administration following the 2003 Iraq invasion. Robert Gates, who succeeded Donald Rumsfeld as secretary of defense in 2006, is a former member of the SAIC board of directors.

The company also has paid millions of dollars in fines for falsifying data in its deliverables under contract to the government (to the EPA in 1991 and to the U.S. Air Force in 1995 and 2005). Whistleblowers from among its ranks have been the source of most investigations regarding SAIC's contract performance irregularities, which have included systematic over-charging as well as outright fraud.

In a joint FBI/Air Force Office of Special Investigations (OSI) case in 2002, the U.S. Attorney in San Antonio, Texas, concluded that:

> *SIAC had, unbeknownst to the Air Force, grossly understated profits [on a $24 million contract to clean up contaminated waste sites at Kelly Air Force Base] . . . rather than the 8 to 10 percent profit the contract allowed, SAIC had realized profits of three times that amount, and had submitted false and fraudulent statements of its expected costs and profits.*[3]

Although SAIC paid a fine in settlement, in a written response to these findings, the company rather blithely characterized its actions as the result of "quantitative risk analysis" it factors into all its contracts "not required to be disclosed under [federal law] based on longstanding legal principles."[4]

The growth of the role of "government contractors" in conducting the actual business of government has increased astronomically since 9/11. SAIC's investors were told in October 2006 that the "war on terror" would "continue to be a growth industry."[5]

Halliburton and its former subsidiary KBR continue to rake in huge profits in their remarkably poorly executed and wasteful infrastructure operations in Iraq.

Perhaps the most worrisome aspect of this is the growth of privatized mercenary armies who sign lucrative contracts with the United States government and then benefit financially from their work in American war zones. The most notable example is Blackwater USA.

Composed of former military officers and highly trained veterans as well as former members of the CIA, Blackwater is being sued by the Iraqi government for allegedly killing civilians without cause, being investigated by the FBI for its activities in Iraq, and under scrutiny for its relationship with the Department of State.

Blackwater is both a symptom of an American military stretched too thin, without the necessary forces to perform all of the tasks an army needs to perform in a war zone, and a government contract system that is completely out of control. Further, it's a striking example of physical security and even military-style operations being conducted under the secrecy of a corporate structure rather than under transparency and the rule of law that are mandated in a government agency.

In their zeal for weapons and action, it's difficult to tell the difference between Blackwater employees wearing fatigues while training in the North Carolina woods from the militias that inspired Timothy McVeigh 15 years ago. Americans should worry that people trained to kill and overthrow foreign governments now work as contractors for the United States, without being accountable to the government that is paying them, to the foreign government hosting their presence, or to the U.S. government agencies—like the State Department—that seem unaware of the potential danger they pose to responsible law enforcement.

Until recent events in Iraq, few Americans had ever heard of Blackwater USA. Established in 1997, it recruited a large number of men who relished playing war games with an assortment of high-powered weapons. But this isn't just any group of weekend paintball enthusiasts itching to pretend they are at war. Blackwater today has in excess of $1 billion in government security contracts. Its founder, Erik Prince, is a former Navy Seal, and its chief operating officer, Joseph Schmitz, was the inspector general at the Pentagon working under former defense secretary Donald Rumsfeld before his departure. It hires former Navy Seals, CIA operatives, and other highly trained military and intelligence community alumni with a penchant for war games and close relationships with their counterparts who are still inside sensitive U.S. government agencies.

Blackwater has been protected by the same wall of secrecy and lack of transparency that characterizes the overall Bush administration's response to the war on terror. An October 2007 congressional report stated that Iraqi officials and U.S. military officers alike have complained that Blackwater employees have taken "an aggressive, trigger-happy approach to their work and have repeatedly acted with reckless disregard for Iraqi life."[6]

Nevertheless, the U.S. State Department, which has paid Blackwater more than $832 million for security services in Iraq and elsewhere, was characterized as exercising "virtually no restraint or supervision of the private security company's 861 employees in Iraq."[7]

On a Baghdad street in September 2007, Blackwater security guards under contract to the State Department opened fire on a group of Iraqis they characterized as militants. Eight Iraqis were killed and 24 wounded. Blackwater claimed the shootings were in self-defense. The State Department dispatched its Bureau of Diplomatic Security to investigate the incident. Their technique (supposedly a standard State Department response for private contractors in war zones) was to grant "limited immunity" to the Blackwater security guards so that they could get cooperation and collect the facts about what actually happened. The immunity grant promised people they would not be prosecuted if their statements were truthful.

The Iraqi government launched its own investigation and found no proof that anyone precipitated an attack on the Blackwater guards. A U.S. Army investigation similarly found "no enemy activity involved."

At least two weeks passed before the State Department referred the investigation to the FBI, by which time many Blackwater employees refused to talk with the Bureau, citing their "limited immunity." The FBI's investigation, ongoing at this writing, has already concluded that some of those killed were actually fleeing the scene.

As part of normal procedure, the State Department inspector general's office also began an internal investigation to determine the facts of what happened. Amid the investigation came allegations from some State Department employees that the department's own inspector general, Howard Krongard, who was responsible for investigating charges of waste, fraud, and abuse, had himself interfered with an earlier investigation into allegations that Blackwater was smuggling weapons into Iraq before the shootings occurred.

During a congressional hearing into the matter, Krongard denied these allegations. Before the House Committee on Oversight and Government Affairs, however, he was confronted by a question that took him by surprise. Asked whether he was aware that his own brother, Alvin Krongard, was employed by Blackwater as a consultant, the inspector general told the committee:

> I can tell you very frankly, I am not aware of any financial interest or position (my brother) has with respect to Blackwater. It couldn't possibly have affected anything I've done, because I don't believe it. . . . But when these things surfaced, I called him and I asked him directly. He has told me he does not have any involvement, he does not have any financial interest."[8]

Congressman Elijah Cummings then produced a copy of an email from Erik Prince to Alvin Krongard that read, ". . . thank you for accepting the invitation to be a member of the board."

Howard Krongard called his brother during a recess in the hearing. Alvin Krongard was attending a meeting of the Blackwater advisory board in Williamsburg, Virginia. He confirmed that he was a paid consultant to Blackwater, and later told the media that he had told his brother, Howard, weeks earlier that he was going to accept the advisory board position. When the recess was over, Howard Krongard removed himself from the State Department inspector general's Blackwater investigation.

The Krongard brothers come from interesting backgrounds. Before he was appointed inspector general, Howard Krongard was a former general counsel at Deloitte and Touche. His brother Alvin was a highly successful investment banker at Alex Brown and Sons, acquired by Bankers Trust in 1997.

In 1998, Alvin went to the CIA as an advisor to CIA Director George Tenet. By 2001 he was the executive director of the CIA. After meeting Erik Prince in Afghanistan in 2002, he put the Blackwater founder in touch with contract officials at the CIA, which led to the company's first security guard contracts with the U.S. government.

The implications of government contractors taking over critical government positions and oversight in the homeland security apparatus doesn't end just with billions of dollars in government contracts going to companies engaged in the war in Iraq. During the Bush administration, the nation's major nuclear weapons laboratories have been "privatized," with contracts going to companies that have heavily supported the Republican Party.[9]

In the aftermath of the "spy" case at Los Alamos National Laboratory (LANL) in the late 1990s involving LANL scientist Wen Ho Lee, Congress created the National Nuclear Security Administration (NNSA) to focus on security and overall management improvements at the nation's weapons labs. Previously the purview of the Department of Energy (DOE), the legislation placed an "Administrator" in charge of the NNSA. The administrator was to have autonomy from the secretary of energy in managing NNSA's interests, but would still need to depend on funding from DOE organizations to complete its work.

But money is power, and this "political" arrangement suffered from opening day. The evolving counterintelligence organization, which had been established within the DOE to deal with the growing problem of foreign espionage and intelligence collection being directed at America's nuclear scientists by foreign intelligence services, was caught in the middle.

In the late 1980s and early 1990s, huge counterintelligence vulnerabilities were created at the national weapons laboratories by politicians who engaged in a number of arms treaties with Russia and China, allowing them substantial access to the country's sensitive labs and the "crown jewels" of the weapons labs: physicists and weapons designers. In the name of preventing the spread of weapons of mass destruction, the cornerstone of American foreign policy became engagement with the enemy, which ended up allowing them far greater access to Americans than our opponents have ever allowed to us.

The arrangement has left America increasingly vulnerable to traditional threats, even as the threat of international terrorism was growing. Within the DOE, the counterintelligence responsibilities were split between two organizations: the DOE Office of Counterintelligence, headed by an FBI official on loan; and the NNSA Office of Defense Nuclear Counterintelligence, headed by a separate "Chief." DOE CI was responsible for providing counterintelligence support to the nation's science labs that did not deal in "classified" information. NNSA ODNCI was responsible for providing the same level of support to the nation's nuclear weapons labs, and, as a result, was concerned with the most sensitive national security efforts.

Sharing common elements of staff at the DOE headquarters level, the early days of this arrangement were characterized by a spectacular level of success and progress brought about by the two personalities who made it work. Highly regarded senior-level FBI official Michael J. Waguespack was brought in from the FBI to head up the DOE CI office, while Catherine Shepard, a ranking DOE and then NNSA official was selected as the chief of the NNSA ODNCI.

Where Waguespack was a seasoned FBI agent who had made his reputation working counterintelligence on the streets of Washington, D.C., busting real "spies," Shepard had come up through the ranks on Capitol Hill, serving in several significant positions in support of congressional leaders prior to her appointment to DOE. What she lacked in counterintelligence experience she more than made up for with her insider knowledge of the ways of Washington, her tireless work ethic, her keen intelligence, and natural instincts.[10]

Shepard and Waguespack immediately embarked on a plan to work together. They jointly developed a counterintelligence strategic plan to guide the work of their growing staff. They astutely realized that international terrorism needed to be addressed by their combined offices, and developed policies and carefully thought out plans to make it happen. Together, they embarked on developing and staffing positions that would comprise the foundation of the DOE/NNSA counterintelligence effort: awareness, analysis, cyber, investigations, and training. They held yearly conferences and called in all of the senior counterintelligence officers working in the labs around the country to seek their guidance and wisdom in moving forward.

Although he was aware that his position in the parent organization of DOE/OCI held the moneybags, Waguespack never misused his authority or sought to diminish the NNSA side of the "house" when it came to budget allocations. He knew the counterintelligence threat, and he dealt with Shepard in a professional and effective manner. They became true "partners" in implementing and growing the DOE/NNSA CI program. Together they took to the road to meet the lab directors and senior counterintelligence officers, and they greatly enhanced the effectiveness of the CI mission at the national nuclear weapons labs.

Only two years after he moved into the position, Waguespack started seeing changes at the FBI that concerned him, and like so many others, decided to retire. His departure was a significant loss to the FBI, and an even greater one to the DOE/NNSA mission. Replaced by another senior FBI official, who would also leave within two years, the relationship and coordination that had characterized his tenure with Shepard and NNSA ODNCI changed dramatically and almost overnight. Waguespack's FBI successor had almost no contact with senior counterintelligence officers in the field, did little to nothing to engage the lab directors, and embarked on an aggressive effort to re-consolidate the two programs under his own DOE/OCI roof. Congress had created the bifurcation in the first place because the Department of Energy had proven incompetent to handle security at the nation's labs. Now, the department fought daily behind the scenes to spread divisiveness and negative energy in the bifurcated CI mission. Gone were the common grounds to secure the best interests of the nation and protect the labs from the foreign threat. Tightening up on the funding Congress provided for both CI components, the new FBI official had one goal: getting everything back under his control. Morale sank as the Field came to realize this.

When conditions couldn't get any worse, Secretary of Energy Samuel Bodman and his deputy[11] went to Congress with a plan to completely restructure the DOE and NNSA counterintelligence efforts. Using his authority as the secretary, Bodman created the Office of Intelligence and Counterintelligence, appointing one common director who would report to the deputy secretary. Both the FBI official and Shepard left their positions and were replaced by a former high-ranking senior CIA official, Rolf Mowatt-Larssen, who assumed control of both the counterintelligence and intelligence functions within DOE.

As Congress stood idly by, watching work from years earlier neutralized and mocked by the partisan political operatives in charge, Mowatt-Larssen wreaked havoc in the position, turning the counterintelligence effort based on awareness and the establishment of trust between the scientists and counterintelligence officers into a secret and "walled" society dominated by intelligence analysis and sensitive operations. With great style and aplomb, Larssen and an array of loyal cronies who came with him from the CIA demolished the careful foundation that had been built to effectively work counterintelligence within DOE. In one meeting after another, it became painfully obvious that Larssen's goal was not the furtherance of an effective counterintelligence effort to protect America's scientists and secrets. Rather, his vision was one of building within DOE a "mini" CIA. His other goal was to please his masters in the Washington, D.C., political establishment.

On more then one occasion, senior counterintelligence officers serving in the field (at the labs) heard their mandate loud and clear: the counterintelligence program needed to produce information that would land Larssen the recognition he most coveted: to be included in the President's Daily Brief or "PDB." Meanwhile, Larssen expressed frustration at the many "rules" he had to follow. His frustration led to his leadership role in working behind the scenes in the intelligence community to modify Executive Order 12333, which, if implemented, will give the CIA far more flexibility to operate within the United States.

One important example illustrates the "code blue" that America's misguided strategy to deal with international terrorism is already taking its toll inside the United States. Bad judgment born of prior training and complete lack of wisdom has cost the Sandia National Weapons Lab a great deal in both funding and prestige.

One former high-level CIA officer—who believed that torture was the only effective technique to secure information from terrorists[12]—employed coercive techniques of his own against a lab employee who was an American citizen helping the FBI in a computer intrusion investigation called "Titan Rain." "Rain" was primary in eventually identifying the PRC as the origin of intensive attacks on sensitive U.S. government computer networks nationwide.

The Sandia lab employee was ordered by the lab not to help the FBI in its investigation. When he helped anyway, he was fired. The employee subsequently sued Sandia and won. Here is his description of his encounter with former CIA officer and Sandia Senior Counterintelligence Officer Bruce Held:

> *During my last meeting with Sandia management, a semicircle of management was positioned in chairs around me and Bruce Held [Sandia's chief of counterintelligence]. Mr. Held arrived about five minutes late to the meeting and positioned his chair inches directly in front of mine. Mr. Held is a retired CIA officer, who evidently ran paramilitary operations in Africa, according to his deposition testimony.*
>
> *At one point, Mr. Held yelled, 'You're lucky you have such understanding management . . . if you worked for me, I would decapitate you! There would at least be blood all over the office!' During the entire meeting, the other managers just sat there and watched.*
>
> *At the conclusion of the meeting, Mr. Held said, 'Your wife works here, doesn't she? I might need to talk to her.'[13]*

A jury awarded the Sandia employee, Shawn Carpenter, close to $5 million. During the trial, Held explained that he had learned his coercive interrogation techniques during his time in the CIA. He remains at Sandia National Laboratory as the senior counterintelligence officer, and Director Rolf Mowatt-

Larssen often points to him as representing the standard for DOE/NNSA counterintelligence and intelligence collection.

The ultimate result of all of this has been a complete and utter breakdown of the counterintelligence mission within the DOE/NNSA complex, and the development of an intelligence component that has primacy and authority over the CI mission. This is neither healthy nor desirable, given the fact that it mirrors the re-structuring of government under the Bush administration that has led to the lawless and unbridled romp of intelligence at the expense of law and civil liberties. Unfortunately, the carefully cultivated years of work that led scientists at the labs to trust their counterintelligence colleagues and thus report potential CI problems is turning into an environment where that trust and credibility are being destroyed.

The unhappy specter of torture now haunts America as we grapple with terrorism internationally in this post–9/11 era. Held's techniques will haunt Sandia lab to the tune of $5 million, and will impact the level of trust between the DOE/NNSA CI program and lab employees for more years than it took to build.

Ironically, in the midst of the unfortunate transition to a mini CIA inside of DOE, both the Lawrence Livermore National Laboratory (LLNL) and the Los Alamos National Laboratory (LANL) contracts transitioned from the University of California (which had held the contracts for 50 years) to a consortium of private industry, led by Bechtel Corporation. Today the university and its reputation for excellence is out at LLNL, over 500 lab employees have been or are facing layoffs, and private industry is in charge of one of our nation's premier weapons labs. A vice president from Bechtel Corporation is second in command at LLNL, another vice president from Bechtel is in charge of operations and business at LLNL, and a former Army general and vice president from the private Batelle Corporation is in charge of "global security" there. It doesn't take a rocket scientist to sort out the complex web of political relationships and the development of corporate wealth that accompanies (and likely motivates) such decisions. In choosing Bechtel to lead the new contracting team managing two of the nation's weapons labs, Secretary of Energy Samuel Bodman was merely continuing the networking trend already begun years ago in the dark and murky field of placing financial and political interests ahead of the nation's best interests.

In October 2003, The Center for Public Integrity issued a report that concluded:

> *More than 70 American companies and individuals have won up to $8 billion in contracts for work in postwar Iraq and Afghanistan over the last two years. . . . Those companies donated more money to the presidential campaigns of George W. Bush—a little over $500,000—than to any other politician over the last dozen years. . . Bechtel Group, a major government contractor. . . was second at around $1.03 billion.*

In first place was Kellogg, Brown and Root (KBR), then a subsidiary of Halliburton, whose former CEO was Vice President Dick Cheney. The revolving doors between government service and private enterprise are disturbing enough when viewed in the context of powerful Washington firms that lobby for their constituents to the future partners of those constituents while they are still in government. But there is a real danger to the national security of all Americans when the profit motive of business is directly involved with both the military and the intelligence community in a time of serious conflict and international terrorism. The addictions to power—and the financial benefits that adhere to that power—compromise even the most intelligent and skilled in government service.

Incredibly, it is FBI agents today who are ordered to train and assimilate into the CIA "culture" rather than maintaining their own—which is constrained by and built around the law and which has served American justice for 100 years. Americans can thank the White House and Washington politicians of both parties for the dangerous road the Bureau is being forced to travel with the CIA and its political and corporate partners in the post–9/11 era.[14]

CHAPTER SEVENTEEN

THE INTELLIGENCE GAME

Torture and Other Tactics

FEDERAL BUREAU OF INVESTIGATION

To: Director's Office   *Date: 09/02/2004*
From: Inspection–Office of Inspections

Title: GTMO
COUNTERTERRORISM DIVISION (CTD)
INSPECTION SPECIAL INQUIRY

*Synopsis: Request approval to designate captioned matter as an
Inspection Division (INSD) Special Inquiry.*

*Details: Based upon a request from OGC [FBI Office of General
Counsel], INSD conducted a survey of all Bureau personnel who had served in any capacity at GTMO since
09/11/2001. This survey. . . . requested personnel to
advise INSD if they observed any aggressive mistreatment, interrogations or interview techniques of GTMO
detainees. . . The survey resulted in identifying nine
employees who observed this treatment and they provided*

short summaries of what they observed . . . In order to commence with the interviews [of these employees], it is requested that the Deputy Director designate and approve this matter as an INSD Special Inquiry" [1]

After the invasion of Afghanistan in late 2001, captured enemy combatants were placed into prison camps at the U.S. military facility at Guantanamo Bay (GTMO). FBI agents joined CIA officers and military intelligence personnel, and began conducting interviews of the "detainees."

In 2002, some of the agents who had been working at GTMO began reporting to FBI headquarters that they were concerned about the tactics being used during interrogations by some of the military intelligence and CIA personnel.

After the 2003 invasion of Iraq and the re-opening of Saddam Hussein's notorious prison, Abu Gahrib, for use by coalition forces, FBI agents were again on the scene in connection with interrogations of detainees. FBI personnel were again troubled by the coercive interrogation techniques being employed there. In July 2003, the head of the national security law unit at the FBI wrote in an email to FBI executives on the seventh floor of the J. Edgar Hoover Building:

Beyond any doubt, what they are doing (and I don't know the extent of it) would be unlawful were these enemy prisoners of war. [2]

Soon after, FBI Director Mueller withdrew FBI agents from participating in the interrogations of "detainees" at both locations.

As allegations of torture by military personnel surfaced in the media worldwide, several military members who were assigned as guards at Abu Gahrib were court martialed. Amid the building concerns that some of the interrogations had gotten out of hand, President Bush, Secretary of Defense Rumsfeld, and the CIA all denied that torture techniques were being used in either camp.

At the same time, the CIA and the White House denied that captured terrorists were being detained and flown around the world in an "extraordinary rendition" program, pending their confessions or cooperation. Allegations that the CIA had secret locations in various European countries where the terrorists were held without the knowledge of those countries prompted protests from foreign governments and further denials from the United States.

In 2007, pursuant to a Freedom of Information Act (FOIA) request from the media, an FBI report that detailed observations of agents who had been embedded with the CIA and military in locations where torture had been alleged was made public. The report included examples of non-FBI interrogators impersonating FBI agents and using questionable techniques against the captives: placing lit cigarettes in the captives' ears; playing loud music; depriving prisoners of sleep; beating the detainees with sticks; and leaving them to lie on cold floors for extended periods of time without access to a toilet facility.

The FBI had provided its report to the secretary of defense and the Department of Justice, but nothing further was done. The word was that Secretary Rumsfeld had authorized the tactics and that President Bush had signed an executive order approving the techniques in order to obtain information that would protect America from future acts of terror.

FBI agents who had opened a "war crimes" file on the incidence of torture at GTMO were ordered by FBI Headquarters to close the file, because "investigating detainee allegations of abuse was not in the FBI's mission."[3]

On May 20, 2008, the Office of the Inspector General of the U.S. Justice Department released a 437-page review of an exhaustive report on the objections—beginning in 2002—of FBI agents to the torture tactics being used at GTMO. It depicts a clear and dangerous division between the concern for the rule of law by FBI agents in the field and political manipulation of the information provided by senior officials at the FBI, the Justice Department, the Department of Defense, and the National Security Council.

The rift between the FBI and the Pentagon over coercive interrogations was reported to then attorney general John Ashcroft, but senior Justice Department officials later told investigators that "they did not recall that any changes were made at GTMO as a result."[4]

Expecting that torture will be effective in securing information relevant to terrorist acts is misleading and misguided. With over 100 years of work in the most complex criminal and intelligence cases facing the nation, the FBI's experience in penetrating conspiracies and gleaning confessions and admissions to the most heinous crimes has demonstrated repeatedly that torture is unnecessary to both solve or prevent acts of crime and terror. Resorting to torture dehumanizes the victim, making the information he provides less reliable and the chance a connection may be built with him far less likely. Once torture is used as a technique, any possibility of establishing a trusting relationship with a former adversary that can be turned back against the main terrorist enemy is gone forever.

In "Rethinking the Psychology of Torture," released in November 2006, a group of former interrogators and research psychologists arrived at several significant conclusions:

Torture does not yield reliable information and is actually counterproductive in intelligence interrogations, which aim to produce the maximum amount of accurate information in the minimum amount of time. In fact, popular assumptions that torture works conflict with the most effective methodologies of interrogation, as well as with fundamental tenets of psychology.

A common argument for torture is the 'ticking time bomb' scenario, in which a terrorist who knows the location of a bomb is tortured in a race to save lives. Interrogators stated that the terrorist would know that he only has to keep his secret for the short time until the bomb detonates—a time period known to him but not to the interrogators. Moreover, the torture would offer the terrorist a prime opportunity to deceive interrogators by falsely naming bomb locations of difficult access. In their combined 100 years of interrogation experience, the interrogators had never encountered a true ticking bomb scenario.

According to the interrogators, harsh approaches are typically the first choice of novice and untrained interrogators but the last choice of experienced professional interrogators.[5]

Former New York FBI Special Agent Jack Cloonan, who spent years pursuing al Qaeda and Osama Bin Laden for their many terrorist crimes, had this to say about torture:

I'm telling you there's a good reason to operate within the law, not to engage in torture. We can accomplish what we want. We'll get the actionable intelligence. We'll be better off, and we won't have to worry about revenge.[6]

Resorting to the tactic of torture is not only unlawful, but it places America in the same category as its terrorist enemies. When terrorism changes the fundamental way our nation views the rule of law and we make exceptions out of fear, then the terrorists are on the road to winning the "asymmetric" terror war. When government officials lie to cover up the acts of torture that they claim didn't happen—or if they did, they failed to meet the definition of torture—the country is already moving quickly down that road of no return. FBI agents are recruited, selected, and trained based on the premise that they have the personal skills to develop relationships with anyone and to elicit admissions and confessions from the most deadly criminals, gang members, and corrupt public officials. Done correctly, success leaves open the option of prosecution in any U.S. court where a lawfully obtained confession to a crime is admissible as evidence. Using torture rules out using any confession and eliminates completely the prosecution option.

We are now at a crossroads, where even Attorney General Michael Mukasey could not be frank about the nature of the "water boarding" technique during his approval hearings before Congress. Saying that he doesn't condone torture and that it is against the law, he then carefully added that the president can authorize techniques that are lawful to protect the country without addressing specific examples of what constitutes torture. This was from the prospective top law enforcement official in the United States.

There is a serious divide between the mission, role, and philosophies of FBI agents raised to resolve issues within the law and CIA officers who are trained in the difficult work of staying hidden and surviving in hostile foreign lands. What the Congress and politicians don't seem to understand is that efforts to reconcile these skill sets and functions simply because the FBI and CIA have similar missions that share the word "intelligence" won't work. The only commonality in the two agencies that has the same purpose is analysis, but trying to convert the FBI into a collection agency modeled after the CIA is as unreasonable and doomed to failure as would be any move to remake the CIA into an investigative agency. It's not the CIA's primary skill set, nor is it the reason it exists.

As the debate continues, this much is certain: Lying to foreign allies about the American government's conduct does not build trust and confidence among our friends as we try to convince them of the steps needed to fight the war on terror. And pitting one agency of the government against others engaged in this type of conduct is counterproductive to the building of necessarily enhanced communication in the post–9/11 era.

Most importantly, however, the FBI experience at GTMO illustrates the critical necessity for the independence of the FBI from involvement in the actions of politicians who react in ways that may seem expedient, but that often undermine both the rule of law and the moral center of American life.

Fear of terrorism has led to panic-stricken attempts by politicians in both parties to stay one step ahead in laying a foundation to blame the other for the next inevitable terrorist attack on American soil. In many government agencies, career bureaucrats are afraid to resist the decrees of agency heads who have loyal ties to the administration, no matter how outrageous the instruction. Congress is inevitably involved in this daily play, because it is the home base for both political parties. Anyone who resists doing what the politicians order them to do in the way they want it done is ripe for doing the wrong—and even illegal—thing as a result.

Today, just as during Watergate, the FBI is caught in the middle between performing a national security mission with its intelligence colleagues and, at the same time, pursuing investigations of their questionable conduct, brought on by the serious lack of political independence in the CIA, military intelligence agencies, and the U.S. Justice Department itself.

If reorganizing the intelligence community to suppress a diversity of opinions and adding layers of secrecy to government oversight is one way misguided officials are ensuring a high degree of homeland insecurity, applying questionable techniques against the enemy at the street level of the terror war is another. On this issue, the Bush administration has excelled at double talk, deceit, and stupidity. Even as a new attorney general was in the process of congressional hearings to determine whether his nomination would be approved, the president and his loyal intelligence appointee allies were engaged in a convoluted debate about what does—and what does not—constitute torture.

Indeed, when evidence of these tactics became public, the supreme arrogance and conviction of the rightness of their approach was vividly apparent in the Washington leadership. CIA Director General Michael Hayden told a U.S. Senate committee, "we used it [torture] against . . . three detainees because of the circumstances at the time."[7]

Vice President Dick Cheney declared: "It's a good thing we had them in custody, and it's a good thing we found out what they knew."[8]

Because of a lawsuit by the American Civil Liberties Union (ACLU), a U.S. district court judge ruled in May 2008 that a 2002 CIA memo justifying the use of torture should be made public. If it is, Americans will finally realize why the FBI, and not the CIA and military intelligence organs, should be firmly in control of the war on terror.

Amazingly, the Bush administration continues to defend torture, peddling the line that using these techniques prevented other terrorist attacks and was thus justified. During a trip to the San Francisco Bay Area, President Bush's Secretary of State Condoleezza Rice had this to say in response to a question about the torture technique of waterboarding:

The fact is that after Sept. 11, whatever was legal in the face of not just the attacks of Sept. 11, but the anthrax attacks that happened, we were in an environment in

*which saving America from the next attack was para-
mount . . . Now there has been a long evolution in American policy about detainees and about interrogations. . . .
We now have in place a law that was not there in 2002
and 2003. . . So the ground is different now.*

There is a huge problem with this. Torture is torture, and
just because a U.S. president decrees that a specific technique is
not torture doesn't make it so. Breaking any law in favor of a
hastily reasoned expediency makes the rule of law essentially
irrelevant.

Today, the doubts expressed by Americans in the prosecution of the war on terror prove the futility of questionable tactics
employed by amateurs at interviewing. Current Secretary of
Defense Robert Gates recently told the Senate Appropriations
Committee, "We're stuck in Cuba at the detention center." CNN
reported:

*There were several detainees who cannot be freed, but
who are also ineligible for prosecution under the military
courts set up by the Bush administration. Gates did not
elaborate on why those detainees would not be charged.*[9]

What is the right—and lawful—course of action when any
possible option rests on the basis of illegality?

While American politicians feverishly debate on what they
knew about torture and when they knew it, al Qaeda and other
terrorist organizations throughout the world are free to use the
revelations of torture at the hands of America's CIA and military intelligence as highly effective recruitment tools, ensuring
that America will be fighting terrorists for decades to come. It's
difficult to spread democracy and the uniqueness of the rule of
law when setting an example to the contrary.

The post–9/11 tactic of the Bush administration was to place the primary responsibility for the "war on terror" in the hands of an enhanced intelligence community and the military. With a passion matched only by their terrorist adversary, they have aggressively moved to fight international terrorism abroad— and sometimes at home. The reach of the CIA and other intelligence operations does not currently stop at the U.S. border. With the new intelligence structure established by the Bush White House, it now reaches into every corner of American society.

The first casualty of the growing influence of America's newly revamped intelligence community was the FBI. With the establishment of the National Security Bureau inside the FBI, led by a former CIA analyst, the FBI was changed forever. For the first time in its history, an outsider with little understanding of the Bureau's law enforcement mission was now in charge. The Bureau's previous independent voice in counterintelligence and intelligence collection matters is a thing of the past. The new intelligence paradigm has the former CIA official working within the greater intelligence community, historically (and currently) under the beck and call of politicians.

The resulting changes are coming fast and cloaked in secrecy. Only when it is too late will American citizens realize what has happened to the country's rule of law in the face of the terrorist attacks on 9/11. There's little doubt that we will someday find ourselves debating which was worst for us: the devastating and deadly attacks of that terrible day, or the political machinations which resulted, and which now threaten America's economic, social, and political future. The primacy of the rule of law, that heretofore sacrosanct and uniquely American creation, is being directly assaulted by politicians who are leading the country headlong into a prolonged and misguided "war on terror."

If any one man has had to contend directly with all of the symptoms of the disappearance of the rule of law in America, it has been FBI Director Robert Mueller. Mueller landed on the FBI's doorstep just days before the 9/11 terrorist attacks. All he had to do was walk across the street from the Department of Justice, where he was serving in a very similar capacity as the unfortunate Nixon loyalist L. Patrick Gray had served several decades earlier.

Before his assignment at Justice, Mueller was a no-nonsense United States Attorney in Northern California. Working out of his office in the Federal Building in San Francisco, Mueller was actively involved in every major investigation his office took on, and he quickly identified proactive initiatives unique to the San Francisco Bay Area.

On one occasion, he traveled to the Silicon Valley with the San Francisco FBI associate special agent in charge to meet with executives from high-tech companies. He listened intently as they explained the impact on their industry of the theft by foreign countries of their intellectual property. He sympathized with their plight, and easily recognized the significance of focusing on the priority of economic espionage. As a result, U.S. Attorney Mueller endorsed a specialized squad within the San Francisco FBI office—the first of its kind anywhere in the nation—to focus on high-tech espionage and theft of intellectual property.[10]

Mueller grasped the importance of national security matters and their effects on various aspects of American society. During his career as one of the nation's most high-profile prosecutors, Mueller worked on the investigation and trial phase of the infamous terrorist bombing of Pan American Flight 007, blasted out of the sky over Lockerbie, Scotland, by a bomb placed by Libyan intelligence agents. He knew firsthand the handiwork of sophisticated terrorists supported by the intelligence networks of state sponsors of terror.

So it's not surprising that Mueller was the choice for FBI director to succeed Louis Freeh, who left to return to private life in June 2001. Mueller was highly experienced, highly intelligent, and had a work ethic that would get him through the long days and nights he would be spending as the Bureau's newest employee. He was also—unlike Louis Freeh—both politically connected to the U.S. Justice Department under Attorney General John Ashcroft, and a former Marine whose personal values included a high degree of loyalty to the administration.

For Mueller, things started off—quite literally—at an explosive pace. That pace has never slowed. As Congress looked for blame in the wake of 9/11, Mueller was forced to agree to the establishment of the National Security Bureau (NSB)—under a career CIA officer and analyst—within the FBI. Had he failed to compromise in this, it would have meant the immediate transfer of counterintelligence and counterterrorism responsibility from the Bureau.

Most FBI agents we have spoken with believe that the FBI's director should have fought harder against the forceful intrusion of the CIA into the FBI's balance between law enforcement and domestic security. They wish he had been able to draw the line sooner.

The Bush administration and the bipartisan 9/11 commission used selective information to support their thesis of what did—or didn't—happen that allowed al Qaeda terrorists to execute a successful series of attacks within the U.S. on 9/11. It is widely recognized within the FBI that NSB will be transferred directly to the CIA if there is another successful terrorist attack. We spoke with one current FBI agent in Washington who smiled ruefully as he told us that the CIA was already quietly making the rounds of politicians in the capital, trying to convince them that NSB should be moved out of the FBI now.

Director Robert Mueller continues to steer the FBI through the choppy waters of political interference in both its mission and its management. But the Bureau pays a heavy price each time it defies the president or powerful politicians in Congress.

When information about military and CIA use of torture first began to surface in 2004, FBI agents present at interrogations where questionable tactics occurred made their feelings known to Director Mueller. One FBI agent reported "aggressive treatment and improper interview techniques," while another FBI official declared that the "tactics have produced no intelligence."

These concerns from field agents came in during the same time frame that an Egyptian cleric claimed he had been kidnapped by the CIA in Italy (the Italian government later indicted 26 Americans and 5 Italian agents allegedly involved) and amid reports that the CIA was operating secret prisons in Poland and Romania. The U.S. government either denied or failed to comment on the allegations until 2007, when President Bush announced that America "does not torture people."

The President is working with Congress to pass legislation that will protect CIA officers from prosecution for having engaged in the very activities the CIA and White House once denied. All of this was done in the name of expediency in fighting terrorism, and it is all in defiance of the rule of law.

The FBI was, and continues to be, caught in the middle. Even as the public continues to lose faith in the credibility of the administration to wage the "war on terror," CIA Director Michael Hayden has lashed out at the CIA's own inspector general, accusing him of being too aggressive in pursuit of the torture allegations. Hayden has initiated an internal investigation of the CIA inspector general himself in response.

Jane Mayer, in an article for *The New Yorker*, August 13, 2007, wrote:

The CIA knew even less about running prisons than it did about hostile interrogations. Tyler Drumheller, a former chief of European operations at the CIA, and the author of a recent book, On the Brink: How the White House Compromised U.S. Intelligence, *said, 'The agency had no experience in detention. Never. But they insisted on arresting and detaining people in this program. It was a mistake, in my opinion. You can't mix intelligence and police work. But the White House was really pushing. They wanted someone to do it. So the CIA said, 'We'll try.' George Tenet came out of politics, not intelligence. His whole modus operandi was to please the principal. We got stuck with all sorts of things. This is really the legacy of a director who never said no to anybody.'*

At this writing, the CIA has confirmed that it destroyed tapes of CIA interrogation videos in 2005 despite the order of a federal judge to preserve evidence "regarding the torture, mistreatment, and abuse of detainees now at the United States Naval Base at Guantanamo Bay." The Justice Department has asked the judge not to "institute a judicial inquiry" of the destruction of the tapes, and has responded to a congressional attempt to gather information on the event by saying that "action responsive to your request would represent significant risk to our preliminary inquiry."

CIA Director Michael Hayden has said that the CIA inspector general (the one he is investigating for stubbornly pursuing the torture allegations) "described the tapes as a mere administrative look at the agency's detention and interrogation practices." The FBI has been called in to sort out the mess.

CHAPTER EIGHTEEN

REALITIES OF INTELLIGENCE
The FBI and the CIA

*There is, fortunately, a fundamental cultural chasm
that divides the FBI from the CIA. That's the good news,
says intelligence expert John Pike, director of GlobalSe-
curity.org. The FBI enforces the law, and the CIA breaks
the law.*[1]

In 2002, the Pentagon approved a plan hatched by former Navy
vice admiral John Poindexter (President Reagan's national
security adviser who was indicted, convicted, and then pardoned for his role in Iran Contra) to develop "technologies to
predict terrorist attacks by mining government databases and
the personal records of people in the United States."

Called Total Information Awareness (TIA), the plan was
supposedly shelved after Congress discovered its existence and
Poindexter was forced to resign as its chief. Recently, information surfaced to suggest that it simply underwent a name
change and, in 2004, was moved to a secret hiding place at NSA
under General Hayden, currently director of the CIA.

Improving the FBI's analytical capability is a step in the
right direction if the nation is to be effective in deterring and
preventing future acts of terror. Changing the FBI "culture" to

prioritize analysis over investigations and to treat analysis as a separate but equal FBI mission, however, is the wrong way to implement such an improvement. It is doomed to failure. Unfortunately, the FBI has taken its cue in developing analysis from Congress and politicians—who equate intelligence operations primarily with the CIA—rather than educating them about how analysis can be enhanced in the unique environment of the FBI.

Despite the statement by FBI Director Robert Mueller at a recent FBI Academy graduation that agents are "collectors" for analysts, FBI agents—who gather evidence of crimes, terrorist acts, and espionage, and then use it to build cases that stand up in court, resulting in long-time prison terms for the perpetrators—are not "collectors." They are not CIA officers, analysts, or investigators in just any other federal agency. They are FBI agents, and they have an identity that has become a legacy: a "brand name" known and respected worldwide.

Collecting evidence and interviewing both good and bad guys to gather the fruits of a crime or to prevent future acts of terror require very similar skill sets. Accurate analysis of the information is vital if the right people are to be identified as responsible for a crime, or patterns of behavior are to be connected with a pending terror attack.

But analysis of information is most often subjective; whereas the standard for the presentation in an American court of law is set far higher. All analysts, regardless of the caliber and extent of their training, are affected by their own natural prejudices, egos, overall personality, and the level of their competition. Investigators, on the other hand, follow the trail of facts to the door of the offender. If they are wrong, or if the case they develop is lacking in evidence, they will pay the price of a loss in open court that is visible to the public.

Investigators have a reputation for tenacity and independence. Without these skills and personal qualities, they would be unable to perform within the challenging American justice system, which, after all, puts them to the test in open court.

There is a central flaw in analysis and "intelligence collection" as it applies to the CIA and throughout the government in other agencies with an intelligence function. The flaw concerns the fact that analysis starts with "collection priorities."

Collection priorities are established based on the current "groupthink" about the nature of the threat. Far too often in American history, the threat is determined by the politics of the time. For example, prior to the fall of the Soviet Union, the CIA's priority was providing American policy makers with updated and critical information on the thinking and intentions of Soviet leaders, how they would react in a variety of scenarios and situations, their succession planning in the event of an emergency, the state of their military readiness, and their economic strength.

The CIA was established to take advantage of thousands of pieces of information from human and electronic sources in order to assess and analyze and come up with the right answers for U.S. presidents and policy makers. Inasmuch as this was the CIA's most important cold war mission, and they had spent hundreds of millions of dollars to develop this primary analytical skill set, it came as somewhat of a shock to most of us that their analysis didn't see coming one of the most important events in the history of the world: the sudden collapse and fall of the Soviet Union.

It's always surprised us that so little public discussion ever occurred regarding how and why this happened. It's even more astonishing that so many politicians are now insisting that the CIA analysis model be instilled within the FBI in order to supposedly deal more effectively with the threat of terrorism.

In the studies that *were* done concerning the reason(s) the CIA missed the imminent demise of the USSR, there is little doubt that "groupthink" and the "collection requirements" mentality contributed in great part to that rather large error. But it's also interesting to look at what happened *after* the Soviet Union crumbled.

Within the U.S. government, political leaders of both parties hailed a new era in which Russia and the United States would become key allies around the world in taking on many issues of strategic importance. Agreements were signed and contracts negotiated that actually placed America's "crown jewels"—its nuclear weapons scientists—in touch with their Russian counterparts to work on programs that would exchange information, disassemble nuclear warheads, and put Russia's nuclear scientists to work so that they would not be encouraged to sell secrets to the highest terrorist bidder.

Through it all, FBI agents on the street saw little change in the behavior of former Soviet—now Russian—spies, who continued working as diligently and aggressively as usual to penetrate American government agencies and steal vital technology and weaponry.

During the 1990s, on countless occasions, worried FBI officials brought this information to the attention of policy makers and congressmen. The response was always the same. The Bureau was regarded as old-fashioned and out of date, old cold warriors looking to the past rather than to the promising future with Russia as a trusted partner.

Today, Russian Federation President—and former KGB officer—Vladimir Putin courts alliances with the People's Republic of China and Iran, misuses the democratic processes that were put into place in Russia after the Soviet Union's fall, and has reinstituted the primacy of the KGB—now the Russian FSB—in every factor of Russian life. Stories of intrigue, mystery, and murder surround his new Russia, such as the case of the fatal poisoning of former Russian spy-turned-dissident, Alexander Litvinenko, in a London apartment building in 2006.

Although the FBI didn't buy into the grand entry of Russia into the world club of free and democratic nation states—since they saw no evidence of much change—the CIA was already moving on to new collection priorities and away from their focus on the former Soviet Union. They laughed at the Bureau for continuing its obsession with a threat that American policy makers—politicians all—clearly no longer wanted to hear about.

This is the heart of the problem with intelligence collection, analysis, and "groupthink": it is grounded in political debate rather than in a conclusion based on clear and impartial examination of the evidence.

Whenever there are public discussions of FBI intelligence "failures" and the dire necessity for the establishment of the National Security Branch—run by a career CIA officer—within the FBI to deal with intelligence and terrorism issues, the debate ignores the distinctions between strategic and tactical analysis.

The CIA was established to deal with long-term strategic analysis. The FBI, on the other hand, is best served by tactical analysis that can change and adapt to the fast-moving pace of a criminal or intelligence-related investigation.

The real point is that both kinds of analysis are necessary if the wider intelligence community—that includes the FBI—is to be effective in preventing terrorist attacks. Tactical analysis integrated within investigative task forces with their components on an equal footing in receiving information, accessing management, and sharing opinions offers the best formula for success in the FBI environment. Such a structure best complements the products, skill levels, and strategic analysis that CIA partners can offer in any intelligence endeavor.

The analytical lessons the FBI learned in managing the UNABOM and Olympic terrorist bombing investigations a decade ago were invaluable. They offer the best real-life examples of how the most complicated terrorism cases can effectively integrate analysis with investigation.

In the early 1990s, the Bureau didn't have sufficient analytical support to staff the needs of complicated and long-unsolved cases like UNABOM, which had gone nearly 18 years without resolution. Between 1994 and 1996, an investigative strategy was created that marked a departure from the FBI's normal management of this type of case. A new management structure was developed where the special agent in charge of the San Francisco Field Office, his assistant, and several supervisors—representing the FBI as well as its partners in the UNABOM Task Force, the Bureau of Alcohol, Tobacco and Firearms and Explosives, and the Postal Inspection Service—combined in daily managing the investigation. Each morning and again each evening, the management team held meetings to review the results of the overall investigation on that day.

The information brought to the table was correlated through a single analytical product. All of the investigators, all of the analysts, and indeed every employee of the UNABOM Task Force (from secretaries to temporary-duty agent personnel working on the Unabom 1-800 number) were provided updated copies of this document on a regular basis. Decisions directing resources, establishing priorities, and changing course were made based on the collective input that resulted. Every agent investigator was encouraged to become an analyst in the context of his or her investigative projects, and every analyst was encouraged to think like an investigator. There were no wrong answers. There were no bad opinions. Every task force member was regarded as valuable, regardless of his or her varying core skills and responsibilities.[2]

The break came when the Unabomber demanded the publication of a lengthy "manifesto" by the mainstream media. The task force recommendation was that the manifesto be published, specifically because analysis and investigation to that point showed it would be the likely key to identifying the elusive bomber. Five months and 50,000 phone calls after *The New York Times* and *The Washington Post* jointly published the document whose words so compellingly reminded the Unabomber's brother of his estranged family member, 18 years of investigation were resolved without any further loss of life. Two years later, the case was so solid that Theodore Kaczynski pled guilty as charged rather than stand trial for all of the UNABOM crimes.

In much the same way, the integration of analysis with investigation and the work of a team of 25 federal, state, and local agencies concentrated the search for Eric Robert Rudolph in a 500,000-square-mile region of the Nantahala National Forest in western North Carolina. Five years after he'd gone to ground, Rudolph emerged from the mountains to rummage through a dumpster for food and was caught by an alert police officer from Murphy, North Carolina. He pled guilty before his trial(s) to the 1996 bombing of the Atlanta Olympics, two bombings in Atlanta in 1997, and the murder of a Birmingham police officer in 1998.

Nevertheless, today it is the FBI that is under intense pressure from the White House, Congress, and the CIA to "reform" its analytical capability. The pressure has led to the expenditure of millions of dollars appropriated to create Field Intelligence Groups (FIGs) within each FBI office.

In 2003 Director Mueller brought Maureen Baginski, a career analyst from NSA, with great fanfare into the FBI fold. Her mission, according to an article in the November 8, 2004, edition of *The New Yorker*, was "to reinvent the Bureau's intelligence program."

Baginski, who had spent 24 years at NSA before coming to the FBI, was highly recommended to Mueller for the job by then NSA director General Michael Hayden. Baginski was quoted as saying her job at the FBI was the same as what she had done at NSA.

It was later revealed that NSA had failed to forward to the intelligence and law enforcement communities intercepted communications between al Qaeda terrorists in a timely fashion just before 9/11, giving NSA its own black eye in the furor of politicians to place blame on anyone but themselves. For her part, Baginski left the FBI after less than two years on the job.

The problems with the structure she left in place are immediately apparent to those of us familiar with how the FBI works in real-world situations, based on our experience in the 1990s and earlier.

A Field Intelligence Group (FIG) has its own supervisor and is not integrated into any particular operational unit. FIG takes its marching orders from both the office special agent in charge and the headquarters entity that sends it its tasking.

From the moment they were created, FIG organizations in the field have received no consistent guidelines on what they should be doing and how they should be doing it. A FIG may engage in strategic or tactical analysis or both, but it lacks consistency in implementation, skill level, and manpower from one office to another. Several agents and analysts we have talked with say the same thing with great frustration: there's no guidance, and there's no true integration of information.

In line with congressional insistence that the FBI "culture" must change, the Bureau has mandated that analysts have equal footing with agent investigators in determining priorities. As a result, and since the "intelligence community" banner waves so insistently over the FBI mission since 9/11, investigations for the most part take a backseat to analysis in the Bureau.

There has been a 30-percent reduction in criminal investigations conducted by the FBI. High-level FBI managers are leaving in record numbers, and many street-level FBI agents are leaving the minute they are eligible for retirement, which is either when they reach their 50th birthday or have 20 years of service.

This exodus is unheard of in the history of the FBI. In one congressional hearing after another, FBI officials are asked why this is happening. The answers they give have never satisfied the congressmen who ask. Maybe that's because the true answer is never given, or discussed, in public. FBI agents are leaving the FBI in record numbers when they are able to retire because they are weary of the effect that political interference in the mission of the FBI has had on their careers.

FBI Director Mueller recently ordered that experienced FBI field supervisors either come to Washington, D.C., to serve a designated period of time and supervise terrorism and other cases from there, or step down from their field supervisory desk. This is exactly the opposite of the successful formula established in UNABOM, the Olympic bombing case, and other significant international terrorism investigations where the matter was run from the field with FBIHQ support and assistance. The results are devastating, but they are certainly changing the FBI "culture":

> *The FBI Agents Association, which represents about 80 percent of the bureau's 12,000 agents, conducted a survey of nearly 1,000 supervisors assigned at 56 field offices affected by the order and found that more than 50 percent of them intended to leave management or retire as a result of the order.*[3]

As determined and well-intentioned as FBI Director Mueller has always been, the necessary independence of his position is continually demonstrated to be sorely lacking in the post–9/11 era. President George W. Bush refers to him as "a member of my administration." His political ties with the Bush administration are strong, and he's valued as a loyal warrior in the "war on terror."

With the establishment of the CIA-run National Security Branch within the FBI, the Bureau is in prime position to lose its counterterrorism mission when it takes the fall for the next terrorist attack on American soil. Although Washington politicians are responsible for the decisions to remake FBI analytical capabilities in the CIA/NSA image, Director Mueller continues to attend the White House staff gatherings at Camp David and appears to have surrendered the independence of the FBI—which is decidedly against the best interests of the nation—to political control for the duration of the "war on terror."

In the current day, highly trained FBI agents with 100 years of successful history behind them in bringing criminals and spies to justice in American courts of law have been supplanted in the "war on terror" by political loyalists to either one party or the other. They've been replaced with CIA "analysts," who sit at desks in Washington and reach subjective opinions after reviewing information hard won in the field by investigators and case officers, rendering analytical judgments that are based on whatever political agenda is primary at the time.

FBI executives, who are called to openly testify before Congress about the mistakes the Bureau has certainly made from time to time, have been relegated since 9/11 to subordinate positions in the overall intelligence community by members of the CIA, NSA, and the military, many of whom have lied and destroyed documents during official investigations. These intelligence community members are loyal to—and answer to—the powerful politicians who put them in their positions. Politicians call the plays based on bad or compromised intelligence, poor judgment, dishonesty, and divisiveness.

This is the situation every FBI director since Watergate has faced. In the present day, the American government is involved in a "war on terror" that could last for decades—and even then remain unresolved. Citizens will become ever more fearful of the threat, and government will continue down the road of less transparency and heightened secrecy as a result.

Any addiction corrupts a rational thought process, and the addiction of Washington politicians to power at the same time that terrorism threatens the nation has given both parties unprecedented power to disrupt and negatively impact American lives. The president and the intelligence chieftains who surround him haven't hesitated to grab what power has become available to them up until this point. What's next?

In October 2007, President Bush told the nation that if Iran obtained nuclear weapons, it could lead to a new World War. Several days later, Vice President Cheney said:

> *The Iranian regime needs to know that if it stays on its present course, the international community is prepared to impose serious consequences. . . . The United States joins other nations in sending a clear message: We will not allow Iran to have a nuclear weapon.*[4]

How sure can we be that any future military action the U.S. government takes will be based on accurate and factual information, when the intelligence community is dominated by political loyalists who are determined to give the White House and its staff of true believers the same kind of flawed analysis that led us into Iraq? Will we have a politically independent FBI to pick apart the trail of lies, deceit, and cover-ups that mark the path to a "war on terror" both inside and outside the U.S.?

It's no secret that Democrats and Republicans alike will blame the FBI for the next terrorist attack on America. At that point, a domestic intelligence program under the control of the CIA and NSA—and possibly including even military intelligence—will potentially be unleashed. American civil liberties will be severely affected, while at the same time no greater protection from acts of domestic or international terror will be attained.

The United States Congress relishes the connecting of the dots in the post–9/11 world. But they haven't required themselves to answer a critical question—a question far more important to the future security of the United States than the location of Osama Bin Laden and his terrorist thugs: why have politicians of both parties acquiesced to the White House strategy of placing the lead role in the war on terror in the hands of the intelligence community and especially the CIA?

Both before 9/11 and after, the work of the CIA has been guided by politicians who seek support for their view of what's important to secure their own power. As a result, the secrecy and lack of transparency that are endemic to the very nature of the CIA and NSA have been the cornerstones of the American strategy to deal with worldwide terrorism, supplanting law enforcement, the FBI, and the rule of law.

CHAPTER NINETEEN

POLITICAL INDEPENDENCE AND THE RULE OF LAW

The Real Power Behind Our Republic

The drive for power can be an unquenchable thirst, addictive in itself. Senator William Fulbright, in his popular bestseller of the 1960s, The Arrogance of Power, *masterfully described the essence of power-hungry politics as the pursuit of power; this he conceived as an end in itself. 'The causes and consequences of war may have more to do with pathology than with politics,' he wrote, 'more to do with irrational pressures of pride and pain than with rational calculation of advantage and profit.'[1]*

Washington politicians take an oath to protect the nation and uphold the Constitution. All too often, that oath takes a back seat to the personal agendas that can be furthered by holding an elective office. Advancing the needs of a variety of donors, financial sponsors, special interest advocates, and close confidantes becomes the job; and without even being aware of it, politicians lose sight of what should be a constant: the clear perspective that their service should be in the national interest.

The entourages who support—and surround—a politician serve to isolate him or her further. In their own addiction to the power game that is Washington, they enable and further the addiction to power of prominent politicians who deal with crucial decisions every day in an atmosphere clouded by that unacknowledged addiction.

Human beings in the grip of an addiction are quick to rally their defenses when they're eventually confronted. In the psychological literature, the list of psychological defenses and symptoms that attend addiction read like a shopping list of many of the behaviors we've described in this book: denial, displacement, anger, manipulation, concealment, lying, deception, poor judgment, and poor choices.

An addict is quick to blame others for his or her problem and will say or do just about anything to avoid having a direct confrontation. Behavior is geared towards feeding the addiction and refusing treatment.

President Nixon denied his involvement in Watergate and became engaged in illegal acts to cover it up. President Clinton denied having an affair with a White House intern. President George W. Bush is in denial about the status of al Qaeda in Iraq prior to the American military invasion.

The constant anger expressed by politicians of both parties plays itself out almost every night to the American public, compliments of the evening news, and every day in the blogosphere. Blaming the "other" political party for the unsolved problems experienced by everyday Americans is a convenient form of displacement (a psychological defense) designed to help one addicted personality outdo the other. Unfortunately, everyone suffers while the addict makes his grab for a bigger dose of power.

Concealment, lying, and deception have characterized nearly every American presidency since President Eisenhower left office. Presidents Nixon, Reagan, Bush, Clinton, and Bush

II have lied to and misled the American people, protected by their political machines, loyal party structures, and occasionally even the news media itself. Dozens of convictions in public trials for obstructing justice, lying to Congress, to a Federal Grand jury, or to the FBI, illustrate the strength of loyalty in those who surround the White House, who are in the grip of the same addiction to power as they act to insulate and protect those who inhabit it from the inevitable consequences.

During the past 40 years, dozens of congressmen from both parties have been indicted and convicted of the same categories of crimes generally reserved for members of the Mob.

Every once and a while, the bond of loyalty in America's political elite is broken and the real essence of what goes on behind the scenes spills out into the open. During these rare episodes, vivid aspects of the addiction to power are on display for all to see.

Dick Morris was a close friend and important political consultant to Bill and Hillary Clinton. Morris left his comfortable White House office one evening and instead of going home to his wife spent the night with one of Washington, D.C.'s many ladies of the evening. She had no idea of the lofty status of her visitor until he decided to prove to her the level of his reach in Washington. He picked up the phone, called the White House, and got President Clinton himself on the phone.

This might have been funny in a movie about a college fraternity, but in Washington, D.C., where dozens of hostile intelligence agencies at any one time are constantly looking for vulnerabilities to exploit in the hopes of finding an American Achilles heel, personal peccadilloes are always fodder for exploitation, and therefore a danger to national security.

As the years went by and President Clinton's own bad judgment and poor choices were exposed, Morris' phone call made perfect sense in the context of a call from one privileged, addicted person to another. After Morris was forced to leave

White House service because of the incident, he became a political commentator for Fox News. He hasn't had anything good to say on the air about either of the Clintons since the exposure of his shenanigans cost him his cozy position with them and ended his access to his primary drug of choice: power.

Enablers who serve an addict of high stature always play an important supporting role to his or her addiction. In Washington, enablers are everywhere: junior and senior staff who cater to the whims of politicians for a whiff of reflected importance; media representatives who foster special connections with politicians to score information that can advance their own careers; lobbyists and special interest groups with enough money and special treatments to offer a useful political contact and ensure his or her support on one committee or another; big business representatives who open doors to big corporate salaries to politicians who are nearing a break in, or departing, government service. Needless to say, the cadre of Washington attorneys is its own privileged (and power-addicted) class, making profits whenever politicians run afoul of the law in their rush to grab as much power and as many perks as they can.

The terrorist attacks on America in 2001 put huge levels of stress on all institutions of government in the United States. Aspects of social, economic, military, political, and legal "business as usual" were shaken to the core.

Under stress, weaknesses in any organism that may have been previously hidden or ignored are likely to appear in clear relief against a newly created background of heightened activity and confusion. Since the events of 9/11, the pre-eminent stressor of terrorism itself—whether foreign or domestic—has made the dysfunctional and divisive behavior by politicians who are addicted to power even more apparent.

President Nixon's White House feared the massive domestic protests to the war in Vietnam, and confused peaceful dissent with the dangerous activities of the Weather Underground and other incipient terrorist organizations. Determined to connect the opposition (Democratic) party with domestic terrorist activities that were gripping the country, Nixon's men committed burglaries, obstructed justice, attempted to misuse the CIA and other government agencies, and in the end condoned and committed extensive domestic spying activities which went far beyond lawful limits. The specter of domestic terrorism was used to label the permissive policies of Democrats as enabling and encouraging violence in the streets. Waving that flag ensured that Nixon and his entourage could continue feeding their addiction to power.

President Gerald Ford's pardon of Nixon set the tone for future presidents to use the pardon as a means to protect loyalists in their entourages who ran afoul of the law during their service. Without that protection, those addicted to power are left vulnerable in a town like Washington, D.C., when opposing addicts with the same problems and needs come to power. The pardon is the ultimate tool to guarantee continued loyalty, and clearly establishes that there are people who are above the law. Presidents have appreciated and used that tool for as long as it's been available to them.

President Ronald Reagan watched as loyal political appointees and overzealous military officers working near the White House engineered a military- and intelligence-related scenario that allowed the United States to covertly ship arms to Iran for money they then used to fund an attempted overthrow of the Nicaraguan government by the Contra rebels. The problem was that Congress had passed legislation prohibiting such funding. After a lengthy investigation by the special prosecutor, high-ranking members of President Reagan's cabinet, CIA officials, and a host of political appointees and military officers were indicted and convicted for their role in the affair that became known as Iran Contra. The majority ended up being pardoned by President George H.W. Bush before he left office.

Just days before leaving office in 2001, President Bill Clinton granted a full pardon to a violent domestic terrorist from the Weather Underground. President George W. Bush granted a commutation of sentence to Vice President Dick Cheney's chief of staff, Lewis "Scooter" Libby, after he was convicted by a trial jury of lying and obstructing justice in the investigation into the leak of the identity of a CIA operative to the public as it related to the president's handling of the early days of the war with Iraq.[2]

It's well known that, however intelligent and accomplished an addicted person is, the force of that addiction generally renders him or her unable to break it on his own. Washington politicians who are addicted to power are therefore highly unlikely to think it's in their interest to admit they need some sort of treatment to counter the effects of the power they hold that makes them feel that they're the most important people in the country doing the most important job in the world.

If it's likely to be left untreated, then, is there any antidote to the toxic effects of the addiction to power of Washington politicians?

The pre-eminent rule of law is the only antidote. And as we've repeatedly said, the primary countervailing force to the impact that the power-addiction of American politicians has on American life is enforcement of the law by a politically independent FBI.

There are three times as many police officers serving New York City's five boroughs as there are FBI agents working within the United States and around the world. Responsible for organized crime, public corruption, crimes on government and Indian reservations, civil rights enforcement, espionage, domestic and international terrorism, and a wide variety of complex interstate frauds and white collar crimes, the FBI's mission takes it deep into the hiding places of America's most violent and corrupt criminal enterprises.

With historic responsibilities in two specific areas, criminal law enforcement and national security, over its 100-year history, the FBI has become one of the premier law enforcement organizations in the world. There is no organization anywhere with its reach, its competencies, and its role in society. Not MI-5 in Britain, where intelligence officers are collectors without firearms and lack the authority to serve search warrants and make arrests. Not the UK's Scotland Yard, where the emphasis is on countering criminality with little role in national security matters. Not the old KGB or its successor, the SVR, where acting as the guardian of civil rights is far from relevant or applicable to the Russian social order. Even within the United States, it would be difficult to come up with an example of another government agency with the FBI's massive and diverse range of jurisdiction, investigative reach, and power to enforce the law.

The development of a public mythology around the Bureau—some of which it actively encouraged in decades past— holds that FBI agents and officials may wield so much power that it presents a danger in itself to the civil liberties and freedoms of Americans. Images from the tragic events at Waco and Ruby Ridge, showing an apparent army of black-clad paramilitary operatives with the letters "FBI" on their backs, evoke a level of fear and anger in Americans who are wary of and regard the Bureau as a sort of national "secret police."

Although politicians have never understood or dealt well with issues of terrorism, whether domestic or international, Senator Arlen Specter, in particular, used the fear of "secret police" to lead a political charge against the FBI's conduct at Ruby Ridge and Waco, with substantial help from Senator Larry Craig, Senator Charles Grassley, and Senator Patrick Leahy.

Specter had announced his decision to seek the 1996 Republican nomination for president of the United States against Bill Clinton. Just as Frank Church had attracted attention to his presidential bid in 1975 with hearings on the FBI and its COIN-TELPRO effort, Specter hoped to use hearings on Ruby Ridge as an opportunity to win the White House. Joining with Senator Craig, Specter pressed for immediate hearings:

> *We sit on a powder keg, with a lot of anxiety and anger welling up across the country as to excessive action by the federal government.*

An article in *The Washington Post* on July 14, 1995, noted:

> *Criticism of the FBI mounted on Capitol Hill and among citizen militias in light of revelations that bureau officials may have destroyed records and misled authorities as they reviewed federal agents' actions.*

In a letter to Specter by fellow Senator Orin Hatch on May 8, 1995, Hatch asked that Specter refrain from using his Subcommittee on Terrorism, Technology and Government Information to hold hearings on Waco and Ruby Ridge. Hatch believed that they were more appropriately addressed by the Committee on the Judiciary for an obvious reason:

> *. . . The hearing you propose is an important one, but I believe that it is unrelated, in any true sense, to the broader issue of the prevention of domestic terrorism. Accordingly, to hold the hearing as you propose at this time will serve only to confuse these important issues. Indeed, by linking the Waco incident to the terrorism issue through hearings at this time, the Committee could inappropriately, albeit unintentionally, convey the wrong message regarding the culpability of those responsible for the atrocity in Oklahoma City. We must not do this.*

Specter replied curtly:

Hearings on Waco and Ruby Ridge, Idaho, should be held promptly. . . . My Subcommittee . . . has clear cut jurisdiction. . . I categorically reject your assertions that the . . . scheduled hearing will serve only to confuse these important issues since I have had and am continuing to have media inquiries on these hearings. . . . I am releasing this exchange of correspondence.

Specter's making a public show of his ire at the FBI, in full view of the media and in apparent solidarity with "citizen militias" that were worrying law enforcement officials all over the country at the time, appeared to trump any more measured response he might have made to Hatch's proposal.

Senator Hatch was right, however, to advocate evaluating the events at Ruby Ridge in the broader context of domestic terrorism.

Had the Senate Committee on the Judiciary succeeded in holding hearings on Ruby Ridge, perhaps there would have been increased and necessary focus on the dangers posed by isolated bands of white supremacists and anti-government activists, who fancied themselves as independent rebel patriots rather than as the potential domestic terrorists they actually were. Perhaps Americans would have learned why a U.S. marshal trying to do his job was murdered by people who didn't think the law applied to them and who interpreted the right to bear arms as the right to use them for any defense they deemed appropriate, irrespective of law. Perhaps a nation evaluating Ruby Ridge as a variant of domestic terrorism would have been more educated and alert to the terrorists who followed, like Timothy McVeigh and Eric Robert Rudolph. Future terrorist acts might have been prevented, or at least dealt with more conclusively if the nation had been alerted to the definition and practical realities of terror, rather than encouraged to regard the FBI as the problem.

Specter's subcommittee completed extensive public hearings on Ruby Ridge. The tone of the hearings was markedly negative towards the Bureau, which had provided them with ample evidence that operations at Ruby Ridge had not been well-conducted. New FBI Director Louis Freeh made an opening statement to the subcommittee on October 19, 1995, setting the factual record straight and taking responsibility for the Bureau's actions even though he had not been the FBI director when Ruby Ridge occurred:

> *At Ruby Ridge, the FBI did not perform at the level which the American people expect or deserve from the FBI. Indeed, for the FBI, Ruby Ridge was a series of terribly flawed law enforcement operations with tragic consequences.*
>
> *There was a trail of serious operational mistakes that went from the mountains of Northern Idaho to FBI Headquarters and back out to a federal courtroom in Boise, Idaho.*
>
> *. . . The FBI has, however, learned from its mistakes there. I have changed almost every aspect of the FBI's crisis response structure and modified or promulgated new policies and procedures to address the flaws and shortcomings apparent from the FBI's response.*

The widow of the U.S. Marshall who was killed at Ruby Ridge, Karen Degan, was quoted in *The New York Times* on September 16, 1995, as saying that the night before his death her husband told her Randy Weaver was "probably the most dangerous guy I have ever had to deal with." She wondered what message the government had sent to her two sons by paying the Weavers "millions of dollars for the events at Ruby Ridge."

Politicians like Arlen Specter have never addressed the fact that their grandstanding opposition to FBI counterterrorism operations in the militia-happy era of the 1990s may have encouraged the domestic terrorism of that time.

David Koresh, who appeared to be delusional and suffering from some sort of mental disorder, held his own followers captive and was solely responsible for their being burned to death at Waco in 1993, resisting any attempts by the federal government to end the standoff peacefully. Timothy McVeigh murdered hundreds of innocent civilians inside the Murrah Federal Building in his April 1995 terrorist bombing to "avenge" the deaths at Waco and spark a new American revolution. Eric Robert Rudolph attacked America through the venue of the 1996 summer Olympics in Atlanta, protesting, in his view, the "one-world" policies of then president Bill Clinton. Even Randy Weaver appeared again. First, he showed up with his former Army commander, Bo Gritz, to offer assistance ending the siege at Waco. They showed up together again at the Freeman standoff in Montana in 1996 to make the same offer. In the summer of 1998, Gritz and Weaver created a flurry of publicity for themselves when they traveled to the rural and rugged mountains of western North Carolina to "join" the law enforcement search for Eric Robert Rudolph.

More recently, Weaver offered support to New Hampshire tax protester Ed Brown and his wife, Elaine. In April 2007, the Browns were convicted and sentenced to five years in prison for refusing to pay more than a million dollars in federal income tax. They sought refuge on their 110-acre property and were in a standoff with federal marshals from June until that October.

Packing a pistol and declaring that federal agents were "guns for hire," Brown proclaimed the tax law unlawful, saying further:

There are no longer any lawful courts. The Free-
masons have taken over our nation . . . and all nations on
the planet.

Randy Weaver traveled to New Hampshire in support of
Brown and his wife. He was quoted in the press as saying:

I'd rather die on my feet right here than die on my
knees under this de facto government. . . Bring it on.

On October 4, 2007, Brown and his wife were peacefully
arrested and are now serving prison terms in federal correc-
tional institutes.

Senator Specter didn't call any public hearings to evaluate
what went right with federal law enforcement's handling of the
Brown event. That's consistent with his lack of reaction to the
peaceful resolution of the Freeman standoff in Montana, the
convictions secured by guilty pleas in the cases involving Theodore Kaczynski and Eric Robert Rudolph, and the restrained
response to a rifle attack on investigators working to find
Rudolph in the mountains of North Carolina that occurred on
Veterans Day, 1998.[3]

On the other hand, there are those who actually champion
the idea of a national secret police force. To address this dangerously misguided notion, we second a recent statement from
former FBI director Louis Freeh:

Establishing in effect a secret police to monitor, col-
lect, and keep under observation those whom a nontrans-
parent agency believes to be a threat to the republic is a
dangerous and dumb idea . . . the practical dysfunction of
such a secret-police agency is apparent to those who
would be charged with the annoying details of executing
such a knucklehead plan.[4]

There is no question that the FBI has an image as a huge and powerful government agency, and it's understandable that some Americans have come to see it as menacing and dangerous, given its numerous depictions as such in Hollywood films and other media over the years.

The reader might be interested to know, however, what was hammered into us when we were new agent trainees at the FBI Academy in Quantico, Virginia.

We were in different classes, but the same message was drilled into all of us. Our legal instructor stood at the head of the class, looking up at an array of former police, military officers, high school teachers, accountants, and lawyers. All of us had left these professions to join the FBI as prospective agents of the FBI, and all of us were intrigued by the prospects of becoming involved in major investigations of interstate crime, violations of the espionage statute, and numerous other high-profile cases. Not everyone in every class made it through to graduation, but those who did all remembered clearly what our legal instructors told us during training:

You're training to become Special Agents, and you might not know what that term actually means.

(A long, serious look at the audience)

You are called Special Agents because your investigative authority is very specifically defined, and limited. You are permitted to investigate violations of specific federal statutes. You cannot investigate anything you want to—you are NOT general agents. You are part of the law enforcement community, not above it, and if you're smart, you'll have successful careers working with other law enforcement officers from the cities and states you're in as well as with other federal agencies.

We never forgot that lesson. No FBI agent is allowed to forget it—or if they do, it's not for long.

Navigating the maze of federal jurisdiction within the FBI used to require that that every agent was trained to do multiple tasks. The process was constant and dynamic, a formal and informal tapestry of training, mentoring, experience, coaching, persistence, and patience. Added to the mix with each passing decade was a new emphasis, a different focus, a significant mandate requiring enforcement of a chosen government priority designed to fix a special problem.

From chasing members of criminal gangs and saboteurs to hunting down spies, dismantling organized crime organizations to dissecting intricate savings and loan frauds, taking on public corruption as well as both domestic and international terrorism, no other agency of this or any other government has adapted itself to so many missions, while preserving its core values and organizational structure. No other agency has had the capabilities, competencies, and culture to answer the call to action, nor been so successful on nearly all of the occasions it has done so.

Since it's comprised of fallible human beings, however, the FBI has suffered like any other organization from crime and corruption from within its ranks, and it has made mistakes as an organization that have shaken the public trust.

There was a day when the Bureau could boast that none of its agents or employees had ever been bribed by the Mob or recruited by a foreign intelligence service. That day is gone. Four FBI special agents have been prosecuted for committing espionage after they provided classified information to agents of foreign powers.

A Los Angeles FBI agent named Richard Miller was arrested in 1984 as he prepared to travel to Europe to meet with the KGB. He had already been targeted and compromised by a Russian émigré named Svetlana Ogorodnikova, who was working on behalf of Soviet intelligence.

Supervisory Special Agent (SSA) Earl Pitts was arrested in 1997 after an investigation showed he had been giving the Russians information from the Bureau's counterintelligence files.

During 16 of the 27 years he spent in the FBI, SSA Robert Hanssen compromised the identities of American intelligence agents directed at Moscow, as well as divulging the identifies of several Soviet intelligence officers who had been recruited by Americans, which led to their executions at the hands of the KGB.

SSA J. J. Smith, a Bureau supervisor and "China hand" in the Los Angeles division of the FBI, compromised counterintelligence information while he was engaged in an affair with a female agent of intelligence services of the People's Republic of China.

The crimes committed by FBI employees haven't been limited to espionage. Both agents and support personnel have been arrested for a variety of crimes, including murder. The Boston field office of the Bureau has been rocked by an organized crime scandal involving some of its key agents working with the Mob. And the outcomes of several high-profile FBI investigations (such as the convoluted espionage case involving the Los Alamos scientist Wen Ho Lee) have resulted in serious questions about FBI capabilities and collective judgment.

No human endeavor is without human frailty, and we don't pretend that FBI agents and support personnel are better people than the personnel of any other organization.

What sets the FBI apart from the addiction to power that plagues American political life, however, is that the behavior of its personnel is constrained by law.

This is a far cry from the permissiveness that pervades the halls of Congress and the White House, where politicians addicted to the heady drug of political power repeatedly violate their oaths of office in the service of attaining higher and higher levels of the seemingly limitless climb to the highest reaches of power in Washington. Not all of them make it to the summit—to the presidency—but they're all a lesser or greater part of the club that puts each individual president there.

The terrorist organization al Qaeda was solely to blame for the 9/11 tragedy. Indicators of their desire to perpetrate an attack of these dimensions existed for years prior to the events of that day, and were reported consistently to politicians on both sides of the congressional aisle.

Despite the efforts of the FBI and other law enforcement and intelligence agencies to disrupt the conspiracies that were behind the attacks, on that terrible day a number of factors converged to enable al Qaeda to strike its catastrophic blows. Investigations ongoing in several regions of the United States to clarify and develop related pieces of information, to effect intelligence exchanges between America's security services and their foreign counterparts, and the dogged determination of hundreds of law enforcement and intelligence professionals all ran out of time as 9/11 neared. What appears so visible in tragic hindsight was a normal day in a shadowy world that most Americans never knew was a direct threat to Americans on their own soil.

But American politicians knew it. They have consistently evaded their responsibility for it, and their most recent posturing to remove the responsibility for domestic security from the FBI and charter it with their political allies in the CIA and elsewhere is a dangerous threat to both the security and the civil liberties of all Americans.

We cannot afford to let those addicted to power deprive us of hope for America's future. That future is in our hands, not in theirs. We should remember that politicians are not evil—their addictions are. By recognizing this, we can deal with the problem.

A great nation reflects on itself through the words and insights of its artists. John Steinbeck, in his 1966 book, *America* and *Americans*, captured the thought process we can all share to deal with any problems that confront us. Let's remember his words as we enter this new and complicated age of terror:

From the beginning, in hindsight at least, our social direction is clear. We have moved to become one people out of many. At intervals, men or groups, through fear of people or the desire to use them, have tried to change our direction, to arrest our growth, or to stampede the Americans. This will happen again and again. The impulses which for a time enforced the Alien and Sedition Laws, which have used fear and illicit emotion to interfere with and put a stop to our continuing revolution, will rise again, and they will serve us in the future as they have in the past to clarify and to strengthen our process. We have failed sometimes, taken wrong paths, paused for renewal, filled our bellies and licked our wounds; but we have never slipped back—never.

ENDNOTES

INTRODUCTION

[1] Comparisons between the late Roman Empire and the current American hegemony are increasingly prevalent. Robert Paine, in his book, *Ancient Rome,* described the state of the Roman Senate:

> *All of the advantages were on the side of the Senate . . . virtually unlimited power was at the disposal of the Senate . . . it was not burdened with the sense of responsibility to the people . Having little or no respect for the laws, the senators dominated Rome as though it were a conquered city . . . Family ties bound them together, they rejoiced in their secrecy . . . 'we are servants of the law in order that we may be free,' Cicero remarked. [But] the Romans failed to live up to this concept . . . When the framers of the United States Constitution erected what they termed a 'government of laws, not men,' they were in effect reasserting Rome's better self.*

In *The Decline and Fall of the Roman Empire*, Edward Gibbons called attention to a number of factors that led to the collapse of Roman civilization over many years, including, "the domestic hostilities of the Romans themselves," and the development of an environment where, "none could trust their lives or properties to the impotence of the law."

CHAPTER ONE

[1] Columbia Pictures, 1939, Directed by Frank Capra.

[2] Vladimir Lifschitz, Gottesman Family Centennial Professor in Computer Sciences, University of Texas at Austin website: http://www.cs.utexas.edu/users/vl/.

[3] Ibid.

[4] from *The Selfish Brain: Learning from Addiction*, by Robert L. DuPont, 2000, Hazelden Press.

[5] In his 1995 book *Emotional Intelligence* (Bantam Press), Daniel Goleman, a Harvard psychology Ph.D. and a *New York Times* science writer, brought together a decade's worth of behavioral research into how the mind processes feelings. His goal was to

redefine what it means to be smart. His thesis: when it comes to predicting people's success, brainpower as measured by IQ and standardized achievement tests may actually matter less than the qualities of mind once thought of as "character" before the word began to sound quaint." (Nancy Gibbs, from her *TIME* article "The EQ Factor," October 2, 1995.)

CHAPTER TWO

1 Robert Dallek's *Partner in Power, Nixon and Kissinger,* looks behind the scenes as Watergate was destroying the Nixon presidency from within:

Kissinger was appalled at apparent leaks to the press from the FBI. 'I think it is murderously dangerous, and I think the FBI must be brought under brutal control,' he told Stewart Alsop. 'This has the objective consequence of subverting the whole machinery of government.'"

It is strong evidence of the self-delusion of those addicted to the pursuit of power that Henry Kissinger, a man of considerable intellect and worldly experience, never understood during Watergate and still fails over three decades later to realize that it was the Nixon presidency itself that subverted the 'whole machinery' of government, not the ensuing FBI investigation.

2 Directed by Alan J. Pakula for Warner Brothers, 1976.

3 In her book *Richard M. Nixon,* Elizabeth Drew captured the personalities of the Plumbers. She described E. Howard Hunt as "a former CIA agent . . . a character out of his own adventure novels . . . dashing and daring." G. Gordon Liddy, a former FBI agent, "often carried a gun and could confuse a suggestion to 'go after' a Nixon 'enemy' as an order to kill him."

4 Ibid.

5 Testimony of L. Patrick Gray at Senate Judiciary Committee hearings, February 1973, on his nomination to succeed J. Edgar Hoover as Director of the FBI.

6 In a review of the 2007 book by Tim Weiner, *Legacy of Ashes, the History of the CIA* for the *Washington Post,* David Wise wrote:

Although most of Weiner's research is superb, he unfortunately perpetuates the legend that CIA director Richard Helms stood firm against Richard Nixon's Watergate cover-up. Not so. In an odd footnote, Weiner says Helms "complied with the president's order to go along with the cover-up for sixteen days at most." But the author, who quotes extensively from dozens of CIA documents, curiously make no mention of the damning memo that Helms wrote to his deputy, Vernon Walters, on June 28, 1972, about the FBI investigation of the break-in: "We still adhere to the request that they confine themselves to the personalities already arrested or directly under suspicion and that they desist from expanding this investigation into other areas which may well, eventually, run afoul of our operations." It was a bald-faced lie, exactly what the White House was demanding that Helms tell the FBI.

7 When the tapes were eventually released, they painted a picture of a President who had been knowingly lying to the public, obstructing justice, and misusing government agencies. They also portrayed a sad portrait of their pet FBI Director, L. Patrick Gray:

P - . . . after going through the hell of the hearings, he [Gray] will not be a good Director, as far as we are concerned.

D - . . . I think he will be a very suspect Director. Not that I think Pat won't do what we want . . . Like he is keeping in close touch with me. He is calling me. He has given me his hot line. We talk at night, how do you want me to handle this, et cetera? So he still stays in touch, and is still being involved, but he can't do it because he is going to be under such surveillance by his own people . . . Not that Pat wouldn't want to play ball, but he may not be able to.

P- I agree. That's what I meant.

D- Pat has already gotten himself in a situation where he has this Mark Felt as his number two man. These other people have surrounded him.

Chapter Three

1 *Operation SOLO: The FBI's Man in the Kremlin,* John Barron, 1997.

2 Kelley's release of these documents was accompanied by his characterization of the serious concerns about terrorist violence that prompted the FBI to act. During the Vietnam War, prior to Watergate, American democracy had been under continual attack by a combination of homegrown anarchists with allegiances to communist governments and by the intelligence organizations of those governments. While it is true that the FBI seemed to have a difficult time distinguishing between legitimate protests and domestic violence, it is also true to say that many elected officials from both sides of the political aisle had consistently encouraged the Bureau to identify, disrupt, and quell the domestic violence that was taking a toll on institutions of government and established law and order.

Out of campus protests against the war in Vietnam emerged the Students for a Democratic Society or SDS. The SDS preached the Maoist brand of revolution and the end of capitalism. Eventually the SDS would spawn the Weather Underground Organization (WUO). The WUO and its leaders embarked upon a campaign of bombings, attacks on police departments and arsons to bring the U.S. government to its knees. Declaring that a worldwide revolution was coming, the WUO declared war on established order. The war raged throughout the late 1960s, continuing into the mid-1970s even as Watergate rocked American public life.

In 1973 there were bombings at the 103rd Precinct of the New York City Police Department and the headquarters of ITT Corporation in New York and Rome. In 1974, bombings of state offices in San Francisco, the California State Attorney General's Office, the headquarters of Gulf Oil in Pittsburgh, and the Anaconda Corporation reminded local, state, and governmental authorities that they had little ability to quell the violence. In 1975, there were bombings at the Department of State, a Bank of Puerto Rico branch in New York City, and the Kennecott Corporation.

After the Watergate scandal, however, the country was in no mood to agree that domestic intelligence operations were a good tactic against the violence. It was in this atmosphere that the Church Committee began its inquiries.

[3] Ibid.

[4] John Barron writes: *No one could have been more sympathetic to King than the Kennedy brothers. During the 1960 presidential campaign they publicly defended him and demanded his release from an Alabama jail, fearing he might be killed in his cell . . . hoping to save King and the civil rights movement from embarrassment, President Kennedy and Attorney General Kennedy cautioned King that, by personally associating with and relying upon Levison and O'Dell, he was putting himself and the civil rights movement in jeopardy. King equivocated, then continued to associate with O'Dell and Levison, both openly and secretly. Operation SOLO: The FBI's Man in the Kremlin*, 1997.

[5] Ibid.

[6] Ibid.

CHAPTER FOUR

[1] Personal papers of the authors.

[2] Robert Ellis Smith, *FORBES*, January 15, 2007.

[3] Personal papers of the authors.

[4] Personal papers of the authors.

CHAPTER FIVE

[1] Online Transcript of panel discussion "FBI: Troubled House," on the News Hour with Jim Lehrer, PBS, April 16, 1997.

[2] "The Federal Bureau of Investigation's Compliance with the Attorney General's Investigative Guidelines," included information the FBI provided to the Subcommittee on Security and Terrorism of the 98th Congress in 1978.

[3] In 1978 the FBI set up "Abdul Enterprises, Ltd." as an undercover company in a sting operation where FBI agents posing as businessmen from the Middle East offered money to public officials–including a U.S. Senator and five members of the House of Representatives who were ultimately convicted on public corruption charges–in exchange for future political favors.

[4] Turchie Note: On a hot and humid Saturday afternoon in August 1986, Soviet KBG Line X (targeting science and technology) Officer Gennadiy Zacharov went to see a source who had been providing him with sensitive, but unclassified material from a defense contractor. After developing a relationship for months, Zacharov, whose cover job was as a United Nations Secretariat employee, had asked the source to give him classified information.

Unknown by Zacharov, his source had been "doubled" by the FBI and was reporting his every move. My partner, Bill Zinnikas, and I, along with special agent Donna Mathews, were asked late that afternoon to play a small role in the arrest plan for Zacharov, to take place right after he acquired the classified documents passed by the source at a clandestine meeting. Our job was simple: we were to keep an eye out for Soviet surveillance vehicles shadowing Zacharov as he met his source at a local eating spot. In t-shirts and shorts, we blended in with the public in the neighborhood, while teams of agents prepared to move in on the KBG spy and arrest him for espionage.

Things didn't go as planned. Zacharov intercepted the source before he showed up at the restaurant. They walked and talked, covering several city blocks and making it impossible for Bureau surveillance teams to follow them without being spotted. Finally, Zacharov directed the source to a deserted subway platform in Brooklyn Queens and told him to wait on the second level, where he would acquire the documents.

The arrest plans would have to change on the fly. Instead of watching from the sidelines, Bill, Donna, and I were directed to follow the source to the subway location, blend in with the crowd and make the arrest as soon as Zacharov received the documents.

Although it was early on a summer afternoon, the subway platform was empty as we followed the source to his rendezvous point. Zacharov appeared from a distance on the platform, his eyes searching for possible surveillance. Bill dove behind a nearby subway door and Donna and I instantly became a devoted couple in a passionate clinch.

"Go ahead, kiss me," I told her with my back to Zacharov on the other side of the platform. "And tell me when he starts to handle the documents."

"Terry, I've never arrested anyone before," she whispered.

"Donna," I whispered back. "I haven't either." Her eyes widened in horror, and I quickly told her I was only joking. Flashing through my brain was everything my friends and mentors had taught me during arrests of fugitives and bank robbers in Portland, Oregon. It was another aspect of the FBI culture that would now serve me well. "Just do what I do," I said.

Seconds later, she saw Zacharov take the sheaf of documents from the source. We had edged a few feet away from them by then, so we abruptly split and I yelled, "Gennadiy Zacharov, FBI, you're under arrest for espionage!"

The Soviet tossed the documents toward the subway tracks and started to run. I tackled him and we both crashed against the hard concrete floor of the platform. As we rolled around the platform, inventing the first iteration of the Ultimate Fighting Championship, he mouthed, "We need to talk."

When I was finally able to hold onto him, Bill and Donna applied the handcuffs–three sets—to his wrists. Just as we were wrapping it up, dozens of agents came charging up the platform, just like in the movies. It was the FBI culture to the rescue. And such was the life of the street agent, the life I surrendered when I left New York and went to FBI Headquarters in 1987, trading dealing with spies for dealing with politicians. I would conclude very shortly that I much preferred dealing with spies.

5 Turchie Note: Also present at this meeting, I told Geer, Stukey, and Geer's deputy, Tom DuHadway, that I thought there was a lot of misinformation out there about this program, and I didn't see how we could stay out of libraries visited by known Soviet intelligence officers. I also didn't see how we could ever agree to something where we were prohibited from interviewing an entire class of people. DuHadway agreed:

We have little choice but to tell Edwards we will be happy to attend his hearing and try to explain this, but his conditions are not acceptable. I spoke with Jim Fox [the FBI Assistant Director in Charge in New York and probably the most respected courterintelligence authority in the FBI at the time], and he has already talked to some of the librarians previously contacted by the FBI. There telling him that not everyone agrees this is an issue.

Don Stukey said:

*I think we need to go to Edwards with some pretty clear and con-
crete facts as to why we feel strongly about this from a national security perspective, and make certain that the librarians realize we
aren't interested in reading lists of American citizens–we're interested
in what these Soviet intelligence officers are up to.*

6 Personal recollections of the authors.

7 *My FBI,* by Louis Freeh, 2006.

CHAPTER SIX

1 *FIREWALL–The Iran-Contra Conspiracy and Cover-Up,* Lawrence
E. Walsh, W.W. Norton & Company, 1997.

2 Ibid.

3 In 1984, controversy over U.S. assistance to the opponents of the
Nicaraguan government (the anti-Sandinista guerrillas known as
the "contras") led to a prohibition on such assistance in a continuing
appropriations bill. This legislative ban is summarized below:

"The continuing appropriations resolution for FY1985, P.L. 98-
473, 98 Stat. 1935-1937, signed October 12, 1984, provided that:
"During fiscal year 1985, no funds available to the Central Intelligence Agency, the Department of Defense, or any other agency or
entity of the United States involved in intelligence activities may be
obligated or expended for the purpose or which would have the effect
of supporting, directly or indirectly, military or paramilitary operations in Nicaragua by any nation, group, organization, movement or
individual."

This legislation also provided that after February 28, 1985, if the
President made a report to Congress specifying certain criteria,
including the need to provide further assistance for "military or
paramilitary operations" prohibited by this statute, he could expend
$14 million in funds if Congress passed a joint resolution approving
such action." [Congressional Research Service, Congressional Use of
Funding Cutoffs Since 1970 Involving U.S. Military Forces and
Overseas Deployments, January 10, 2001, pg. 6.]

4 *The New York Times,* October 12, 1986.

5 *Foreign Affairs,* Iran-Contra Affair, 1985-1992 "Irangate," ushis-
tory.com.

[6] Address to the Nation on the Iran Arms and Contra Aid Controversy," March 4, 1987.

[7] From the final report of the Independent Counsel for Iran/Contra Matters, Lawrence Walsh, August 4, 1993.

CHAPTER SEVEN

[1] Oral statement of Senator Patrick Leahy at the hearing on the nomination of Robert S. Mueller, III, to be Director of the Federal Bureau of Investigation, July 30, 2001.

[2] "Grassley Fervent as Critic of FBI," Jane Norman, *Des Moines Register,* July 5, 2002.

[3] Senator Leahy and Representative Edwards allied with the Electronic Frontier Foundation in drafting their version of the Digital Telephony bill.

The Electronic Frontier Foundation (EFF) is an international non-profit advocacy and legal organization based in the U.S with the stated purpose of being dedicated to preserving free speech rights such as those protected by the First Amendment in the context of today's digital age. Its stated main goal is to educate the press, policymakers and the general public about civil liberties issues related to technology; and to act as a defender of those liberties. (from Wikipedia)

Daniel Weitzer, the Deputy Policy Director for EFF said of the legislation, "the fact that law enforcement has to take a case to court in order to get permission to access records is a major new privacy protection which will benefit all users of online communications systems." Jerry Berman, EFF's Policy Director, described the bill as ". . . substantially better from a privacy, technology policy, and civil liberties standpoint than the draconian measures offered in the past by the [first]Bush Administration."

Berman vowed that the "EFF will work to ensure that privacy and public process provisions are strengthened, and that the scope remains narrow-continuing to exclude the Internet, electronic bulletin board systems, and online communication services such as America Online, Prodigy and Compuserve."

Senator Leahy and Representative Edwards agreed with EFF's position that government should not be allowed to acquire and sort through transactional information to conduct traffic analysis, and that the standard of proof for any acquisition of these types of records, toll records, and pen registers must involve a United States Attorney or District Attorney convincing a judge that there is a law enforcement reason to ask for the records.

[4] Jay Nordlinger, *National Review*, July 9, 2001.

CHAPTER EIGHT

[1] *Rats in the Grain: The Dirty Tricks and Trials of Archer Daniels Midland, The Supermarket to the World*, James Lieber, 2000, Four Walls Eight Windows Press, NY.

[2] Ibid

[3] There is apparently no financial limit to the resources of mammoth corporations in protecting themselves, with cadres of highly paid attorneys as well as huge budgets for propaganda. In a chapter called "Brinkley Shills for Corporate Criminals," authors Russell Mokhiber and Robert Weissman in their 1999 book *Corporate Predators– The Hunt for Mega-Profits and the Attack on Democracy*, note that after ADM paid their $100 Million dollar fine for criminal price fixing in 1996, they hired respected newsman David Brinkley to film a series of TV promos to repair the company's image with the public.

[4] Personal conversation with the authors, January 2008.

[5] *Rats in the Grain: The Dirty Tricks and Trials of Archer Daniels Midland, The Supermarket to the World*, James Lieber, 2000, Four Walls Eight Windows Press, NY.

[6] Ibid

[7] Ibid

CHAPTER NINE

[1] In his 2006 book *My FBI*, Louis Freeh had this to say about President Clinton's interest in the case:

> *As 1998 wore on, Bill Clinton was pursuing rapprochement with the Iranians and finding himself in increasingly hot water domesti- cally. Ken Starr was dogging the president; Monica Lewinsky had become maybe the best-known White House intern in history. Mean- while, Khobar Towers was sliding further and further toward the back burner . . . Sandy Berger . . . had come out of the political side of the Clinton machine. He'd been part of the campaign. Even when he was deputy national security adviser, he sat in on the once-a-week political meetings at the White House, and they weren't discussing foreign policy . . . Don't get me wrong: Sandy did have a very sincere*

interest in foreign policy–of that I'm certain—but the lens through which he seemed to view everything was the politics of getting Bill Clinton reelected and, later, of preserving Clinton's legacy and the Democratic party's hold on the presidency. Among other things, that meant shortchanging the needs of the Khobar Tower families.

[2] Final Report of the National Commission on Terrorism, June 2000.

[3] Turchie Note: I was part of the FBI group on this whirlwind international anti-terror tour with the Director, with whom I had had considerable contact during my work on the UNABOM Task Force (1994–1998) as well as heading up the Fugitive Task Force for the Southeast Bomb Task Force that was hunting Eric Robert Rudolph, the Olympic Park Bomber (1998—1999). By this time, I was serving as Deputy Assistant Director of the new FBI Counterterrorism Division.

[4] Turchie Note; I was the FBI Deputy Assistant Director present at both at the Wye River Conference in June 2000 and the Shay Committee in July 2000.

[5] "The Clinton Legacy," from *The Progressive Review* (last updated in 2000).

[6] Susan Rosenberg had been under investigation for her possible role in the robbery of a Brinks armored car in Nyack, New York, in 1981. A Brink's guard and two Nyack police officers were murdered during the robbery. Weather Underground member Kathy Boudin was connected to the crime. Ten years earlier Boudin and Cathy Wilkerson were in a terrorist safe house in Greenwich Village in New York City when there was an accidental explosion while they and other members of the Weather Underground were preparing for an attack on Fort Dix, New Jersey. A witness saw Wilkerson running from the apartment.

In 1985, Rosenberg and Linda Evans were caught with 740 pounds of explosives and subsequenly admitted they were planning additional terrorist attacks within the United States. Evans went to prison for 40 years and Rosenberg for 58. No further charges were filed against Rosenberg for the 1981 Nyack murders after her sentencing on the explosive charges. As President Clinton pardoned Rosenberg and Evans before he left office, the San Francisco Police Department was working steadily to tie the pieces together that would connect the Weather Underground to the murder of a San Francisco Police Officer in a bombing of the Ingleside Station in February 1970.

In late 1970, former special agent Donald Max Noel was one of the San Francisco FBI agents assigned to work a Weather Underground investigation that was declaired an "office special." The investigation was initiated within days of the accidental explosion in

Greenwich Village that killed three members of the Weather Underground. Several members fled to the west coast from New York, becoming federal fugitives. The FBI knew that among the fugitives were Kathy Boudin and Cathy Wilkerson. Both were believed to be in the San Francisco Bay Area.

In the investigation, the Bureau looked at the records of deceased infants, compared a variety of public records to deceased infant identities and submitted the results to the Department of Motor Vehicles, asking for copies of DMV photographs. Checking everything from library cards to Pacific Gas and Electric utility records, the FBI hoped to identify Weather Underground fugitives using deceased infant identities and thereafter trace them to their safe house addresses, with the firm belief that they were hiding out in San Francisco.

Weather Underground members became aware that the FBI was hot on their trail and looked for a way to escape the Bay Area. In need of money to affect their fugitive run, they turned to the National Lawyers Guild in Chicago for help. The NLG arranged to send funding through Western Union, and the FBI knew the time, location, and name of the person who was supposed to pick up the money.

The agreed upon approach was to use criminal and counterintelligence agents working in teams with differing objectives. The criminal agents would collect evidence related to the bombings and other crimes being committed by the Weather Underground, while the counterintelligence agents would assess and analyze information collected that might serve to tie the organization to foreign sponsors such as the Russians and Cubans. A plan was introduced that was relatively clear cut—the agents would follow " whoever came to pick up the money."

As the agents watched, an old Volvo sedan appeared on the scene. The occupants were a man and a woman. The FBI knew that the NLG expected to give a check to an unknown male. The unidentified male walked into the Western Union location. An agent observing him let others know, "that it looks like Jeff Jones." (Jones was a highly sought after Weather Underground fugitive). Another agent, referring to the female companion staying in the truck, said that she "looks just like Cathy Wilkerson."

The two sped off after collecting the money. They were lost by their hunters, disappearing into a maze of San Francisco streets. Documents they handled at Western Union were processed for fingerprints, and surveillance photographs were developed. The unidentified subjects who had appeared in person at Western Union were two of the most notorious Weather Underground fugitives of their day—Jeff Jones and Cathy Wilkerson. Later that evening, agents carpooling out of the city spotted the Volvo parked on Golden Gate Avenue near the Federal Building.

Over the next few days, the car was followed but eventually lost in the vicinity Pine and Taylor Streets. Agents knocked on doors and asked questions of residents in the location. Several days later agents received a call from the owner of an apartment building. He hadn't seen the occupants of one of his apartments for some time. Old newspapers were gathering outside their door. They might match the FBI's neighborhood inquiries. As agents entered the apartment along with bomb experts from the San Francisco Police Department, they found an abandoned bomb factory, complete with personal items, wire, papers, and a trunk with the military explosive C-4. The find was highly important. San Francisco had been the target of repeated terrorist murders and bombings in 1970 and 1971, some still unsolved when President Clinton pardoned Weather Underground terrorist Susan Rosenberg and Linda Evans during his final day in office.

CHAPTER TEN

1   Investigation of Illegal or Improper Activities in Connection with 1996 Federal Election Campaigns, 105th Congress 2nd Session, March 10, 1998

2   Ibid

3   "The Rise of a New Power, A Communist Economic Juggernaut Emerges To Challenge The West," June 20, 2005.

4   "Clinton Calls Arms Dealer's White House Visit Inappropriate," Pete Yost, Associated Press, December 20, 1996.

5   Testimony of Samuel "Sandy" Berger before the Senate Governmental Affairs Committee, September 11, 1997.

6   Statement of Thad Cochran during the testimony of Sandy Berger before the Senate Governmental Affairs Committee, September 11, 1997.

7   (October 7, 1997 Hearings Transcript)

8   *Washington Post*, August 21, 1998.

9   NBC's *Today* show, January 24, 1997.

CHAPTER ELEVEN

1   Walter Pincus and Dana Priest, *Washington Post*, June 20, 2002.

[2] Secretary of Defense Donald Rumsfeld Interviewed on NBC's *Today* show, May 17, 2002.

3 Secretary of Defense Donald Rumsfeld, interviewed on NBC's *Today* show, May 17, 2002.

[4] Murray Waas, *National Journal*, Feb. 15, 2007.

[5] Ibid

[6] NBC News, July 26, 2004, "Senator Shelby the subject of probe on 9/11 intelligence leak".

[7] *National Journal Magazine,* Feb. 15, 2007.

CHAPTER TWELVE

[1] In *All the President's Men* (Carl Bernstein, Bob Woodward, 1974, New York Simon and Schuster, p. 105), Mitchell is quoted as telling Bernstein, *"Katie Graham's gonna get her tit caught in a big fat wringer if that's published,"* referring to an upcoming article planned by the *Washington Post* on the Watergate scandal.

[2] *NYT* February 4, 2000.

[3] Walsh report, Chapter 31 titled, "Edwin Meese, III," November, 1986, note #3.

[4] Testimony of James Comey before the Senate Judiciary Committee, May 15, 2007.

[5] Turchie Note: In 2001, I was present at a meeting at FBIHQ involving representatives of both Britain's MI-5 and MI-6 with FBI Director Freeh. The Brits made clear that their system had weaknesses, and said that they were somewhat envious of the uniqueness of the FBI in its dual role of national security and law enforcement. After 9/11, the Brits reiterated to a U.S. Congressional fact-finding committee that the U.S. should consider the downside of changing the FBI's structure and removing national security from its jurisdiction. Their primary view was that the downside would be a loss of independence and effectiveness.

[6] Thomas Keane and Lee Hamilton on NBC's *Meet the Press*, November 28, 2004.

[7] Turchie Note: I met Powell in the early stages of the Clinton/Bush transition, at least a month prior to the President elect's inaugural. The FBI Assistant Director for Counterterrorism, Dale Watson, was scheduled to join a number of other counterterrorism experts to provide a threat briefing to Powell at the State Department. Watson's wife was expecting and on the day of the briefing, they needed to make an unexpected trip to the Dr.'s office. I had been sick at home

for a week and was planning on returning to work the day after Powell's briefing.

Dale sent a car to get me over to the Hoover Building, and assured me I'd have all the briefing papers I needed. He added that tom Pickard wanted to see me in his office an hour before the briefing to pass along some specifics.

I always got sick trying to read in the car, and wasn't about to try studying the briefing documents two hours before talking to the new Secretary of State. So when I sowed up at Pickard's office, I still hadn't looked at the carefully prepared details the FBI wanted transmitted to Powell during his first meeting on terrorism matters. Pickard was Director Freeh's handpicked choice as Deputy FBI Director. The only time he and I had ever spoken prior to my arrival at FBI headquarters was after the UNABOM manuscript had been received and urgent leads were being worked out of the New York Office. At that time, Pickard was the special Agent in Charge of New York's massive criminal investigation program.

Pickard was in his office early and always left late. He was a quick study on every conceivable issue worked on by the FBI and not the sort of person anyone should try to bullshit. Pickard could spot insincerity ten miles away, and his face could go from genial to stern in milliseconds.

"Turchie, I can't believe we're sending you to brief General Powell," Pickard started out in him most sarcastic tone, "but Watson's out and I can't go, so you're it."

I admitted I hadn't even been able to look at the briefing book.

"Listen," Tom said, "Louie [Louis Freeh's nickname] wants to talk with the new Secretary of State in private about the Khobar Towers bombing. We don't even know whether it will come up today, but there are several people who may be at the briefing who will want to show Powell how much they know and try to engage in details of the Bureau's investigation to impress him. The problem is they don't know the details, and it's better at this juncture to brief him privately. If it comes up, do what you have to, but defer on the topic until Louie can see him personally."

I sat in the State Department conference room at Foggy Bottom along with at least 20 other government employees bringing to the table the interests of their respective agencies in various aspects of counterterrorism. I was amazed at the mission diversity they represented. I was accompanied by the CIA officer on assignment a the FBI as the deputy chief in the Bureau's international terrorism section, headed at the time by Michael Rolince. The officer was highly respected and well-qualified to serve in the position. Both the FBI and the CIA had agreed during Director Freeh's creation of the Counterterrorism Division that the exchange would enhance and

improve communication between the agencies and render the overall government counterterrorism effort more effective. An FBI desig-
nee served a reciprocal role at the CIA.

Before leaving the Hoover Building, I had the opportunity to
review Dale Watson's briefing notes. In the car ride to The Department of State, my CIA colleague highlighted some of the points I
might wish to make. There was little time to dwell on the subject.
Unlike the reputation President Clinton earned for always showing
up late for meetings, Powell entered the conference room precisely
at the scheduled time. He made quite an impression as he entered
the room. Wearing blue jeans, a casual beige sport coat and faint but
friendly smile, he greeted some of those he already knew with an
extra nod and took his chair.

I had only seen Powell at Dick Cheney's side during press conferences about the first Iraq war. To me he was a photograph in magazines and an occasional sound bite on the nightly news. But now he
was in front of me. In just a few minutes in the State conference
room that morning, before he ever spoke a word, it was easy to seen
why people had mentioned him as a possible candidate for the White
House. It was just as easy to conclude why he didn't run for President. Powell was a leader without strings and determined to keep it
that way. He didn't belong to the Democrats or the Republicans—he
belonged to the nation. On that day as he discussed, asked questions, and talked about he terrorist threat to America, he appeared
to do so with caution, deliberation, and wisdom. I was even more
impressed than I'd thought I'd be.

As predicted, someone introduced the topic of Khobar Towers and
the unsolved bombing that killed 16 American servicemen in 1966.
When Powell asked a simple follow-up question, the room was
silent. Since the individual who broached the topic knew nothing
else about it, this was my moment to make the pitch on behalf of
Director Freeh.

I told him that the Khobar Towers bombing was one of the FBI's
most significant investigations, and the information we'd developed
by was highly sensitive. I added that Director Freeh had asked me
to pass along that he would appreciate the opportunity to fully brief
him in person on the case at his earliest convenience. Faces fell
around the room as it became apparent that the FBI investigation
would not be discussed in the meeting. Powell smiled broadly and
asked an aide to make a note to schedule a meeting with the FBI
Director.

8 "The Iraqi Connection: Interview with James Woolsey and Others,"
On the Line, November 24, 2001.

[9] Turchie Note: As the Senior Counterintelligence Officer at Lawrence Livermore Weapons Lab after my retirement from the FBI, I had extensive liaison with the local CIA station. With my co-author, Dr. Kathleen Puckett along during one of our routine meetings prior to the invasion of Iraq, the CIA San Francisco Station Chief told us in no uncertain terms that the agency had proof of Hussein's weapons of mass destruction and emphasized that the day of reckoning for him would soon come. Shortly after the conversation, the Station Chief was transferred to CIA Headquarters to assume a highly placed position in the hierarchy.

[10] Turchie Note: When I made the trip with Director Freeh.

CHAPTER THIRTEEN

[1] PBS *Frontline*, http://www.pbs.org/wgbh/pages/frontline/cheney/view/

[2] "Papers Detail Industry's Role in Cheney's Energy Report," by Michael Abramowitz and Steven Mufson, *Washington Post*, July 18, 2007.

CHAPTER FOURTEEN

[1] "What House Speaker Dennis Hastert Thinks Is Behind ABC Report," May 25, 2006, Fox News.

[2] We are helpless to resist quoting Lord Acton: *Power tends to corrupt and absolute power corrupts absolutely.* Jim Powell, *The Freeman: Ideas on Liberty*, June 1996.

CHAPTER FIFTEEN

[1] "A Lobbyist in Full," Michael Crowley, *Washington Post*, May 1, 2005.

[2] "Case Shines Light on How War Contracts Are Awarded," Sign On San Diego.com, by the *Union Tribune*, February 15, 2007.

CHAPTER SIXTEEN

[1] "Washington's $8 Billion Shadow," Donald L. Barlett and James B. Steele, *Vanity Fair* March 2007.

[2] Ibid

[3] Ibid

[4] Ibid

[5] Ibid

[6] "Report Says Firm Sought to Cover Up Iraq Shootings," John M. Broder, *Washington Post*, October 2, 2007.

[7] Ibid

[8] Testimony of State Department Inspector General Howard Krongard Before the House Government Oversight and Reform Committee, November 14, 2007.

[9] Authors' Note: We both took positions as Counterintelligence principals at Lawrence Livermore National Laboratory as employees of the University of California, until it became apparent that changes at the lab brought on by the "privatization" would result in an ineffective counterintelligence program managed at the Department of Energy by a former CIA official, supplanting FBI officials who themselves did not have the necessary experience to do the job, reflecting the FBI's movement towards satisfying politicians and changing its "culture" to appease them.

[10] Turchie Note: After I retired from the FBI in Spring 2001, I went to work for Shepard, taking the position of Senior Counterintelligence Officer at the Lawrence Livermore National Lab in Livermore, California. I soon found her to be one of the most (if not the most) dedicated person I had ever seen in a management position in counterintelligence and spent four years working for her until she left the position in 2005.

[11] Clay Sell, from Texas.

[12] Turchie Note: I attended a meeting in early 2007 involving the field and headquarters staff of the Department of Energy Office of Intelligence and Counterintelligence. The day before the conference began, I went to dinner with several colleagues, including a former high-ranking CIA official who was my counterpart at another DOE weapons lab. Bright, analytical, and visionary, Bruce Held brought up the topic of torture when we were having a drink in the bar before eating.

Referring to the interrogations of detainees in Iraq and Cuba, he shook his head and motioned with his hands, *I don't see the big deal. It's proven that torture is the only thing that works with these people.*

When I looked at him in disbelief, he repeated his assertion and added, *It's true, besides the President approved it so what's not to like. It works.*

[13] In court testimony, Held admitted using the word "decapitated" and said that he wouldn't contest using the word "blood" although he didn't recall saying it. He also apologized for using those terms.

(Q&A: Reverse Hacker Describes Ordeal, Sandia Put Lab's Interest Over Those of the Country, Security Analyst Says," *Computerworld*, February 26, 2007.)

[14] I was particularly saddened by the lack of any adequate defense to Larsen's moves by the senior FBI official selected (by Larsen) to be the deputy director for counterintelligence interests. On one of his trips to Livermore to meet with my counterintelligence staff, this FBI official lamented that he didn't know exactly how much money he had available to fund the counterintelligence effort for the upcoming fiscal year because he could not get any answers from Larsen or his staff as to what funding there was. Inasmuch as funding was always a constant problem for each individual counterintelligence effort, my colleagues at Los Alamos National Lab and the Sandia National Lab in Albuquerque sent numerous emails to summarize our budget situations and ask for help in advance of potential budget issues. We never received a response from our FBI Deputy Director. In one of the rare two-day meetings we held in Las Vegas, Nevada, to discuss the counterintelligence and intelligence missions, this FBI executive sat silent for both days, contributing nothing of any substance to the get together aside from a canned speech of thirty minutes that he gave on the afternoon of the first day. During the remainder of the conference he said nothing and we were all invited to drink Rolf Mowatt Larsen's kool aid for two days. On the second day, at 4:00 p.m., we were scheduled to have at least an hour alone with our FBI Deputy Director for Counterintelligence. I asked him about the looming budget issues for 2007 and 2008, and reminded him that staffing and performance would be critically impacted if they weren't resolved. His response was to look at his watch and remind us that Rolf was holding a "social" in his room at 5:00 p.m. and that we all should try and be there.

When I left the position of Senior Counterintelligence Officer at Lawrence Livermore National Lab at the end of September 2007, lab management was following a carefully laid plan to bring in a qualified replacement for me. Larsen and his FBI "deputy" got involved with the selection, and as of summer, 2008, there still is no Senior Counterintelligence Officer permanently in place at the lab.

As the lab faced the prospect of losing counterintelligence positions because of budget priorities dictated by DOE headquarters, the head of the Office of Intelligence and Counterintelligence, former CIA official Rolf Mowatt Larsen, departed for a prolonged respite somewhere on a mountain top in a remote section of the world to "find himself."

CHAPTER SEVENTEEN

[1] From the redacted file provided on January 2, 2007 by the FBI under a Freedom of Information Act (FOIA) request by media representatives (see http://foia.fbi.gov/foiaindex/guanatamo.htm).

[2] "Report Details Dissent on Guantanamo Tactics," Eric Lichtblau and Scott Shane, *The New York Times*, May 21, 2008.

[3] Ibid

[4] "FBI Drew Line on Terror Suspect Interrogations, Audit Finds," FOX News, May 20, 2008.

[5] "Rethinking the Psychology of Torture: A Preliminary Report from Former Interrogators and Research Psychologists," November 2006.

[6] "Debating Torture," OnLine Newshour, December 2, 2005, Comments of former FBI Special Agent Jack Cloonan.

[7] "CIA Director Names Waterboarded Detainees," CBS News Interactive: About Global Terrorism, February 5, 2008.

[8] "Cheney Defends U.S. Use of Waterboarding," CBS News, February 8, 2008.

[9] "Gates: U.S. Stuck in Guantanamo," CNN, May 20, 2008.

[10] Turchie Note: I was the Associate Special Agent in Charge in San Francisco at the time.

CHAPTER EIGHTEEN

[1] "FBI, CIA Remain Worlds Apart," Siobhan Gorman, *National Journal*, August 1, 2003.

[2] Turchie Note: When I decided the UTF needed a 24-hour analytical effort to pro-actively identify potential Unabom candidates through computer runs with established criteria, FBI Headquarters balked at sending 50 analysts to San Francisco to work three 8-hour shifts pouring through millions of pieces of computer data collected over 18 years. The Bureau simply didn't have that many analysts. The UTF won out and in a single phone call from then Deputy Director Bill Esposito to Director Freeh, 25 FBI analysts were on their way to California to work Unabom indefinitely. By 1996, the integrated approach had uncovered so many pieces of information that had previously gone unnoticed, that the right information could break the case.

[3] "5 Years Up Costs FBI Top Managers," *Washington Times*, May 23, 2008.

4 "Chaney: Iran Faces 'Serious Consequences' Over Nuclear Drive," Vice President's Speech to the Washington Institute for Near East Policy, October 21, 2007.

CHAPTER NINETEEN

1 From a Counterpunch.org, Essay by Katherine van Wormer, "Addiction, Brain Damage and the President—'Dry Drunk' Syndrome and George W. Bush," October 11, 2002.

2 Professor Katherine van Wormer, a professor of Social Work at the University of Northern Iowa, wrote an essay for counterpunch.org on October 11, 2002 titled, "Addiction, Brain Damage and the President—'Dry Drunk' Syndrome and George W. Bush." In it, she characterizes Bush's "rigid, judgmental outlook" as being symptomatic of a classic addictive thinking pattern that includes an "either you are with us or against us" mentality as well as a constant repetition of thoughts that are the result of organic brain damage caused during the addictive substance use.

3 Despite the firing of eight shots at the Federal Command Post in Andrews, North Carolina, and the presence of over 200 armed local, state, and Federal agents, not a single firearm was discharged on that night or during the intense one year chase for Rudolph by any member of the Fugitive Search Task Force.

4 "Why the U.S. Doesn't Need a Secret Police," Former FBI Director Louis Freeh, June, 2007.

Index

306

History Publishing Company
Books in Print

The award-winning *Hunting the American Terrorist—The FBI's War on Homegrown Terror,* by Terry D. Turchie and Kathleen M. Puckett.

The award-winning *The Words of War—The Civil War Battle Reportage of The New York Times and The Charleston Mercury and What Historians Say Really Happened*, by Donnagh Bracken.

Legerdemain—The President's Secret Plan, the Bomb, and What the French Never Knew, by James J. Heaphey.

A Lovely Little War—Life in a Japanese Prison Camp Through the Eyes of a Child, by Angus M. Lorenzen.

Don't Shoot, We're Republicans—Why the FBI Held Its Fire, by Jack Owens (January 2009)

A Marked Heart—A Spiritual Journey Inspired by Martin Luther King that Brought America the 401(k) Program, by David George Ball (February 2009).

Today's Books Imprint

Career of Gold—Defeat Age Bias by Re-Careering for the Second Half of Your Life, by Don Bracken.

How to Survive in an Organization, by James J. Heaphey.

A Manager's Guide to Surviving a Disaster, by Barbara Hillenbrand (Spring 2009).

Chronicle Press Imprint

Custer Survivor, by John Koster (Spring 2009).